forgiveness
in international
politics

forgiveness

in international politics

politics

... *an alternative road to peace*

William Bole

Drew Christiansen, SJ

Robert T. Hennemeyer

UNITED STATES CONFERENCE OF CATHOLIC BISHOPS
Washington, D.C.

Forgiveness in International Politics: An Alternative Road to Peace is the product of a series of conferences sponsored by the Woodstock Theological Center, with close collaboration by the Office of International Justice and Peace of the United States Conference of Catholic Bishops (USCCB). It was reviewed by the chairman of the Committee on International Policy, Bishop John H. Ricard, SSJ, and has been authorized for publication by the undersigned.

—Msgr. William P. Fay
General Secretary, USCCB

First Printing, May 2004

ISBN 1-57455-574-X

Contents

Foreword

CARDINAL THEODORE MCCARRICK

A lthough this book does not represent any particular religious view, it does bring to light a theme—forgiveness—that was all but synonymous with personal piety until fairly recent times. Most recently, forgiveness has become part of our therapeutic culture, recommended as one way of achieving personal wellness and interpersonal harmony.

This publication, which reflects years of dialogue among theorists and practitioners of conflict resolution, brings forgiveness into the broad context of international politics. Its aim is to present a strong concept of forgiveness that has value as a means of conflict resolution.

Many different voices are presented here, yet they cohere as a call for alternative ways of conceiving what is "realistic" or "strategic" in the arena of international conflict and diplomacy. Forgiveness is one expression of this search for new ways of international engagement. It has potential as an organizing principle of peacemaking, one that focuses on renewing relationships across ethnic, religious, tribal, and ideological boundaries. I believe this book will help us find what the Protestant social ethicist Donald W. Shriver has called a "new home" for forgiveness: the sociopolitical realm.

As one who has been part of reconciliation efforts in a number of conflicts, I appreciate the contributions this book makes to the fields of conflict resolution and peacebuilding. As a religious leader, I appreciate its contribution to religious reflections on peace and societal conflict. I share the hope that forgiveness will not only "act upon the secular policy world, but also 'act back' upon the religious world," as is stated in the Conclusion. All of us, politicians, diplomats, church members, and civil leaders, can learn by listening to the religious traditions that call us to the practice of this special virtue.

For us who are Christians, the call for forgiveness in the Gospels makes clear the relevance of this virtue in every facet of daily life. It would be impossible for Christians to think about their religion without this concept, even if we have not always lived by it. The call of Jesus to forgiveness is a lifelong vocation—a way of life born of the gift of forgiveness that God has given us. The gift and the call to forgiveness grant us the promise and reality of change in our lives.

From a distance or up close, we have seen the forces—and faces—of unforgiveness. Chapter 3 retells a conversation with a Croatian government minister, who shamelessly shared with Fr. Drew Christiansen, SJ, and me the plans for an ethnic cleansing of Serbs from eastern Slavonia to northern Bosnia, which he expected would, in turn, trigger the ethnic cleansing of Catholics and Muslims from the Serb-controlled north. Although this scheme did not materialize, the broader campaign of ethnic cleansing was all too successful: the Catholic diocese of that region has been gutted, and the Muslim population has suffered as well. So many men, women, and children killed; so many houses burned; so many churches and mosques destroyed. So many families thrown off lands they had farmed for hundreds of years and from churches and mosques where they had prayed and celebrated their faith. Here was a straightforward rejection of co-existence, the kind of political posture that makes forgiveness seem far-fetched, if not impossible.

Yet the forces of forgiveness are with us too. Regrettably, they are often overlooked in the midst of, or after, brutal conflict. Two of my heroes from the Bosnian conflict are Cardinal Vinko Puljic of Sarajevo and Bishop Franjo Komarica of Banja Luka in northern Bosnia. Serbian soldiers prevented me from visiting Cardinal Puljic when I came to Sarajevo for the first time during the war. He was stopped at a checkpoint and did not arrive home in time to meet me. But nothing stopped him or Bishop Komarica from speaking out effectively on behalf of forgiveness and especially forbearance from revenge.

Forbearance from revenge is implied in the command of Jesus in Matthew's Gospel. It has become part of the definition of forgiveness adopted by the writers of this book. The other elements of forgiveness include truth telling as a first order of action, as well as empathy and the commitment to repair fractured human relationships. We have seen forbearance, truth, and empathy at work in some of the most miserable conflicts on earth, from Northern Ireland to South Africa. We have seen the genuinely strong power of forgiveness emerge from these conflicts.

I am pleased to note that in these pages, various religious and civil voices have been gathered together to argue for forgiveness as a core value, a realistic if unexpected strategy in the arena of international conflict and diplomacy. Among its contributions, *Forgiveness in International Politics* offers a realistic assessment of the role of religion in both nurturing peace and perpetuating conflicts. This historical ambiguity is constantly contentious, but this book helps us move beyond theoretical debates by examining case studies of explicitly religious initiatives on behalf of dialogue and reconciliation. The examples confirm my conviction that religion can be a force for peace, a distinct part of the solution to intergroup conflict. Although religion can be usurped or perverted by people who have no desire for peace, it can also change lives for the good.

I am grateful that the Woodstock Theological Center under its former director, Fr. James L. Connor, SJ, decided to start a dialogue about forgiveness among people who work on behalf of both governmental and non-governmental organizations. I am also pleased that Woodstock, under its new director, Fr. Gasper Lo Biondo, SJ, has decided to make this conversation available to the wider communities who might benefit. For years, the Woodstock Theological Center has facilitated dialogues on concerns such as business ethics, lobbying, and the impact of global markets on local cultures. These discussions have brought together people of good will across the full range of religious and civil perspectives. As a religiously oriented research and educational center with a global outlook, Woodstock is well positioned to help translate forgiveness into the idiom of international relations.

Admittedly, the notion of forgiveness is foreign to the way we normally think about security and world order. Especially now, it seems counterintuitive—as I write, the United States is struggling to bring order to postwar Iraq. On the eve of that military conflict, many of us gathered to pray at the Basilica of the National Shrine of the

Immaculate Conception in Washington, D.C. We prayed for a miracle, the miracle of peace, but it was not to be.

I would like to end my reflections with the words of Pope John Paul II, who has been one of the most visible witnesses to the need for civil, racial, and religious forgiveness on our global stage. The pope recognizes, as this book does, that peace is more than the absence of war:

> True peace therefore is the fruit of justice, that moral virtue and legal guarantee which ensures full respect for rights and responsibilities, and the just distribution of benefits and burdens. But because human justice is always fragile and imperfect, subject as it is to the limitations and egoism of individuals and groups, it must include and, as it were, be completed by the *forgiveness which heals and rebuilds troubled human relations from their foundations.*[1]

There is, indeed, as the pope has constantly reminded us, "No peace without justice, no justice without forgiveness."

NOTE

1   Pope John Paul II, 2002 World Day of Peace Message "No Peace Without Justice, No Justice Without Forgiveness" (January 1, 2002), no. 3, http://www.vatican.va (accessed in October 2003).

Forgiveness: A Radical New Factor

T he project that produced this book was nearing its final phase when word came of jets crashing into the Twin Towers in Lower Manhattan. The drafting of the book continued through the further anguish of suicide bombings in the Middle East, bloody clashes between Muslims and Christians in several African countries, a spreading war on terrorism, and new doctrines of defense highlighted by the U.S. invasion of Iraq. All of these developments might lend an air of implausibility to any discussion of forgiveness and international conflict resolution, which raises the question: Is it purely imaginary to think of a global strategy that deploys the concept of forgiveness in this time of harsh intergroup conflict?

Even apart from recent events, forgiveness is hardly a traditional value in world affairs. The concept is foreign to most secular political philosophies and peripheral at best to traditional Christian theories of the common good and a just war. Among twentieth-century philosophers, the German-Jewish refugee Hannah Arendt stands out, writing after the Holocaust that she saw forgiveness as one of two human capacities that make it possible to alter the political future. The other is the ability to enter into covenants.[1]

It is not that forgiveness has been a no-show in the wide world. It surfaced after the nightmare of apartheid in South Africa, when then-President Nelson Mandela awakened many to a reality expressed later in the title of Archbishop Desmond Tutu's book *No Future Without Forgiveness*. The magnanimous President Mandela became an effective symbol of forgiveness and reconciliation: he had spent twenty-seven years as a political prisoner, yet he made his white jailer an honored guest at his 1994 inauguration. Through the Truth and Reconciliation

Commission headed by Tutu, a Nobel Peace Prize laureate, South Africa formally abstained from revenge. Devised in the wake of elections that transferred power from a white minority regime to the black majority, the commission in effect gave notorious violators of human rights a choice: tell the whole truth, or face prosecution. The truth came out, with grisly detail about atrocities during the apartheid era, and many violators went free. The two elements—acknowledgment of crimes and conditional amnesty—helped to avert the racial bloodbath that many had predicted.

In Northern Ireland, many Catholics and Protestants have been able to imagine a different future through public acts of mutual repentance and forgiveness. In the Balkans, some voices of forgiveness have transcended obsessive nationalism and ethnocentrism, which drove the region to war on several fronts, and have helped to lay a distant path of co-existence and cooperation. In Cambodia, Buddhist Primate Moha Ghosananda has struggled to release people from a paralyzing past by envisioning a future of forgiveness. He has called for selectively forgiving Khmer Rouge leaders who have repented and renounced violence after perpetrating that nation's unspeakable genocide, but Cambodians need more time.[2]

As these and other conflicts illustrate, forgiveness is not necessarily a discrete transaction between two individuals. It is also a social process that blends elements such as forbearance from revenge and the will to eventually reconcile, according to a definition by social ethicist Donald W. Shriver Jr. Nevertheless, the reigning doctrines of statecraft make scant place for such sentiment. "Realist" theories normally scoff at the idea of fractious peoples' reaching beyond their group interests and horizons, which is the transcendent quality of social forgiveness. Realism seeks instead to negotiate these interests rationally or to strike directly with armed force or political-economic pressure.

One problem with pure "realism," however, is that it seems less than realistic as a strategy in many of today's clashes. Given the changing nature of conflict in the post–Cold War period, some of the most intractable conflicts are rooted not in political ideologies and palpable interests, but in ethnicity, religion, and other intangibles of communal identity. These clashes can be highly resistant to the standard remedies of realism. Often, it is hard to see how such strife can end without the introduction of a radical new factor like forgiveness.

Consider the hostilities in places like the Balkans and Rwanda. Deadly and vicious beyond all expectation, they brought on trauma and resentment that exceeded the capacity of any purely political initiative to resolve them. Since most of these antagonisms were social in nature, peace required more than the cessation of hostilities and crafting of political accords. It required social healing. In the meantime, however, the international community took an uncertain stance. The major powers were reluctant to engage in these conflicts and were determined to limit involvement once the engagement became unavoidable. This created a strategic opening for non-military, non-political agents, including non-governmental organizations (NGOs). Such settings allowed room to explore the healing role of forgiveness in traumatized societies.

One unforeseen effect of such strife, then, has been the emergence of conflict-resolution programs from the lagoons of academia into the mainstream of international diplomacy. Riding close behind this wave has been an upsurge of programs that feature forgiveness as a crucial factor in moving from hostility to reconciliation in divided, post-conflict societies. The Woodstock Theological Center's project "Forgiveness in Conflict Resolution: Reality and Utility" grew out of this new international context, at a time when there was also renewed interest in the role of religion in world affairs. Originating with a Woodstock forum that featured Shriver and his book *An Ethic for Enemies: Forgiveness in Politics*, the project also owes greatly to the pioneering work of Douglas Johnston, Cynthia Sampson, and their collaborators in the volume *Religion, the Missing Dimension of Statecraft*.[3]

To look at forgiveness in this framework is to look away from some conventional wisdom. For one thing, forgiveness in politics is never about forgetting, but about remembering in a certain way, as the South Africans chose to do in establishing a truth commission after apartheid. ("The past is never dead; it's not even past," William Faulkner wrote in his play *Requiem for a Nun*.) Forgiveness is not simply about personal piety, but about social cooperation. ("For to be social is to be forgiving," Robert Frost wrote in "The Star-Splitter."[4]) Forgiveness is not a denial of human responsibility; rather, it rests on the moral judgment that an act was wrong. Forgiveness is compatible with justice, never with vengeance. (Hannah Arendt also said, "Men cannot forgive what they cannot punish."[5])

Some theorists and practitioners have reintroduced forgiveness in this textured, political sense. In *An Ethic for Enemies*, Shriver defined "forgiveness" as "an act that joins moral truth, forbearance, empathy, and commitment to repair a fractured human relation."[6] Based on that definition (which will be examined in Chapter 3), Woodstock's "Forgiveness in Conflict Resolution" project set out to clarify the concept of forgiveness as used in conflict-resolution programs. It sought to illuminate the process of bringing antagonists to the verge of forgiveness, within the overall movement toward conflict resolution.

Though nearly universal, the concept of forgiveness carries different weight and finds varied expressions from one tradition to another. This diversity raises questions about how well forgiveness can travel across cultural boundaries. An enlarged concept of forgiveness, however, can accommodate and even facilitate these multiple expressions. It can help to organize the voices of forgiveness that have already risen in regional conflicts around the world. In this enlarged view, forgiveness is a process—a set of interrelated conditions and components, as suggested in Shriver's definition. Essentially, it is a process of relationship building that progresses toward (but may not represent) actual reconciliation.

Some may well object to making "forgiveness" a catchall term for this process. This is a legitimate reservation, but the reality is that the language of forgiveness is already part of a growing international conversation, despite the multiple forces of *unforgiveness* (a concept defined in Chapter 1). What often appears lacking in this conversation is a dynamic understanding of what forgiveness means in the sphere of social conflict. That is largely because forgiveness has typically entered the political realm with bulky baggage from the interpersonal realm. The emerging task is to put forgiveness squarely on a social plane—to give it "a new home," in Shriver's words.[7] The specific challenge is to join this discussion more closely to understandings of conflict prevention and resolution.

THE PROJECT AND THE PUBLICATION

This book is the culmination of seven years of dialogue about forgiveness in the midst of corrosive social conflict. The conversations began in the 1990s, when the Woodstock Theological Center sponsored an initial forum followed by series of colloquia that assembled distinguished scholars, religious leaders, government officials, diplomats, and practitioners in the field of conflict resolution. The Center published proceedings of the colloquia in four reports[8] that explored the utility of forgiveness in transforming conflict, with special attention to Northern Ireland and Bosnia as well as the experiences of various truth commissions. Afterward, the Center continued tracking the work of original participants and others in this fledgling field and reconstituted an informal working group to analyze themes and to review drafts of a final text. This volume is the fruit of those conversations; but it is also, in a sense, a conversation itself—a presentation of diverse voices from the communities in conflict as well as the professional arena of conflict resolution.

The eight chapters of *Forgiveness in International Politics* move from the contexts of conflict today to an understanding of societal forgiveness, through an examination of the central components of societal forgiveness and its various acts and agents:

- What are the forces of unforgiveness? How do distorted memories, for example, contribute to these unforgiving forces? (Chapter 1)

- Why is forgiveness emerging as a strategic consideration in today's international political context? (Chapter 2)

- What are the constitutive elements of forgiveness in the sociopolitical field? (Chapter 3)

- How are transactions of forgiveness conducted in politics, and what are the strengths and weaknesses of different potential agents of forgiveness? (Chapter 4)

- What role might truth commissions and facilitated small groups play in institutionalizing a forgiveness-based approach to transforming intergroup conflict? (Chapter 5)

- How can religious communities in the midst of conflict transcend ethnic divisions and help to build a "new home" for forgiveness in the political arena? (Chapter 6)

- How can faith-based non-governmental organizations (NGOs), acting as third parties, help to mine the peace-building assets of organized religion? (Chapter 7)

- What should peacebuilders and policy makers know about religion and culture as systems of meaning and interpretation? (Chapter 8)

Finally, in conclusion, how shall we summarize the lessons to be learned from practitioners who have worked with tools of forgiveness in conflict resolution? (An initial glance at highlighted lessons in the Conclusion may give readers a better grip on the discussion through-out the text.)

Underlying the analyses are this book's assumptions, or propositions, about how to understand forgiveness as a social and political reality. The book's most transparent assumption is that familiar notions of forgiveness as a personal virtue or therapeutic exercise do not easily translate to societal forgiveness. Such notions often entail an image of forgiveness as a single act or utterance, a one-time gesture that occurs usually between two people or in the heart of the forgiver. The conviction in these pages, however, is that forgiveness in politics is, above all, a process consisting of interrelated elements that might eventually contribute to reconciliation.

As commonly understood, forgiveness is something one can identify more or less by seeing it: one person says, "I'm sorry," and the other says, "You're forgiven." While that surely has happened in the political world, societal or political forgiveness is more usefully understood as a reality inversely related to the famous remark by U.S. Supreme Court Justice Potter Stewart, who defined "obscenity" in a 1964 case: "I know it when I see it." In a textured political understanding, we can define forgiveness as a compound of properties including truth and forbearance—but apart from that understanding, we do not always "know it when we see it." For example, without a Desmond Tutu to lend interpretation, the world might not clearly recognize a truth commission as part of the politics of forgiveness. If our idea of forgiveness extends no further than hearing somebody say, "You're forgiven," we will probably overlook many other instances of forgiveness in the international field. It is also helpful to keep in mind that even in the broader political understanding, a particular transaction of forgiveness—say, a public act of forbearance from revenge—does not in itself constitute forgiveness. It is one step in a process.

Perhaps the whole thrust of forgiveness is to move beyond narrow perceptions, interests, and desires, in a process aided by the search for truth as well as forbearance, empathy, and the commitment to repair relationships. Further, to be a genuinely political reality, the pursuit of forgiveness must also come with a collection of motivations that are essentially social values such as justice, human rights, social development, and cooperation or solidarity.

For the most part, these assumptions and propositions operate below the surface of the text. Overall, *Forgiveness in International Politics* aims primarily to glean lessons from and for the field of conflict resolution and peacebuilding. The intention is to advance this work by informing those who work on both the official and unofficial tracks of diplomacy and conflict resolution—that is, people in government as well as in the civil/societal realm of non-governmental organizations, including religious communities. We hope these experiences and reflections might make it possible to apply principles of forgiveness in settings where—without the introduction of this radical new factor—we can otherwise expect only stalemate and instability for years to come.

ACKNOWLEDGMENTS

We owe a debt of gratitude to all of those who participated in the Woodstock conversations on forgiveness and conflict resolution, including those who shared their experiences and expertise in interviews; many are quoted in this text. (They represented organizations that are listed, among others, in the Appendix on institutional resources.) But there are two people without whom this text and project would not have come into being: James L. Connor, SJ, the Woodstock Theological Center's immediate past director, who conceived of the project; and Donald W. Shriver Jr., who literally wrote the book on forgiveness in politics. In addition to initiating the conversation, Connor and Shriver provided critical guidance throughout the drafting process, as did Gerard F. Powers, John P. Langan, SJ, and Brandon Grove.

In addition, Woodstock received a generous grant from the United States Peace Institute that helped launch the formal dialogues on forgiveness and conflict resolution. The institute's executive vice president, Harriet Hentges, offered her time and thoughts at a crucial stage of drafting. Connor, Shriver, Powers, Langan, Grove, and Hentges attended meetings of an informal working group that evaluated drafts and advanced the discussion (referred to in several notes in the text as the "Forgiveness Working Group"). An earlier permutation of that group, which evaluated the forgiveness colloquia, also included Douglas Johnston and Alan Geyer. We are grateful to them, and we are grateful to, among others, Olga Botcharova, for her insights into the cycle of revenge and the road to healing and reconciliation. In addition, versions of several passages of this book appeared originally in *America* magazine, *Our Sunday Visitor*, and the *National Catholic Reporter*; we thank the editors of those publications.

We are especially grateful to the Office of International Justice and Peace of the United States Conference of Catholic Bishops (USCCB) for its close collaboration on this project from its inception, and to USCCB Publishing for offering to publish this book. Paul Henderson was quick to see the significance of publishing a work on forgiveness for a Church that is actively promoting peace and reconciliation around the world, and Jeanette M. Fast expertly and patiently shepherded it through the publication process.

At the Georgetown offices of Woodstock, Matthew Gladden conducted research for the Appendix, while helping to circulate drafts and arrange meetings. Elizabeth Kostelac helped to marshal the administrative resources of Woodstock, from the beginning of the project to the end. Visiting international fellow Cristina J. Montiel helped to distill and analyze material from the original colloquia. Special thanks also go to Adoreen McCormack, formerly of the Woodstock staff, who organized and was largely responsible for the reports on four colloquia addressing forgiveness in politics. The guidance and motivation provided by Gasper F. Lo Biondo, SJ, Woodstock's new director, by Woodstock fellow John Farina, and (again) by Powers played no small part in finally allowing this book to see the light of day. Finally, we thank the author of our Foreword, Cardinal Theodore E. McCarrick, who has carried a message of justice and reconciliation to the ends of the earth.

NOTES

1   Arendt cited in Donald W. Shriver Jr., *An Ethic for Enemies: Forgiveness in Politics* (New York, Oxford: Oxford University Press, 1995), 6.

2   Related in Marc Gopin, *Between Eden and Armageddon: The Future of World Religions, Violence, and Peacemaking* (New York, Oxford: Oxford University Press, 2000), 44-47; and in R. Scott Appleby, *The Ambivalence of the Sacred: Religion, Violence, and Reconciliation* (Lanham, MD: Rowman & Littlefield, 2000), 123-140.

3   Douglas Johnston and Cynthia Sampson, eds., *Religion, the Missing Dimension of Statecraft* (New York, Oxford: Oxford University Press, 1995).

4   Quoted by Shriver, in Woodstock Theological Center Forum "An Ethic for Enemies: Forgiveness in Politics" (November 15, 1995), *Woodstock Report* (March 1996), http://www.georgetown.edu/centers/woodstock/report/r-fea45.htm (accessed in October 2003).

5   Quoted in Appleby, *The Ambivalence of the Sacred*, 196.

6   Shriver, *An Ethic for Enemies*, 9.

7   Shriver, *Woodstock Report* (March 1996).

8   The reports from these four colloquia and all Woodstock publications cited in this book are available online at *www.georgetown.edu/centers/woodstock*.

CHAPTER 1

The Forces of Unforgiveness

Cycles of revenge, distorted memories, "victimhood," and
institutional breakdown are signs and symptoms of unforgiveness.
Yet in the post–Cold War era, these forces have propelled the
notion of forgiveness into the international conversation.

H uman beings have been settling scores for all of recorded
history. Yet while vengeance and retribution are ancient
themes in international affairs, since the dissolution of the
Cold War these and other unforgiving ways have found a new and
permissive environment. In this geopolitical atmosphere, the nature
of conflict itself has shifted. Scrimmages in the superpower struggle,
driven by the material interests of conventional politics and ideology,
have given way to conflicts entangled in the intangibles of culture,
identity, ethnicity, and religion. These new spirals of conflict, often
rooted in historic animosities, have helped to unleash some old forces
of unforgiveness.

For many in the Western world, the terrorist challenge has only
recently brought home the hard reality of identity-based violence. For
nearly a decade, however, practitioners exploring forgiveness as a
strategy have stressed the significance of this new order of antagonism. With the passing of East-West rivalry, most conflicts "will derive
from clashes of communal identity, whether on the basis of race, ethnicity, nationality, or religion," Douglas M. Johnston predicted in the
early 1990s. "Such disputes tend to occur at the fault lines between
rival nationalities or in situations where societies are suffering from
the strains of economic competition and rising expectations. These
are the most intractable sources of conflict, and they are the sources

with which conventional diplomacy is least suited to deal."[1] At the time, Johnston—a former nuclear submarine commander who now conducts faith-based conflict resolution—was writing against the backdrop of inter-ethnic hostilities, including the conflicts in the Balkans. Today, his observation applies just as freshly to extreme cultural-religious clashes that have given rise to violence and terror.

Clearly, other kinds of corrosive conflict can be found today, removed from fundamental issues of identity, as witnessed in the bloodshed surrounding the oil and diamond trades (notably in Africa). Still, it is often hard to separate these tangible interests from the less tangible issues of ethnic, tribal, religious, and cultural identity.

This chapter identifies voices of forgiveness, speaking to the forces of unforgiveness. These forces are arrayed here in four sections: cycles of revenge, dangerous memories, the exaggerated sense of victimhood, and the institutional abyss—all of which contribute to a culture of unforgiveness. As destructive as these forces continue to be, they also explain why forgiveness has entered the international political conversation.

CYCLES OF REVENGE

The "cycle of revenge" has become almost clichéd in the chronicles of international conflict; yet this evil is anything but banal (especially for those in its grip), and it calls for fresh consideration. To better conceptualize this vicious cycle, we can think of it as just one of the forces of unforgiveness—indeed, probably the most acute or visible mark of an unforgiving society. In this light, a direct opposite of revenge is forbearance, although other opposites include the willingness to co-exist.

Perhaps we could see the revenge cycle more clearly through the eyes of people in the throes of such conflict. Consider two voices from a struggle predating the post–Cold War era: the Northern Ireland conflict. At a June 1997 colloquium sponsored by the Woodstock Theological Center, retired Cardinal Cahal B. Daly, of the Archdiocese of Armagh, testified that "one of the most destructive forces in society is the spirit of vengeance. It creates a spiral of evil which can be broken only by repentance, followed by forgiveness."[2] The Rev. Douglas R. Baker of the ecumenical Corrymeela Community, which promotes reconciliation between Protestants and Catholics, added, "In Northern Ireland we know all too much about the power, the negative power of resentment and bitterness, and scorn and hatred. . . . And that has all led to a downward cycle of revenge, of tit for tat killings, all in the name of getting even, paying back, settling the score."[3]

The cycle of retribution leads fractious groups toward a radical rejection of the other in their midst. If forgiveness involves a commitment to achieving eventual social reconciliation, then vengeance can be taken as signaling the refusal to co-exist. Paul B. Mojzes, an expert on religion and ethnicity in Eastern Europe, offers one telling image of these ingrained animosities:

> Imagine that you give a magic wand to an Orthodox person in the former Yugoslavia and you tell that person, "How would you use it against the Catholics and the Muslims?" My guess is, if you gave the wand to a basically good person, they would use it simply to make the other two communities disappear. . . . This is, if they are well-intentioned. If they are not well-intentioned, they would accompany this act of disappearance with a degree of pain and torture.[4]

While clearly a broad generalization, Mojzes's point seems to throw light on other conflicts as well:

> I think there is a basic reluctance on the part of people of the Orthodox, Catholic, and Muslim traditions in the former Yugoslavia to have the others in their presence. They would really wish them away. I have seen statements in print where they say they wouldn't mind living among the Chinese or among people from Nigeria, but they do mind living among their Balkan neighbors. The problem is, they have to live right next to these people.[5]

The most frightful measure of this refusal by some to co-exist is the toll of dead and missing. After the worst of the Bosnian strife, William F. Vendley, secretary general of the New York–based World Conference of Religions for Peace (formerly the World Conference on Religion and Peace), reported the assessment that twenty thousand persons were still missing in Bosnia, many of them probably in mass graves. Extrapolating from figures released by international agencies, he estimated that every person there knew thirty-five missing people and that every family had "some connection to the missing."[6]

DANGEROUS MEMORIES

Donald W. Shriver Jr. recounts a television news interview with a Serbian soldier at the onset of war in the former Yugoslavia. The American television reporter asked the soldier, "Why are you fighting this war?" The soldier replied, "Because of what they did to us at Kosovo." Here Shriver interjects, "Battle of Kosovo, 1389."[7]

Dangerous or distorted memories help to fuel the cycle of revenge, especially in inter-ethnic struggles. Even the casual observer understands that memory is no small part of the problem in clashes like the one that tore through Bosnia and Herzegovina after the breakup of Communist Eastern Europe. When people say there is no way to resolve inter-ethnic conflicts with deep historical roots, they are testifying to the lethal power of collective memory. Undoubtedly, memories can be dangerous; a potent and often skewed sense of memory has fueled many of today's confrontations. This is *memory as a force of unforgiveness*. However, memory is a bipolar phenomenon; it can be deadly but also be crucial to reckoning constructively with past evils. This is *memory as a path to forgiveness*, which begins with truth and requires a sense of empathy that often results from an open accounting of the past.

Not surprisingly, people caught in the middle of ancient conflict are often acutely aware of how memory can take societies down the first road, the road of unforgiveness and revenge. During dialogues on forgiveness in recent years, representatives of communities in Northern Ireland have tended to stress this destructive side. In the view of Paul Arthur, a political scientist at the University of Ulster, a quote from Nobel laureate Czeslaw Milosz is highly applicable to the Irish conflict: "It is possible that there is no other memory than the memory of wounds."[8] Referring to the founding declaration of the provisional leaders of the Irish Republican Army, Arthur notes, "In the 1916 proclamation, they made the point very clearly that they were the vanguard of the Irish people, speaking with God's will for all the Irish people, and they said this was the seventh time since 1798 that the Irish people had revolted against oppression. This sense of memory, I think, has been one of our deadliest problems."[9]

Yet even in settings where memory is clearly lethal, few (upon reflection) would disregard the value of cultivating authentic memories. In other words, few would suggest that forgetting is generally the reliable road to long-lasting forgiveness and reconciliation. Baker, a Presbyterian who has ministered in both Northern Ireland and the United States, explains, "Forgiveness is not forgetting; it has more to do with how something is remembered. It's not remembered with bitterness."[10] The experiences of truth commissions lend powerful testimony to the extreme need for a certain construction of memory. This is particularly urgent in societies on the road to recovery from terrible atrocities and mass oppression.

Whether memory is one of our "deadliest problems" or the first step toward resolution of conflicts, one thing is certain: memory matters. It can hardly, without serious danger to social stability, be dismissed as "a preoccupation with ancient history."[11] That would miss the evidence for truth once written by William Faulkner in *Requiem for a Nun* (as quoted in the Introduction): "The past is never dead; it's not even past."[12] Memory matters the most in typical ethnic conflicts, such as when the Serbian soldier said on television that he was exacting revenge for the 1389 Battle of Kosovo.

"Mytho-History"

Some precision is required when speaking of the problem of memory in intergroup conflict. The problem is more specifically distorted memory, which is retrieved and recycled for use in the current confrontation.

Through such distortions, people in conflict cultivate a mythological past, or "mytho-history." This mytho-history, in turn, reinforces the distorted recollection of atrocities and an exaggerated sense of victimization. Often in such conflicts, each side accuses the other of falsifying history. Furthermore, according to Mojzes, each side tremendously exaggerates its losses. This tendency is hardly limited to actual combatants in civil warfare. In one of the Woodstock colloquia, Mojzes, who teaches religious studies at Rosemont College in Pennsylvania, told of a conference in Budapest in which a Serbian Orthodox theology professor reported that thousands of Serbian churches had been destroyed during war in Bosnia from 1992 to 1995: "I think the number is probably much closer to three hundred, which is still plenty of destroyed churches, but each side tends to just add another zero to figures and obviously that puts the other side immediately into a defensive position. Establishing the facts would be extremely helpful."[13]

In the process of making their mytho-history, victimized groups typically "forget" aspects of their own history that do not conform to images of victimization and might actually fit the profile of an aggressor. Thus, real memories are ignored. Daly has addressed this obstacle, urging Catholics of Northern Ireland to understand and take seriously the fears of their Protestant neighbors. The cardinal has referred to historical episodes largely forgotten by Catholic nationalists (who want to be part of the Republic of Ireland) but vividly remembered by Protestant unionists (who support British rule). Among those he cites are atrocities committed against Protestants during the 1641 rebellion, episodes almost completely forgotten by Irish Catholics.[14]

What is forgotten can be as consequential as what is remembered. So at the opposite pole of the problem of memory is historical amnesia or denial, especially by perpetrators and their groups. Two illustrations of this obstacle are the processes of reconciliation in Chile and South Africa. In Chile, amnesia was institutionalized with an amnesty law enacted by the regime of former dictator Augusto Pinochet—a law that allowed the regime, in effect, to forgive itself for the political crimes of the military junta in the 1970s. A truth commission set up in the post-Pinochet years documented many shocking abuses, including deaths and disappearances. However, in what was considered yet another indication of historical amnesia, the commission's final report in 1990 omitted crimes of torture (except in cases that led to death). In South Africa, in contrast, the stricter provisions of the Truth and Reconciliation Commission made it extremely difficult for the accused to achieve amnesty through amnesia. Still, efforts to uncover truth led to many expressions of denial by former members of the white minority regime. Though the two countries' efforts represent qualitatively different experiences of truth commissions, in both Chile and South Africa the lack of authentic memory presented a roadblock to healingand reconciliation.

Failure to grapple effectively with a group's memories can become a barrier to collective mourning and therefore to healing and peace. Rabbi Marc Gopin, a practitioner of international conflict resolution and a professor at Tufts University in Medford, Massachusetts, suggests that reconciliation in the Middle East will depend in part upon whether Arabs and Jews acknowledge each others' memories of loss in a mutual mourning process. Citing his own extended family as an example, Gopin noted that many Jews have never been able to or invited to mourn the destruction of European Jewry, which he believes accounts for an "obsess[ion] with Jewish survival" and Israeli security in particular: "with all the surface vitality and wealth of the Jewish community, I often feel that we are walking among the dead, haunted by loss."[15]

Gopin's point is all the more poignant when one considers that Jews have held the gravest memories of the past century. In remembering, they testify that "there can be no reconciliation without memory," as Richard Freiherr von Weizsacker, president of the former Federal Republic of Germany, explained to the people of his country in 1985.[16] That many Jews are unable to remember in a way that permits mourning is indicative of the complexities of social memory. Shriver summarizes:

> Pain can sear the human memory in two crippling ways: with forgetfulness of the past or imprisonment in it. The mind that

insulates the traumatic past from conscious memory plants a live bomb in the depths of the psyche—it takes no great grasp of psychiatry to know that. But the mind that fixes on pain risks getting trapped in it. Too horrible to remember, too horrible to forget: down either path lies little health for the human sufferers of great evil.[17]

Both individually and collectively, imagination factors into the process of distorted or discarded memories. "Often, what makes these conflicts unsolvable is that people are in the grip of imaginative pictures," notes John Langan, SJ, a moral and social philosopher at Georgetown University in Washington, D.C.[18] These "imaginative pictures" not only reflect a group's sense of social reality but also shape the reality and begin to form (or deform) identities—a factor that can become corrosive when fixed entirely on a history of hurts and grievances.

VICTIMHOOD

When we think of victimization, we point a finger at the oppressors, not the victims themselves—and rightly so. To do otherwise would be to "blame the victim." Yet what happens in the course of intergroup conflict when each side sees itself as the historically aggrieved party—when victims become perpetrators and perpetrators become victims in a cycle of retribution? Often, in such surroundings, we cannot help but point to victims as part of the problem, as potential agents of unforgiveness themselves.

Put more precisely, what begins to take shape is an identity of victimization, or victimhood. The self-understanding of victims can easily merge into a collective conceit that leads one group to progressively disregard the welfare, even the humanity, of the other. Arthur calls this "the egoism of victimization, a society without empathy. . . . the subjective and elusive barriers to peace in Northern Ireland."[19]

The Northern Ireland struggle has, in fact, been one of the longer-running theaters of victimhood in the Western world, as dramatized by the hunger strikes. Arthur observes, "It is not surprising that the people of Northern Ireland suffered from a political economy of helplessness, a victim-based society in which memories of past injustice and humiliation are so firmly entrenched in both communities and the sense of entrapment so complete that the hunger strikes are a metaphor for the entrapment of the larger society."[20] In addition to venting these feelings of helplessness, the Catholic hunger strikes also sanctioned implicitly the mindset of victimhood and the violent struggle. This, in turn, perpetuated the cycle of victimization that drove violence by Protestants and unionists.

Feelings of victimhood are inflated when, as in Northern Ireland, both communities have strong claims to victimization. Victimhood becomes a primary form of identity, and one thing that enemies have in common. In various ways, the two sides begin to seek the maximization of victimhood. Consider further the process of victimization in Northern Ireland, as articulated by Anthony Cary of the British Embassy in Washington, D.C.: "I think the great difficulty now is that there are those in both communities who, far from seeking forgiveness, are actively nurturing grievance and seeking not reconciliation, but maximum victimhood. . . . there's a tremendous self-righteousness about that."[21]

On the individual level, victimhood develops differently according to circumstances. However, psychologist and conflict-resolution trainer Olga Botcharova has pinpointed some common tendencies that illustrate the vengeance cycle that erupts with an act of aggression. Her "stages of victimhood development" should be required reading for those seeking to understand the sources of perpetual violence. The following seven points offer a condensation of those stages, from injury to aggression.

1. INJURY, PAIN, SHOCK, DENIAL. The pain triggered by an abuse often comes with shock, which "separates us from reality, makes us unable to experience the loss, to think or to act."[22] The first reaction after shock is denial.

2. REALIZATION OF LOSS. Recognition happens gradually, with denial continuing between moments of realization.

3. SUPPRESSION OF GRIEF AND FEARS. One is afraid to unleash one's emotions, but these suppressed feelings eventually rise to the surface in predictable ways, such as nightmares, fatigue, phobias, and psychosomatic disorders.

4. ANGER; WHY ME? "The sad truth is, we will never find an answer to this tormenting question: nobody deserves to be a victim, to be humiliated or treated unfairly."[23] More pain must be let go from the suppressed anger, which is projected onto a real or imaginary perpetrator. One hates not only the individual perpetrator but also "everybody and everything associated with him or her . . . family, community, religious group, etc."[24]

5. DESIRE FOR JUSTICE AND/OR REVENGE. Punishing the perpetrator becomes the way to deal with grief and loss. This desire, however, is rarely satisfied, for two reasons. First, even the most severe justice does not compensate a victim for the suffering brought on by the loss of a family member or the destruction of an entire community. Second, the structures of legal justice are often lacking in these contexts of conflict. In other words, the suffering of the victim goes unrecognized, which increases the desire for revenge.

6. CREATION OF MYTHS OR HEROES; THE "RIGHT" CONFLICT HISTORY. Often, the victim pauses to create myths that reinforce his or her "rightness"—and sets in place the justification for retaliatory aggression: "Thinking of a violent action of revenge, the victim attempts at the same time to preserve his [or her] image as a sufferer by all means—the task is very complicated and hardly realistic."[25]

7. ACT OF "JUSTIFIED" AGGRESSION. This act completes the retribution cycle, "with the roles reversed: the former aggressor

screams in pain and appeals for justice, the former innocent victim celebrates the victory. The conflict becomes more and more complicated with every turn of the vicious spiral."[26] From this point on, victim and aggressor repeatedly change roles, thoroughly mixing the identities of the two: "Both sides are tremendously victimized by each other, and, in fact, leave no other possibility for the outsiders to stop the conflict but by force— by introducing more violence. The history of the Balkans is a classic example of this."[27]

Having worked closely with people traumatized by war in the Balkans, Botcharova has concluded that these dynamics are not exceptional but rather are typical reactions to an act of violence. She describes this as a kind of survival mechanism, which operates also at the group level, though in a more complicated way: "Unfortunately, it is a dominating tendency in the development of contemporary ethnic conflict among nations, communities, and tribes."[28]

THE INSTITUTIONAL ABYSS

As the seven-year United Nations peacekeeping efforts in Bosnia and Herzegovina wound down at the end of 2002, one top official looked back at the international engagement and saw the first inklings of an emerging global doctrine. Paddy Ashdown, high representative for the international community there, predicted in October 2002 that Bosnia would be seen as a "new model of international intervention— one designed not to pursue narrow national interests but to prevent conflict, to promote human rights and to rebuild war-torn societies."[29] Among the successes of that intervention, he counted the return of refugees, the establishment of a professional police service, and the fact that the peace was kept.

However, Ashdown also acknowledged mistakes that bring to light the broader conditions of political forgiveness, which can be easily overlooked in the course of conflict resolution. The international community believed that democracy was the highest priority, and it measured democracy in the number of elections organized. Yet Ashdown commented, "In hindsight, we should have put the establishment of the rule of law first. For everything else depends on it: a functioning economy, a free and fair political system, the development of civil society, public confidence in police and the courts." He added, "We would do well to reflect on this as we formulate our plans for Afghanistan and, perhaps, Iraq."[30]

In a word, Ashdown was speaking of institutions. The forces of unforgiveness thrive in an institutional vacuum, that is, in the absence of political, juridical, economic, civic, and other social structures. These structures and institutions are essential to managing conflict, facilitating dialogue, and generally nurturing the conditions of social peace. The next several pages look into the institutional abyss by discussing (1) the rule of law, (2) civil society, and (3) other institutions, including those at the global level, that are often barely functional in post-conflict societies.

Rule of Law

Ashdown's comment highlighted the rule of law, which is not a new insight in the field of conflict resolution. Two years before the international community began its engagement in Bosnia and Herzegovina, the United States Institute of Peace launched its Rule of Law initiative, based on the premise that the rule of law demands "far more than mechanical application of static technicalities; it requires an evolutionary search for those institutions and processes that will best bring about authentic stability through justice."[31] (See Appendix, under heading "United States Institute of Peace, Rule of Law Program.")

Often, these "institutions and processes" aren't entirely lacking in societies that have fallen into extreme conflict; but they have been corroded, corrupted, or commandeered in one way or another. Although some have spoken loosely of the "anarchy" that supposedly characterized pre-genocide Rwanda, even in that country the state and social institutions did function, albeit in an atmosphere of deep suspicion and age-old tribal hatred. In Burundi as well as Rwanda, the organizational social structures were present—state, police, army, and so on—but they were either subverted or paralyzed by profound tribal hostility. In Rwanda, the Hutus who planned or joined in the genocide had taken control of the institutions.

In the case of Chile, a period of intense and brutal repression amounted to an interruption of the rule of law, a breakdown of political and juridical institutions. One telling illustration of this breakdown can be gleaned from statistics published by the commission that later investigated abuses by the Pinochet regime. Juan Laval, of the Central Bank of Chile, notes,

> In 1974, for example, you can see that the Socialist party board was killed person by person. In 1975, you can see how the Communist party suffered the same fate, and that went on and on. At the beginning, perhaps, you could say the military junta lost control of the whole process, but after that, you can clearly see a policy designed by the state to exterminate its adversaries.[32]

The number of those exterminated adversaries ran into the thousands. They represented institutions—independent sources of power—that might have otherwise served as social and political countervailing forces.

Institutional failure creates the need for transitional forms of justice in post-conflict societies. Important among these have been truth commissions, which arise in the absence of judicial and political structures that can channel vengeance into justice. Even more profoundly, the need for such a body betrays a failure to agree on elemental truths: observable facts about a conflict. Such agreement is usually crucial to eventual reconciliation, and it relies heavily on institutions, such as impartial courts and independent mass media, to help create a common picture of reality. An inability or unwillingness to reach agreement on truth tends to solidify stalemates through the perpetuation of mytho-history.

Civil Society

The absence of strong central governments is a clear cause of instability or even international terrorism, as seen in the disarray of Afghanistan before September 11, 2001, or in the international crisis caused by Somali warlords. In the work of conflict resolution, many practitioners have focused on another crucial yet missing element: what sociologists call "social capital," or what Vendley has referred to as "social assets": "traditions, customs, and institutions, including assemblies of religious believers, schools, organs of communication, specialized societies within each of the communities."[33] Through the World Conference of Religions for Peace, Vendley conducted reconciliation efforts in Bosnia and found that these assets reached into every town and village there. The existence of social assets gives communities (he was speaking especially of religious communities) an ability to be creative in solving problems. However, in Bosnia-Herzegovina,

> as in many other parts of the world, cataloging these assets in terms of their potential for forgiveness brought us face-to-face with how damaged the institutions are. It is not simply that these assets are not imagined in relevance to a new challenge, but that in fact there are profound legacies that at the present time compromise their free use. Clearly, in Bosnia there's a legacy of previously unrequited suffering—suffering that has not been managed under a rubric of forgiveness.[34]

For one source of institutional decay in the Balkans, Vendley points to a "history of enfeeblement" paralleling fifty years of state socialism. In private conversations with him, leaders of religious communities acknowledged that their communities had been "enfeebled. They have a weak sense of spirituality. They were systematically undercut; they were, to use a slogan, 'sitting ducks,' to be picked up and manipulated in the vacuum of the [dissolution] of Yugoslavia itself."[35]

Consequently, in Bosnia, civil society institutions had been reduced and undermined before the eruption of ethnic hostilities. The post–Cold War cycle of vengeance made communities even less likely to "reach for the language of forgiveness" and muster their social assets for the sake of reconciliation.[36]

Vendley's account suggests also that institutions can be not only corroded by brute repression but also corrupted by extreme social polarization. Some have pointed to religious institutions that run the risk of being co-opted in places where religion and nationality are inextricably tied. An example frequently cited by Vendley is Bosnia, where, in many minds, being a Serb is synonymous with being Orthodox, and being a Croat is synonymous with being Catholic. This close identification of religion and ethnicity "allowed a co-option of religious symbols by a national program," Vendley recalls. "Consequently, there has been an extreme nationalization of religious symbols and a consequent loss of credibility. . . . [In that sense] religion was implicated in the conflict."[37]

Global Institutions and Human Needs

The forces of unforgiveness multiply in the absence of institutions that can promote human rights, development, solidarity, and world order. Drew Christiansen, SJ, has enumerated these four elements of a positive conception of peace, which is more than simply the absence of war or even the avoidance of war. Human rights, development, solidarity, and world order are clearly wanting in many strife-torn countries, and the causes go beyond those countries and their institutional voids.[38]

Internationally, structures and institutions may be weak or lacking. Such an institutional deficit will hobble efforts to defend human rights or promote other elements of social peace, including equitable development. The struggles to create an international criminal court are perhaps one illustration; another might be found in complaints about global financial institutions and their imbalanced representation.

At all levels, when institutions fail, it becomes harder to provide for human needs, which must be minimally satisfied in order to ensure social peace. Existential psychologist Abraham Maslow's hierarchy of needs includes basic needs for physical survival as well as relational or social needs for connectedness and group identity. The frustration of these needs, often for lack of an adequate social infrastructure, may be essential to "understanding the genesis of political conflict in general and of ethnic and sectarian conflict and violence in particular," according to Joseph V. Montville, of the Center for Strategic and International Studies in Washington, D.C.[39]

CULTURE AND THE "HOTHEAD FACTOR"

Cycles of revenge, distorted memories, victimhood, and institutional breakdown—these forces, especially when acting together, will bring about the emergence of a culture of unforgiveness. As seen all too frequently, this culture can take hold even when there are competing forces of forgiveness, of dialogue and reconciliation. In this connection, clinical psychologist Everett L. Worthington Jr.'s description of the "hothead factor" is useful. In short, society will always include "hotheads" who "aim to keep people apart by violent and hateful acts. Of course, there are also cool heads and passionate promoters of peace."[40]

But which prevails: the hothead or cooler-head factor? In suggesting the social obstacles, Worthington extrapolated from research in developmental psychology focusing on marital tensions. For example, studies have found that it takes five or six "positive events" to compensate for a single negative event; in troubled marriages, the ratio must be ten to one or higher to reverse the tide of the negative.[41] The psychological research brings into sobering view the elaborate social resources needed in order to counter the culture of unforgiveness.

An atmosphere of polarization can reach such depths that people may no longer speak a common language—in something more than a metaphorical sense. Conflicting atmospheres often eliminate the vocabulary of civil relations, namely, the first-person plural. "Sometimes, when societies are very badly fractured, the ability to say 'we' pretty much vanishes . . . [and] that leads to secession or to the breakup of a society," observes Langan of Georgetown University. "That is, I think, a very important part of what went wrong in the Yugoslav case. It may be that the difficulty of achieving a stable sense of 'we' is one of the most baffling and perplexing aspects of the conflict in Northern Ireland, where there are temptations to say 'we' to different configurations, depending on history, ethnicity, economy, and culture."[42]

The need for an atmosphere of forgiveness is not confined to the world's trouble spots. In the United States, a growing number of observers see the importance of what Christiansen calls a "public philosophy of forgiveness," which is needed to foster in turn the social conditions of forgiveness and reconciliation. For example, Christiansen points to the "culture wars," which have revealed the sight of a less forgiving America. He also points to the political culture of blame and recrimination, which leads to a hardness of heart and injects vengefulness into the search for justice, especially criminal justice: "A society driven by those qualities is heading towards its own dissolution, because it has ceased to have the kind of moral balance and center which understands the equilibrium between justice and forgiveness."[43]

These advocates of forgiveness could easily sound like voices in the geopolitical wilderness, seemingly distant and isolated when weighed against the multiple forces of unforgiveness. Cycles of revenge and other unforgiving ways might serve as grounds for dismissing the possibilities of forgiveness in the realm of international conflict transformation. Yet these very conditions have drawn the notion of forgiveness—with its components of truth, forbearance, empathy, and the will to reconcile—into the post–Cold War conversation.

NOTES

1   Douglas Johnston, "Introduction: Beyond Power Politics," in *Religion, the Missing Dimension of Statecraft*, ed. Douglas Johnston and Cynthia Sampson (New York, Oxford: Oxford University Press, 1995), 3.

2   Cardinal Cahal B. Daly, in Woodstock Colloquium *Forgiveness in Conflict Resolution: Reality and Utility—The Northern Ireland Experience* (June 18, 1997) (Washington, DC: Woodstock Theological Center, n.d.), 8.

3   Rev. Douglas R. Baker, in Woodstock Colloquium *Forgiveness in Conflict Resolution: Reality and Utility—The Northern Ireland Experience*, 48.

4   Paul B. Mojzes, in Woodstock Colloquium *Forgiveness in Conflict Resolution: Reality and Utility—The Bosnian Experience* (October 24, 1997) (Washington, DC: Woodstock Theological Center, n.d.), 22.

5   Mojzes, in Woodstock Colloquium *Forgiveness in Conflict Resolution: Reality and Utility—The Bosnian Experience*, 22.

6   William F. Vendley, in Woodstock Colloquium *Forgiveness in Conflict Resolution: Reality and Utility—The Bosnian Experience*, 15.

7   Donald W. Shriver Jr., in Woodstock Theological Center Forum "An Ethic for Enemies: Forgiveness in Politics" (November 15, 1995), *Woodstock Report* (March 1996), http://www.georgetown.edu/centers/woodstock/report/r-fea45.htm (accessed in October 2003).

8   Paul Arthur, Woodstock Colloquium *Forgiveness in Conflict Resolution: Reality and Utility—The Northern Ireland Experience*, 19.

9   Arthur, in Woodstock Colloquium *Forgiveness in Conflict Resolution: Reality and Utility—The Northern Ireland Experience*, 19.

10 Baker, in Woodstock Colloquium *Forgiveness in Conflict Resolution: Reality and Utility—The Northern Ireland Experience*, 66.

11 Shriver, *An Ethic for Enemies: Forgiveness in Politics* (New York, Oxford: Oxford University Press, 1995), 4.

12 Cited in Shriver, *An Ethic for Enemies*, 4.

13 Mojzes, in Woodstock Colloquium *Forgiveness in Conflict Resolution: Reality and Utility—The Bosnian Experience*, 52.

14 Daly, in Woodstock Colloquium *Forgiveness in Conflict Resolution: Reality and Utility—The Northern Ireland Experience*, 11.

15 Marc Gopin, *Between Eden and Armageddon: The Future of World Religions, Violence, and Peacemaking* (New York, Oxford: Oxford University Press, 2000), 173; cf. 171-174.

16 Quoted in Shriver, *An Ethic for Enemies*, 110; cf. 108-112.

17 Shriver, *An Ethic for Enemies*, 119.

18 John Langan's comment during meeting of working group (May 2002) held as part of the Woodstock Theological Center's project "Forgiveness and Conflict Resolution: Reality and Utility."

19 Arthur, in Woodstock Colloquium *Forgiveness in Conflict Resolution: Reality and Utility—The Northern Ireland Experience*, 23.

20 Arthur, in Woodstock Colloquium *Forgiveness in Conflict Resolution: Reality and Utility—The Northern Ireland Experience*, 22.

21 Cary, in Woodstock Colloquium *Forgiveness in Conflict Resolution: Reality and Utility—The Northern Ireland Experience*, 27-28.

22 Olga Botcharova, in Woodstock Colloquium *Forgiveness in Conflict Resolution: Reality and Utility* (December 9, 1996) (Washington, DC: Woodstock Theological Center, n.d.), 39.

23 Botcharova, in Woodstock Colloquium *Forgiveness in Conflict Resolution: Reality and Utility*, 40.

24 Botcharova, in Woodstock Colloquium *Forgiveness in Conflict Resolution: Reality and Utility*, 40.

25 Botcharova, in Woodstock Colloquium *Forgiveness in Conflict Resolution: Reality and Utility*, 41.

26 Botcharova, in Woodstock Colloquium *Forgiveness in Conflict Resolution: Reality and Utility*, 41-42.

27 Botcharova, in Woodstock Colloquium *Forgiveness in Conflict Resolution: Reality and Utility*, 42.

28 Botcharova, in Woodstock Colloquium *Forgiveness in Conflict Resolution: Reality and Utility*, 42; cf. 39-43.

29 Paddy Ashdown, "What I Learned in Bosnia," *New York Times*, October 28, 2002: opinion page.

30   Ashdown, "What I Learned in Bosnia."

31   United States Institute of Peace, "Rule of Law," http://www.usip.org/rol/rol.html (accessed in January 2004).

32   Juan Laval, in Woodstock Colloquium *Forgiveness in Conflict Resolution: Reality and Utility—The Experiences of the Truth Commissions* (March 11, 1998) (Washington, DC: Woodstock Theological Center, n.d.), 68.

33   Vendley, in Woodstock Colloquium *Forgiveness in Conflict Resolution: Reality and Utility—The Bosnian Experience*, 7.

34   Vendley, in Woodstock Colloquium *Forgiveness in Conflict Resolution: Reality and Utility—The Bosnian Experience*, 8-9.

35   Vendley, in Woodstock Colloquium *Forgiveness in Conflict Resolution: Reality and Utility—The Bosnian Experience*, 9.

36   Cf. Vendley, in Woodstock Colloquium *Forgiveness in Conflict Resolution: Reality and Utility—The Bosnian Experience*, 7-9.

37   Vendley, in Woodstock Colloquium *Forgiveness in Conflict Resolution: Reality and Utility—The Bosnian Experience*, 10.

38   Drew Christiansen, SJ, "Catholic Peacemaking: From *Pacem in terris* to *Centesimus annus*" (presentation, United States Institute of Peace, February 5, 2001).

39   Joseph V. Montville, "Justice and the Burdens of History," in *Reconciliation, Justice, and Coexistence: Theory and Practice*, ed. Mohammed Abu-Nimer (Lanham, MD: Lexington Books, 2001), 115-128.

40   E. L. Worthington Jr., "Unforgiveness, Forgiveness, and Reconciliation in Societies," in *Forgiveness and Reconciliation: Religion, Public Policy, and Conflict Transformation*, ed. Raymond G. Helmick and Rodney L. Petersen (Philadelphia: The Templeton Foundation Press, 2001), 188.

41   Worthington, "Unforgiveness, Forgiveness, and Reconciliation in Societies," 188.

42   Langan, in Woodstock Colloquium *Forgiveness in Conflict Resolution: Reality and Utility—The Experiences of the Truth Commissions*, 97.

43   Christiansen, "Some Preliminary Theological Reflections on Forgiveness in Politics" (unpublished essay, December 2000).

CHAPTER 2

Why Forgiveness?

Shifting global realities are leading some theorists and practitioners of conflict resolution to speak of forgiveness as a strategic international value.

T hose who see forgiveness as a potential instrument of conflict resolution are acting not solely on moral, ethical, or religious convictions. While these concerns are central, so are strategic considerations and political circumstances. Indeed, this new attention to the dynamics of political forgiveness has far less to do with moralism (in the "holier-than-thou" sense) than with a gathering sense of global realism. In these quarters, the case for the utility of forgiveness rests primarily on a reading of geopolitical realities today and the experiences of many who have grappled with those realities on the front lines of peacebuilding and conflict transformation. Among them are counselors and small-group facilitators who have worked with victims in need of healing and reconciliation.

"A society . . . heading towards its own dissolution"—as articulated by Drew Christiansen, SJ—is one way to express the urgency of a strategic ethic of forgiveness. The same sentiment is communicated emphatically in the very title of Anglican Archbishop Desmond Tutu's book *No Future Without Forgiveness*, which underscores the pragmatic dimension of forgiveness. In this chapter, we glance at the "why" of forgiveness through four separate windows: (a) the reconciliation process in South Africa, (b) the rise of identity-based conflict, (c) the forces of globalization, and (d) interpersonal healing.

A FUTURE IN SOUTH AFRICA

To understand why Tutu sees forgiveness as considerably more than a dreamy notion, one must look at the South Africa experience through the lens of that country's Truth and Reconciliation Commission, which he chaired.

Much of the apartheid past came to full light as a result of the truth commission, appointed in 1995 by prisoner-turned-President Nelson Mandela. The commission served as a way to reveal the evils of the old order, the system of racial subjugation, without salting the wounds with an onslaught of political trials (though the process did include a few high-profile prosecutions). It offered amnesty to those responsible for atrocities during the long nightmare of white-minority rule. But to be cleared, perpetrators had to come forward, apply for amnesty—and confess all. Many did, in the grisliest detail. In one testimony, an officer of the Security Police, the ferocious arm of the former white-supremacist government, told of a young black anti-apartheid activist who was drugged, shot in the top of the head, doused with gasoline, and burned all through the night: "The chunks of meat, especially the buttocks and the upper parts of the legs, had to be turned frequently during the night to make sure everything burnt to ashes," so there would be no body to discover, the officer testified. He added— even more sickeningly—"Whilst that happened, we were drinking and even having a braai [barbecue] next to the fire."[1]

To this exegesis of evil, Tutu adds two levels of moral reflection. The first is visceral, the second hopeful:

> [First] you are devastated by the fact that it could be possible at all for human beings to shoot and kill a fellow human being, burn his body on a pyre, and while this cremation is going on actually enjoy a barbecue on the side. What had happened to their humanity that they could do this? How were they literally able to stomach it? Burning human flesh has an odor which is stomach-turning for most normal

people. Is it that they had to split themselves into two personalities to be able to go on living? How was it possible for them to return from such an outing to their homes, embrace their wives, and enjoy, say, their child's birthday party?[2]

This very brutality, however, leads eventually to a more hopeful set of questions, turning on the fact that there was no bloodbath in the twilight of apartheid rule in South Africa, contrary to much forewarning. After the 1994 elections that ushered Mandela and the African National Congress to power, blacks, for the most part, did not do unto whites as whites had done unto them during the apartheid era. How did so many people, who by rights might have been spitting with revenge, choose to look away from vengeance, or even to forgive their oppressors? What encouraged some of the perpetrators, whites as well as blacks who perpetrated terrorist acts, to plead for forgiveness from victims and families? Could other people at each other's throats, from Northern Ireland to the Middle East, follow the example of so many South Africans?

The officer who gave the account of the barbecue/cremation had applied for amnesty and presumably received it. In a strictly legal sense, the truth set him free. He was repentant, but he didn't have to be, in order to parry prosecution. The essential requisite was full disclosure of crimes, including where the bodies were buried. With that, victims and families lost the right even to make a civil claim against their violators. This forgiving arrangement raised some international eyebrows. Explaining it in his book, Tutu points in part to political circumstances: no negotiated settlement, no peaceful transition to multiracial democracy, would have been possible if black leaders had insisted on bringing white abusers to trial. They could only have had justice, and a South Africa "lying in ashes—a truly Pyrrhic victory if there ever was one."[3]

In that respect, there really was no future without forgiveness, or at least a fair measure of forgiveness, in South Africa.

NEW DYNAMICS OF CONFLICT

Another approach to the question "Why forgiveness?" is suggested by the altered states of conflict in the post-superpower age. The ascendance of identity-based antagonism calls for new responses, unlike those of the Cold War period. Referring to the various forms of negotiation and other strategies, Douglas Johnston, formerly of the Center for Strategic and International Studies (CSIS), writes,

> These measures are normally quite suitable for dealing with conflicts that relate to power politics and tangible material interests. Such interests are inherently divisible and thus subject to compromise. Non-material "identity-based" conflicts, on the other hand, are often not well understood by practical-minded diplomats accustomed to operating in the old East-West context of nation-state politics. What is required is not a shrewd understanding of the interests of both sides, but rather an understanding of the emotional stakes of the parties, which are often deeply rooted in history, and their respective interpretations of first principles such as self-determination, justice, and freedom.[4]

What are some implications here for strategies aimed at resolving conflicts in regions such as the Balkans? One general proposition is that the non-material dimension, which includes forgiveness, might be unavoidable when attacking the root causes of intractable conflict. That lesson was learned as well as taught by Johnston and his team at the CSIS in their efforts toward reconciliation in Bosnia. "When we undertook this work, we walked in with eyes open. We had no notion that what we were going to do would in any way affect the then-existing hostilities. Our goal was to plant the seeds for long-term reconciliation,"[5] recalls Johnston, who has since launched a new organization, the International Center on Religion and Diplomacy in Washington, D.C. "Certainly no diplomatic or military solution will ever break the cycle of revenge. Unless one can introduce a spiritual component that gets to the business of forgiveness and reconciliation, the same drumbeat is likely to repeat itself for the next three centuries."[6]

GLOBALIZATION'S CHALLENGE

Globalization, in its cultural, political, and economic forms, points to other urgencies of forgiveness and reconciliation. There is debate over whether globalization as such is fomenting intergroup conflict, a topic that is contentious as well as amorphous. Nevertheless, it is fair to say that globalization represents the spread of liberal modernity, essentially everywhere. And to many in the field of conflict transformation, it has become clear that these forces are introducing values that challenge the identity of local cultures. Cultures are undoubtedly more porous than might be suggested by the pervasive talk of a "clash of civilizations." Still, it is true that human beings and social groups have a basic need for uniqueness, not just integration.[7] Failure to satisfy unique identity needs can lead to instability, especially when mixed with other sources of social and economic disruption.

To choose one example of volatility, Rabbi Marc Gopin has argued that religious militancy has re-emerged as a "direct response to this assault on uniqueness,"[8] to the resolute march of global materialist trends. These prototypical conflicts may defy conventional diplomacy and call for a deeper process of forgiveness and reconciliation.

Such concerns throw light again on human-needs theory, introduced in the context of institutions in Chapter 1. Joseph V. Montville, who directs the Preventive Diplomacy Program of the Center for Strategic and International Studies, cites one finding that basic physical needs are well secured by no more than 10 or 20 percent of the world's population, and that this places enormous violence-inducing stress on many societies.[9]

Montville himself has focused primarily on identity and esteem needs, which, together with the lack of basic material things, fuel a sense of powerlessness. Esteem needs are intertwined with collective memories because, for many nations and peoples, "traumatic loss dominates their memory of history." Such memories help to engender the psychology of victimhood, which puts people on constant guard against aggression and makes them "strongly resistant to pressures to make peace *before the aggressors acknowledge the victims' losses and ask forgiveness for their violence*" (emphasis added).[10]

PERSONAL HEALING AND RECONCILIATION

Still another way to assess the "why" of forgiveness is through the prism of long-range healing. The clinical research tracked by Everett L. Worthington Jr. led to his observation that "people do not like to feel unforgiveness. While the anger and the revenge motive can energize and empower them, generally people try to reduce or eliminate unforgiveness as quickly as they can."[11] They seek to do so in many active and passive ways, from forgiving to forgetting, as well as through the often elusive search for justice and recompense. From a cold clinical perspective, Worthington also argues that acts of retaliation and revenge can reduce one's feelings of unforgiveness by balancing the scales of (primitive) justice. But as he acknowledges, the recipients of retaliation seldom see any justice in their own comeuppance. And so goes the cycle of vengeance.[12]

Other psychological experts have rejected the suggestion that feelings of unforgiveness can be relieved by the catharsis of retaliation. Conflict-resolution trainer Olga Botcharova, for example, describes what happens when the former victim carries out an act of aggression: "After the moment of triumph he suddenly realizes that though justice is preformed, the pain is still there, the fears of how to cope with loss are not gone, and the anger continues to burn him from inside. Disappointment and feelings of emptiness often come after an immediate relief; life seems even more senseless after the goal is achieved and the enemy is destroyed."[13]

Cathartic effects of revenge aside, there is little doubt that feelings of unforgiveness can impose an unbearable burden on the individual, albeit a burden that might go unrecognized. As one way of inducing dialogue, the CSIS team has made a practice of showing people in workshop settings how they are trapped by their unforgiveness.[14] For many, this revelation becomes the first step toward healing. From the troubles of Northern Ireland have come many such examples. Maura Kelly, for one, lost her only son, Jarrod, who was shot while walking out of Mass in a random sectarian attack nearly a quarter-century ago. She came to realize after severe anguish that, as related by the Rev. Douglas Baker, the "bitterness welling up inside her was destroying her relationships with everyone, including her own family, until she got to a point where either she got rid of it or she destroyed her life. And she found the power to do that."[15] She forgave those who shot Jarrod.

In re-telling that story at a forgiveness colloquium, Baker, of Northern Ireland's ecumenical Corrymeela Community, also pointed to how forgiveness might make it possible for a perpetrator to move on, to be free of his or her exclusive identity as an aggressor. To that end, Baker quoted Hannah Arendt's insight: "Without being forgiven, released from the consequences of what we have done, our capacity to act, would, as it were, be confined to one single deed from which we could never recover."[16] In that light, forgiveness can rob an atrocity of its perpetual power to affect the psychology of human relations and corrode bonds of humanity. It is in this context that Baker cited Arendt's critical insight that forgiveness makes genuine social change possible.

TOWARD A SOCIAL DEFINITION

Specifically, as related in the Introduction, Arendt sees forgiveness as one of two human capacities that allow real social change. The second is the ability to make new promises or covenants. Donald W. Shriver Jr. suggests that the connection between these two conditions of genuine change is inseparable, though few modern liberal-democratic thinkers have noticed it. In the history of political philosophy, few theorists have adequately explained why enemies may not exercise the capacity to enter into agreements. "Hardly any has supposed that one of the reasons is a politics-paralyzing refusal of forgiveness," Shriver observes in *An Ethic for Enemies*.[17]

Still, forgiveness is a largely unexplored tract of the political and international landscape. It is a "strange candidate" for a central place in politics, its strangeness owing to its long association with religion. "The word *forgiveness* has a religious ring in the ears of most modern westerners in a way that *justice* decidedly does not,"[18] Shriver explains, arguing that theologians themselves (notably the apostle of realism, Reinhold Niebuhr) have been most responsible for this separation of forgiveness and politics. "If forgiveness is to escape its religious captivity and enter the ranks of ordinary political virtues, it has to acquire a more precise, dynamic, and politically contexted definition than it has usually enjoyed."[19]

Serious questions arise about the very possibility of escaping this captivity—about what public forgiveness is and how it could be used in practical political affairs. Chapter 3 unpacks the "precise, dynamic, and politically contexted definition" that Shriver has proposed.

NOTES

1   Desmond Mpilo Tutu, *No Future Without Forgiveness* (New York: Doubleday, 1999), 129-130.
2   Tutu, *No Future Without Forgiveness*, 129-130.
3   Tutu, *No Future Without Forgiveness*, 23.
4   Douglas Johnston, "Introduction: Beyond Power Politics," in *Religion, the Missing Dimension of Statecraft*, ed. Douglas Johnston and Cynthia Sampson (New York, Oxford: Oxford University Press, 1995), 3.
5   Johnston, in Woodstock Colloquium *Forgiveness in Conflict Resolution: Reality and Utility* (December 9, 1996) (Washington, DC: Woodstock Theological Center, n.d.), 36.
6   Johnston, in Woodstock Colloquium *Forgiveness in Conflict Resolution: Reality and Utility*, 36.
7   Marc Gopin, *Between Eden and Armageddon: The Future of World Religions, Violence, and Peacemaking* (New York, Oxford: Oxford University Press, 2000), 5.
8   Gopin, *Between Eden and Armageddon*, 205.
9   Joseph V. Montville, "Justice and the Burdens of History," in *Reconciliation, Justice, and Coexistence: Theory and Practice*, ed. Mohammed Abu-Nimer (Lanham, MD: Lexington Books, 2001), 116.
10 Montville, "Justice and the Burdens of History," 116.
11 E. L. Worthington Jr., "Unforgiveness, Forgiveness, and Reconciliation in Societies," in *Forgiveness and Reconciliation: Religion, Public Policy, and Conflict Transformation*, ed. Raymond G. Helmick and Rodney L. Petersen (Philadelphia: The Templeton Foundation Press, 2001), 173.
12 Worthington, "Unforgiveness, Forgiveness, and Reconciliation in Societies," 177.

13   Olga Botcharova, in Woodstock Colloquium *Forgiveness in Conflict Resolution: Reality and Utility*, 44.

14   Cf. Johnston, in Woodstock Colloquium *Forgiveness in Conflict Resolution: Reality and Utility*, 51.

15   Rev. Douglas Baker, in Woodstock Colloquium *Forgiveness in Conflict Resolution: Reality and Utility—The Northern Ireland Experience* (June 18, 1997) (Washington, DC: Woodstock Theological Center, n.d.), 52.

16   Baker, in Woodstock Colloquium *Forgiveness in Conflict Resolution: Reality and Utility—The Northern Ireland Experience*, 53.

17   Donald W. Shriver Jr., *An Ethic for Enemies: Forgiveness in Politics* (New York, Oxford: Oxford University Press, 1995), 7.

18   Shriver, *An Ethic for Enemies*, 7.

19   Shriver, *An Ethic for Enemies*, 7.

CHAPTER 3

Understanding Forgiveness in Politics

Forgiveness in politics "joins moral truth, forbearance, empathy, and commitment to repair a fractured relationship."

An American physician traveling in Bosnia witnesses an unspeakable act: her translator, an ethnic Albanian Kosovar with whom she has traveled for weeks, pulls out a gun in a medical clinic and fatally shoots a surgeon. It turns out that the surgeon, who is a Serb, has committed an arguably less gruesome but serious political misdeed against the translator and his family. This was payback time.

A Croatian woman sees her husband murdered in her home by Serbian attackers. Instead of pleading with the aggressors to spare the lives of her and her children, the mother lets the aggressors know that she will strive to forgive them and that her sons will seek no revenge. With her words, the surprised assailants end the slaughter in that household.

These are, of course, snapshots of the forces of unforgiveness and forgiveness, stories that will be detailed later in this chapter. More deeply, they illustrate constitutive elements of two opposite forces in human social relationships: colliding elements such as truth and myth, forbearance and revenge, empathy and dehumanization.

The shooting at the clinic revealed a rejection not just of forgiveness in general but of forbearance from revenge in particular, along with any thought of eventual reconciliation. What kind of "mytho-histories" or distortions of truth did the translator indulge in his mind before he was mentally prepared to slaughter his former neighbor, the surgeon? In contrast, the Croatian mother's vow of forgiveness offered a glimpse into the power of forbearance as well as the element of surprise that is often built into such an act of forbearance or empathy. How was she, in those horrendous moments, able to envision and articulate a future of co-existence and reconciliation?

Forgiveness as an interpersonal concept is familiar enough among people of many beliefs and cultures, but forgiveness as a political possibility is less widely understood. There is, to be sure, a vast store of popular wisdom about forgiveness. In different cultures, to different degrees, many are versed in the concept of forgiveness and in kindred notions such as repentance and reconciliation. But while this familiarity could work in favor of incorporating forgiveness into politics, it can just as easily work against such incorporation.

Some conventional notions can make forgiveness seem highly unsuitable in the social and political sphere. For example, the maxim "forgive and forget" might imply that to forgive is to abandon moral judgment and a clear-eyed understanding of the crimes of an enemy. It is a fairly quick step from there to conclude that forgiveness is irreconcilable with justice. Indeed, this conventional view has complicated peace efforts in places like Bosnia, where the forgiveness-justice duality "causes really serious blocks in initiating a sincere dialogue on reconciliation, particularly between Christians and Muslims. It also provokes negative attitudes towards outsiders who come to the area vigorously preaching forgiveness as a solution to the people's problems," as psychologist Olga Botcharova points out.[1]

In a radically different conception, however, "remember and forgive" is the more fitting slogan because "forgiveness begins with memory suffused with moral judgment."[2] (In a similar vein, Mennonite peacebuilder John Paul Lederach would replace "forgive and forget" with "remember and change."[3]) Donald W. Shriver Jr. explains:

> The most serious aspect of forgiveness is confronting the evil perpetrated by human agents. We do not forgive hurricanes and floods; we forgive human beings who could and should

have acted differently. We hold them responsible, and we hold them under the judgment of memory, especially so long as the perpetrators do not repent their actions. Even after they repent, the evil we suffered may be too important to forget either personally or culturally. If your parents died in Auschwitz, your father on Iwo Jima, your sister at Hiroshima, or your grandfather at the end of a lynch-rope in Alabama, you are not going to forget. Ethically speaking, why should you? To be forgotten is the final indignity that one's neighbors can impose on you in your unjust suffering.[4]

This is not to say that remembering is a sure path to forgiveness; in the first chapter we saw that memory often moves people in the opposite direction, toward unforgiveness. On the other hand, from a clinical psychological perspective, Everett L. Worthington Jr. argues that forgetting can reduce feelings of unforgiveness: "the passing of time erodes memories," particularly if what is forgotten is a relatively minor transgression. However, he points out that transgressions with large and lasting consequences tend to be "magnified in importance as a person elaborates on the meaning of those events."[5] On this point, the message seems to be that while victims and victimized groups should not forget, neither is it healthy for them to dwell on every hurt or offense.

Similarly, there is growing acceptance of the view that forgiveness and justice are not mutually exclusive. In Shriver's understanding, forgiveness does not require the abandonment of all versions of punishment of evildoers; what it demands is a turn away from revenge.[6] Brian D. Lennon, SJ, has come to the conclusion that a person can forgive but still desire that a perpetrator be punished "for the sake of order and not out of revenge."[7] Lennon, who has coordinated interfaith mediation efforts in Northern Ireland, let it be known that he was not always of that mind. Just a year before the colloquium in which he made that statement, he wrote in a paper that forgiveness means "letting the perpetrator off punishment rightly and justly due to him."[8] This revision goes hand in hand with the even finer distinction he now draws between letting go of all resentment, which is a requirement of forgiveness, and letting go of all anger, which is not.[9]

The Shriver-Lennon concept of forgiveness embraces justice—but perhaps not some conventional notions of justice. Their concept implies, for example, a rejection of justice as being reduced simply to punishment, which may be necessary in itself but does not "address the primary need of the victim, which is healing," as retired U.S. Ambassador Robert T. Hennemeyer relates.[10] Healing, according to Botcharova, is possible through forgiveness, a process of "rehumanizing the enemy, identifying with the very basic human needs of the enemy and understanding the fears behind them, while still respecting my own suffering."[11]

THE DEFINITION(S)

During dialogues on forgiveness sponsored by the Woodstock Theological Center at Georgetown University in Washington, D.C., core participants embraced a definition drawn from Shriver's formulation: "Forgiveness in a political context is an act that joins moral truth, forbearance, empathy, and commitment to repair a fractured relationship."[12] Shriver's exact words in An Ethic for Enemies were "fractured human relation":

> Such a combination calls for a collective turning from the past that neither ignores past evil nor excuses it, that neither overlooks justice nor reduces justice to revenge, that insists on the humanity of enemies even in their commission of dehumanizing deeds, and that values the justice that restores political community above the justice that destroys it.[13]

Lennon arrived at a parallel understanding by way of a question: What is the difference between a person who has forgiven and one who has not? He offered an answer at one of the Woodstock colloquia:

(1) . . . human forgiveness always presupposes a judgment by the victim that an objectively moral wrong has been committed knowingly and freely against oneself or one's group by a responsible agent, and (2) it must always also involve one or all of the following judgments or decisions by the victim: (a) a judgment that the bad act does not define the perpetrator as a person; (b) a decision not to be governed by revenge; and (c) a decision by the victim to seek reconciliation. This means that the victim decides that from her side she will not allow the act of the perpetrator to stand in the way of a new relationship.[14]

In this definition, too, we can see an emphasis of truth, empathy, forbearance, and the commitment to repair a fractured relationship—in that order.

One can imagine other definitions of forgiveness, conceived as a social and political process. Other words, like "repentance," "acknowledgment," and "trust," could well appear in such a definition. Nevertheless, core participants in the Woodstock conversations found Shriver's definition to be more than adequate in analyzing a wide range of conflict situations. Therefore, drawing on experiences in the field of international conflict resolution, the rest of this chapter illustrates the qualities of truth and judgment, the turn from revenge, understanding and empathy, and the resolve to reconcile. The purpose here is not to present case studies (which come later) but to elucidate a definition.

MORAL TRUTH

Forgiveness implies a moral judgment about the truth of a transgression. That is why a person might recoil when told he or she is forgiven: they rightly sense that they are being judged and might not agree with the judgment. "Absent a preliminary agreement between two or more parties that there is something from the past to *be* forgiven, forgiveness stalls at the starting gate," Shriver writes. "Especially between antagonistic groups of humans, consensus on the wrongs that each may have inflicted on the other may take a very long time. Logically forgiveness goes from wrong-sufferers to wrongdoers, but in human societies, and most of all in political conflict, it may have to go both ways."[15]

In other words, forgiveness in politics depends on truth. "You can't get to reconciliation or forgiveness until you have a description of the reality that people don't fight about. . . . You cannot begin to talk about reconciliation until you have the truth. Then there has to be an effort to get people to face the truth," argues John Carr, director of the Department of Social Development and World Peace of the United States Conference of Catholic Bishops.[16] He and others have pointed out that the military in Argentina still harbors an alternative version of the truth about what happened during the so-called "dirty war." Whites in South Africa may find it harder to indulge in such a pseudo-reality, thanks to the truth elicited by South Africa's Truth and Reconciliation Commission.

Truth and reconciliation commissions embody the proposition that the critical first step is a consensus on wrongs, with a wide airing of that consensus. This proposition is not necessarily self-evident. In fact, the once-dominant view of mediators and negotiators held that addressing past atrocities posed an obstacle to resolving conflicts. Truth commissions represent what Neil J. Kritz, an authority on transitional justice at the United States Institute of Peace, considers a paradigmatic change of view, one that stresses the need to account for past abuses. The commissions strive toward reconciliation in part through "a cathartic public airing of evil and pain that has been inflicted."[17]

The need for a full accounting of abuses is often reflected in the experiences and desires of victims: "A common victim comment in many countries is that they may be willing to forgive, but they cannot forgive if they don't know the facts of what happened and if they don't know whom to forgive."[18] In that sense, truth commissions may facilitate the process of interpersonal forgiveness by exposing these facts of cruelty and oppression. As the next chapter will explore, beyond their own healing, victims have a further role to play in advancing the truth about atrocities and resisting public denial or forgetfulness.

Memory and the past, as volatile as they have proven to be, are crucial to any process of reconciliation in the present. Shriver writes that this process is a question of "how we manage our mutual relationships with the past without letting them manage us."[19] Mytho-history and the cycle of vengeance that it propels (as discussed in Chapter 1) are examples of letting the past manage us. A particularly challenging way to manage the past instead is reflected in now-retired Cardinal Cahal B. Daly's call for Catholics in Northern Ireland to remember atrocities perpetrated by their own ancestors against Protestants: "For true forgiveness it is as necessary to recover the memory of our own community's forgotten sins, as it is to be willing to forgive the remembered sins of others."[20]

FORBEARANCE FROM REVENGE

As noted above, while not precluding punishment, forgiveness does rule out revenge. It requires forbearance, which in the dictionary definition means tolerance and restraint in the face of provocation. "Forbearance opens the door toward a future that will not repeat the old crimes," Shriver writes in *An Ethic for Enemies*:

> Forgiveness gets its real start under the "double impetus" of judgment and forbearance. . . . Unaccompanied by forbearance in this very beginning, moral judgment often fuels new enmity. Who are more ferocious in battle than the morally empowered? Who is more tempted to make sure that the enemy pays for its crimes many times over? Moral justifications have been great friends of vengeance from time immemorial.[21]

The choice between forbearance and revenge is stark. The consequences can be seen by nearly anyone who comes into contact with brutal intergroup conflict, as made graphically clear in the stories of forgiveness and unforgiveness related at the start of this chapter.

The first story was told by a prominent American physician, Susan Black of Tewksbury, Massachusetts, to her local newspaper in Lowell, Massachusetts. (She also supplied some details to the authors of this book.) Black had traveled to Kosovo as a volunteer expert in autumn 1999 to help improve medical services in refugee camps. She visited various health-houses or clinics, including one in the divided town of Mitrovitche in northeast Kosovo, where she spoke to doctors about their needs with the help of her translator, Faza, an Albanian Kosovar. Faza seemed to recognize the orthopedic surgeon at the clinic, a Serb. Black later recounted, "All of a sudden, Faza says to me, 'You don't want to see this,' then he shoots this guy. In front of everybody. . . . I didn't know that my translator carried a gun, and I knew him well. We worked together for twelve hours a day, for six weeks. . . . To try to get close to somebody and really feel you understand them. Then to see the hatred in their heart. . . ."[22] The article continued,

> The surgeon had been Faza's neighbor, Black said. Faza's family had been hiding from Serbian police, and the surgeon had turned them in to the authorities. Faza's cousin was shot to death, and the surgeon's wife plundered their home, stealing anything of value, Black said. When she and Faza walked into the health house, Black said, the surgeon was wearing a shirt that had been stolen from Faza.[23]

Black said that the doctor, shot in the head, was killed. As for Faza, his fellow ethnic Albanians whisked him into hiding. Aside from being shocked by the sheer brutality, Black said that she was struck by the nonchalant attitude of U.S. officials, including Marines, who had seen it all before.[24]

Faza embodies the cycle of revenge at the precise point at which the rejection of forbearance reaches its most extreme conclusion. What light can Botcharova's explanation of victimhood development (see Chapter 1) cast on this decision to exact revenge rather than to refrain?[25] One can picture Faza passing through the stages of injury, realization of loss, suppression of grief and fears, anger ("why me?"), desire for justice or revenge, and creation of mytho-history. In that clinic he arrived at the final stage, the act of so-called "justified aggression," in which the cycle of retribution is completed, and the roles are reversed: "the former aggressor screams in pain and appeals for justice, the former innocent victim celebrates the victory."[26]

But another road to the political future is illustrated in the story of the Croatian woman in post-war Bosnia who saw her husband killed by Serbs. The recollection surfaced during one of the small-group seminars held by the Center for Strategic and International Studies and was later related by Botcharova at a Woodstock colloquium. In this case, the women's vow of forbearance had an astounding effect on aggressors who were about to kill her children next, as Botcharova recounted:

> A young Catholic priest from Banja Luka who was at the seminar told the story of what happened to his family during the war. At the time, he was a very young man, maybe twenty-two or twenty-three years old. His family consisted of a father, a mother, and six children. His father was killed in their house right in front of the children and the wife. His life and his brothers' lives were under threat. When there was discussion among the attackers of whom they should kill—all the boys at least, if not the wife—the mother suddenly raised her voice and somehow made them listen to her. His mother said, "You don't understand. We're Catholics and some of my boys are future priests. We're Christians; they are not going to get into revenge. I believe that they will learn and will teach me how to forgive."[27]

Botcharova went on to comment,

> That was one of the moments when God's miracle of forgiveness worked. It may not happen often that aggressors would hear such a plea and not kill, but this time it did happen. As I understand it, this statement by the woman, whose husband had been killed right in front of her eyes, was so powerful that they could not proceed with killing. In a way, it was a victory

of her spiritual identity, which was more than the identity of an angry wife or widow, even more than her identity as the mother of boys who did not beg to save their lives. She simply said, "You don't understand; we're Christians. It means they will forgive and they will teach me how." So they let them go. They were instead expelled and became refugees. When this young man told us this story, his face was twisting and he was struggling not to cry.[28]

This account supports Shriver's observation that the act of forbearance (as well as empathy) contains an element of surprise, since it is a break with the unfortunately ordinary rule of "do unto others what they have done unto you."[29] That the mother did not grant forgiveness on the spot is illuminating; instead, she made a vow to strive for forgiveness, while making it clear to her sons that they should give no thought to exacting revenge and thus imitating their oppressors. Forgiveness in politics, as the mother teaches us, is not a single act but a process in which a number of elements must fall into place.

But how did she open a door to the future in those moments of terror? Could she have somehow transcended the stages of victimhood outlined in Chapter 1 by Botcharova? Could she have instantly passed from "why me?" to "why them?"[30] (This reversal of the victimhood cycle will be taken up in Chapter 5.) In other words, could she have glimpsed an understanding of what made people of that community do this to her family—a question of empathy? Did she already have the wisdom of suffering,[31] the realization that the road of vengeance would never relieve her sorrow?

As far as we can tell, what that woman did was close the door to revenge; she turned away from a possible future that might have swallowed up her surviving family members in the cycle of retribution. Some would call this a prophetic gesture that, while commendable, is not very applicable to politics and warfare. Others, however, are quick to stress the utility of forbearance as a communal ethic. "Forbearance from tit-for-tat revenge is no mere ideal. It is practical politics,"[32] Shriver remarks, pointing negatively to the post–World War I Treaty of

Versailles and positively to the post–World War II Marshall Plan. "Revenge destroys politics; forbearance is the refusal to repeat the enemy's crimes. It anticipates a new political history, as did Lincoln in his eloquent Second Inaugural."[33] He quotes a Holocaust survivor: "When our liberation was at hand, we began to outnumber the guards. We could have killed them all with impunity. Instead we locked two hundred of them up and let the Allies decide what to do with them. They were all murderers, but this was a measure of the difference between them and us."[34]

EMPATHY

The distinction between empathy and sympathy is not sharply drawn in most dictionary definitions, yet this distinction takes on a strong dimension in the context of our morally laden definition of forgiveness. Shriver argues that the moral stance of forgivers, who must exercise judgment about wrongs done to them, precludes sympathy. To underscore the difference, he recalls the journal entry written by Ulysses S. Grant after accepting the surrender of Robert E. Lee at Appomattox: "I felt . . . sad and depressed at the downfall of a foe who had fought so long and valiantly, and had suffered so much for a cause, though that cause was, I believe, one of the worst for which a people ever fought."[35] Shriver follows with commentary: "This combination of moral judgment upon wrong with empathy for wrongdoers may be rare in human affairs, but in fact acknowledgment of fellow humanity lays a groundwork for both the construction and the repair of any human community."[36] Grant had empathy, but not sympathy, for Lee.

Shriver suggests that empathy for enemies may be the most difficult of all attributes of forgiveness, specifically because political conflict is fueled by dehumanization. He cites a Serbian officer who, in the process of killing Muslim men, called them "rabbits," Americans who called the Japanese "monkeys" in the Pacific War, and Japanese who called Americans "demons."[37] Still, humanizing the enemy is critical to any repair of human relationships.

As Botcharova argues, the very possibility of forgiveness arises in re-humanization, in identifying with the enemy's needs and fears, "while still respecting my own suffering. Only then I will be able to understand the suffering of the other side."[38] On a psycho-spiritual level, forgiveness comes from "re-thinking the criminal, that is, perceiving the criminal as in an inner dialogue with God. . . . Then there is a possibility to better understand criminal acts as sins performed by persons who are sinners, persons whom God, at the moment, has disconnected from their own spirituality."[39]

Understanding the humanity of the enemy means seeing him or her as more than just the enemy. This can be done through formal dialogue programs as well as through glimpses of people's lives. The Rev. Douglas Baker, of the ecumenical Corrymeela Community in Northern Ireland, tells of a telephone conversation he had with a Sinn Fein councilor whom he had invited to speak at a seminar.

> This is a person whom I had never met personally and who has probably made some statements by which I would find it difficult to abide. But here's what happened in the course of a two or three-minute telephone conversation. His children were crying in the background; it was near bedtime and they were being fractious. My children were crying in the background, also being fractious. I saw him as a parent, and I could relate to that. He was about to go out to play football—his means of relaxation, not mine—but I recognized that he's not one-hundred percent involved in republican politics all day long. He has a recreational and social life. When I came off the telephone, I had a totally different picture of him than I had previously had.[40]

He added, "It's still rare, however, that we ever enter into situations where we can see each other's humanity."[41]

As Shriver observes, it is not true that "to understand all is to forgive all," but understanding enemies is a step in a better direction.[42] Understanding, in relation to forgiveness, is a step toward learning to live with enemies as fellow human beings, without abandoning moral judgment.

Arguably, in the Middle East, the most momentous step toward peace in the past twenty-five years was preceded by an act of empathy and understanding. On January 1, 1978, in an interview with an Egyptian magazine, President Anwar Sadat displayed this insight into Jewish self-understanding:

> All Israelis are under arms until age fifty-five. They know war and know it is loathsome. . . . Jews are victims of war, politics, and hatred. They have special problems, which we must know so as to understand their positions. Jews have lived in fear for thousands of years, exposed to many massacres and persecutions. When they established Israel, imagination became a reality and fear a certainty. They are strangers in a strange land. They are surrounded by millions of hostile Arabs.[43]

Joseph V. Montville, who spent twenty-three years as a U.S. diplomat with posts in the Middle East and North Africa, argues that it would be difficult to overestimate the impact of Sadat's words on Israeli public opinion at the time. In that interview, cited by Montville, Sadat communicated to the Israelis that he understood them, while educating his own people about the psychology of Jewishness. Montville comments, "This act helped Arabs to understand a little better the vigor of Israeli aggressiveness in defense of the collective self and set the stage for the ultimate Camp David accords [September 1978] by providing a rationale for ending the state of war and making some sort of peace."[44]

COMMITMENT TO REPAIR A
FRACTURED HUMAN RELATIONSHIP

What Shriver called the "fourth dimension" of genuine forgiveness is the renewal of a human relationship. Such renewal builds on truth, forbearance, and empathy and begins with a desire to achieve eventual reconciliation. This means living alongside, if not yet along with, the enemy. It means a willingness to co-exist.

Co-existence is exactly what a Croatian government minister rejected when, over dinner with Drew Christiansen, SJ, and now-Cardinal Theodore McCarrick of Washington, D.C., he unabashedly laid out his plans for the forced transfer of minority Serbs from eastern Slavonia to northern Bosnia, predicting that this repopulation would lead to the expulsion of Catholics and Muslims from that region. "Then he added for our benefit that we needed to reconcile ourselves to the death of the Diocese of Banja Luka in northern Bosnia and the Archdiocese of Sarajevo in central Bosnia," Christiansen recounts.[45] (He notes that while those dioceses suffered terribly during the war, these particular plans were thwarted by international authorities.)

It is easy to make pessimistic conclusions about the prospects of co-existence in regions like the former Yugoslavia. After the brutality that she witnessed in Kosovo, Black, the American physician, said of the Albanians and Serbs, "They will never live together."[46]

With such enmity in mind, Shriver speaks merely of an "intention, however fragile and threatened by despair, of one enemy to go on living alongside another."[47] He finds a pithy expression of that intention in the founding declaration of the World Council of Churches, which brought together separated Protestant churches in 1948: "WE INTEND TO STAY TOGETHER" (capitals original). The seeming impossibility of the hope that enemies in the Balkans and elsewhere will live together is matched by the practical necessity of their at least intending to do so. It might well be "the most practical intention on earth for the twenty-first century. If World War II proved nothing else, it was this: From now on we live or die together."[48]

The challenge of co-existence is to eventually turn "alongside" relationships into "with" relationships.[49] That conversion calls in particular for "interactive co-existence," a step toward engagement between the alienated. Shriver said that another name for that is "civil society."[50]

As agents of civil society, non-governmental organizations (NGOs), including relief and development agencies, can serve as a sign of the desire to repair the social fractures. For that matter, functioning institutions across the board—political, juridical, economic, and civil—can signal the commitment to renew relationships. They can do so, essentially, by nurturing the conditions of social peace, including human rights and development, and by helping to provide for human needs. As noted in Chapter 1, this is the work of the international community as well as local, regional, and national institutions.

Shriver is careful to avoid speaking of "reconciliation" at this stage of the forgiveness process, saying the word is perhaps best reserved for what results from the whole process of forgiveness. "Co-existence may be only the mildest of moves toward reconciliation and only the faintest anticipation of a genuine political connection. It may be little different from passive tolerance," he acknowledges. "But it is a move away from the past towards a new political future."[51]

Indeed, the ultimate thrust of truth, forbearance, empathy, and the will to reconcile is a turn toward the future. Among other possibilities, this turn points to the concrete role of forgiveness in the broader development and progress of people and societies, especially in post-conflict societies. Arguing this exact point in his 2002 World Day of Peace message, Pope John Paul II stated,

> The ability to forgive lies at the very basis of the idea of a future society marked by justice and solidarity. By contrast, the failure to forgive . . . is extremely costly in terms of human development. Resources are used for weapons rather than for development, peace and justice. What sufferings are inflicted on humanity because of the failure to reconcile! What delays in progress because of the failure to forgive! Peace is essential for development, but true peace is made possible only through forgiveness.[52]

TOWARD A DYNAMIC
PROCESS OF FORGIVENESS

In sorting out the elements of forgiveness, it is important to clarify that the steps are not necessarily sequential. They may surface at various points of the process. For example, a particular group may have a vague desire to achieve eventual reconciliation (the fourth dimension), partly out of practical security concerns. But it may frequently regress to acts of vengeance (lacking forbearance) and have little interest in uncovering the truth or little or no empathy for the enemy. One thinks of the Israeli-Palestinian peace process, before it shattered into suicide bombs and political assassinations.

"Not a single one of them comes first," Shriver notes, referring to the elements of forgiveness. At the end of the colloquium in which Botcharova spoke of the Croatian mother, Shriver applied her example:

> When that mother forbears from revenge, predicting that her children will forbear from revenge, she already invites repentance on the other side whether or not it actually happens in the moment. Likewise, the surfacing of some truth about a long-hidden rankling fact of the past is itself at least a signal of possibility that a relationship might be repaired. If not, why would even the truth about its damage be promoted? Similarly with empathy, that surprising capacity of some people who have been damaged to understand why the person who caused the damage might act how he or she did act. This is the human capacity that makes it possible for us to have society between less than perfect people.[53]

What the operative definition does suggest is that forgiveness is a process, not simply an isolated act. As a social process, it goes far beyond the simple asking for or receiving of forgiveness that is characteristic of the interpersonal encounter (though even between two people, forgiveness is often not straightforward or explicit). One distinct advantage of the process notion is that it guards against an instantaneous forgiveness that may be too quick or superficial. Shriver suggests that forgiveness as a process gives people permission to be patient and work out deep differences. Thus, the process helps to define the distance between forgiveness, which goes only so far as a commitment to repair relationships, and reconciliation, which is the hoped-for result.[54]

To look at it this way is also to develop a sense of what Shriver refers to as the "finitude,"[55] or limitations and ambiguities, of forgiveness in politics. The healing effects of forgiveness can be as finite as what was felt by Gordon Wilson, the Northern Ireland legislator who (as we will see in the next chapter) forgave the Irish Republican Army after his daughter died in an IRA bombing, and who visibly struggled with pain and grief until the moment he died. Or forgiveness can be as ambiguous as a public apology that rings hollow, or the fear that enemies might be able to exploit such a public act of acknowledgment.

One illustrative point about the process view is that mediators and fractious groups can operate on each level of Shriver's definition without uttering the word "forgiveness." Indeed, theorists and practitioners of conflict resolution have advised that in some circumstances or stages of reconciliation, it would be prudent not to dwell on the word. Botcharova said that besides the misperceptions (e.g., the forgiveness-justice dualism), a process centered explicitly on forgiveness could promote "a kind of pseudo-dialogue" that fails to focus on the conditions of political forgiveness (truth, etc.) as well as to grapple with underlying sources of conflict. Speaking in the midst of her efforts in Bosnia in 1997, she went further to say, "I would put the word 'forgiveness' on the list of bad terms for the moment."[56]

In his chapter on vengeance and forbearance in *An Ethic for Enemies*, Shriver gives an extensive account of a 1984 speech to the German Bundestag by then-President Richard Freiherr von Weizsacker.[57] At the time, von Weizsacker declared that his fellow Germans must understand that memory is part of Jewish belief and that there can be "no reconciliation without memory."[58] Shriver considers it a classic in the annals of political forgiveness—yet "not once in the Bundestag speech did he use the word forgiveness, and it would have violated the spirit of the whole utterance if he had added the gratuitous note, 'On these grounds, I hope, the nations of the world will forgive Germany.'"[59] The president himself said some years later that it would be pretentious to suppose that nations can be forgiven for their sins, but Shriver notes that his speech did touch on almost all the requirements of political forgiveness as well as repentance. Von Weizsacker accepted judgment, acknowledged the forbearance of the allies after World War II, expressed empathy, and chartered a course of reconciliation: "In this respect it is an authentic beginning of the process by which nations plant their feet firmly on the road to reconciliation."[60]

Sometimes forgiveness dares not speak its name. Sometimes the results of forgiveness will not be beneficial, because forgiveness in politics is, after all, *in politics*, subject to the missteps and uncertainties of that worldly realm. Still, as will be shown further, recent experiences and experiments indicate that forgiveness can be a viable strategy in international politics. And if it is to be so, the bulk of attention will have to focus on the components: truth, empathy, forbearance, and the desire to repair relationships.

Essentially, this process is about building trust and relationships amid intergroup suspicions and about transcending one's own immediate interests or perceptions. Yet how is that done? What are some characteristic ways in which forgiveness is tendered in the arenas of conflict?

NOTES

1   Olga Botcharova, in Woodstock Colloquium *Forgiveness in Conflict Resolution: Reality and Utility—The Bosnian Experience* (October 24, 1997) (Washington, DC: Woodstock Theological Center, n.d.), 89-90.

2   Donald W. Shriver Jr., *An Ethic for Enemies: Forgiveness in Politics* (New York, Oxford: Oxford University Press, 1995), 7.

3   John Paul Lederach, "Five Qualities of Practice in Support of Reconciliation Processes," in *Forgiveness and Reconciliation: Religion, Public Policy, and Conflict Transformation*, ed. Raymond G. Helmick and Rodney L. Petersen (Philadelphia: The Templeton Foundation Press, 2001), 201.

4   Shriver, in Woodstock Theological Center Forum "An Ethic for Enemies: Forgiveness in Politics" (November 15, 1995), *Woodstock Report* (March 1996), http://www.georgetown.edu/centers/woodstock/report/r-fea45.htm (accessed in October 2003).

5   E. L. Worthington Jr., "Unforgiveness, Forgiveness, and Reconciliation in Societies," in *Forgiveness and Reconciliation: Religion, Public Policy, and Conflict Transformation*, 180.

6   Cf. Shriver, *An Ethic for Enemies*, 8; also Shriver, *Woodstock Report* (March 1996).

7   Brian D. Lennon, SJ, in Woodstock Colloquium *Forgiveness in Conflict Resolution: Reality and Utility* (December 9, 1996) (Washington, DC: Woodstock Theological Center, n.d.), 56.

8   Lennon, in Woodstock Colloquium *Forgiveness in Conflict Resolution: Reality and Utility*, 56.

9   Lennon, in Woodstock Colloquium *Forgiveness in Conflict Resolution: Reality and Utility*, 56.

10 Robert T. Hennemeyer, "Forgiveness in Conflict Resolution: Reality and Utility—The Bosnian Experience," in *Three Dimensions of Peacebuilding in Bosnia: Findings from USIP-Sponsored Research and Field Projects*, ed. Steven M. Riskin (Washington, DC: United States Institute of Peace), 40.

11   Botcharova, Woodstock Colloquium *Forgiveness in Conflict Resolution: Reality and Utility—The Bosnian Experience*, 93.

12   Hennemeyer, "Forgiveness in Conflict Resolution: Reality and Utility—The Bosnian Experience," 38.

13   Shriver, *An Ethic for Enemies*, 9.

14   Lennon, in Woodstock Colloquium *Forgiveness in Conflict Resolution: Reality and Utility*, 55.

15   Shriver, *An Ethic for Enemies*, 7.

16   John Carr, in Woodstock Colloquium *Forgiveness in Conflict Resolution: Reality and Utility—The Experiences of the Truth Commissions* (March 11, 1998) (Washington, DC: Woodstock Theological Center, n.d.), 50.

17   Neil J. Kritz, in Woodstock Colloquium *Forgiveness in Conflict Resolution: Reality and Utility—The Experiences of the Truth Commissions*, 5.

18   Kritz, in Woodstock Colloquium *Forgiveness in Conflict Resolution: Reality and Utility—The Experiences of the Truth Commissions*, 12.

19   Shriver, *Woodstock Report* (March 1996).

20   Cardinal Cahal B. Daly, in Woodstock Colloquium *Forgiveness in Conflict Resolution: Reality and Utility—The Northern Ireland Experience* (June 18, 1997) (Washington, DC: Woodstock Theological Center, n.d.), 11.

21   Shriver, *An Ethic for Enemies*, 8.

22   Matt Wickenheiser, "Tewksbury Doctor Treated Kosovo's Neediest, Witnessed Its Most Ruthless," *Lowell Sun*, December 5, 2000.

23   Black, quoted in Wickenheiser, "Tewksbury Doctor Treated Kosovo's Neediest, Witnessed Its Most Ruthless."

24   Wickenheiser, "Tewksbury Doctor Treated Kosovo's Neediest, Witnessed Its Most Ruthless."

25   Cf. Botcharova, in Woodstock Colloquium *Forgiveness in Conflict Resolution: Reality and Utility*, 39-43.

26   Botcharova, in Woodstock Colloquium *Forgiveness in Conflict Resolution: Reality and Utility*, 41.

27   Botcharova, in Woodstock Colloquium *Forgiveness in Conflict Resolution: Reality and Utility—The Bosnian Experience*, 87.

28   Botcharova, in Woodstock Colloquium *Forgiveness in Conflict Resolution: Reality and Utility—The Bosnian Experience*, 87-88.

29   Shriver, *An Ethic for Enemies*, 8.

30   Botcharova, in Woodstock Colloquium *Forgiveness in Conflict Resolution: Reality and Utility—The Bosnian Experience*, 92.

31   Botcharova, in Woodstock Colloquium *Forgiveness in Conflict Resolution: Reality and Utility*, 48.

32   Shriver, *Woodstock Report* (March 1996).

32   Shriver, *Woodstock Report* (March 1996).

34   Shriver, *Woodstock Report* (March 1996).

35   Quoted in Shriver, *An Ethic for Enemies*, 8.

36   Shriver, *An Ethic for Enemies*, 8.

37   Shriver, *Woodstock Report* (March 1996).

38   Botcharova, in Woodstock Colloquium *Forgiveness in Conflict Resolution: Reality and Utility—The Bosnian Experience*, 93.

39   Botcharova, in Woodstock Colloquium *Forgiveness in Conflict Resolution: Reality and Utility—The Bosnian Experience*, 93.

40 Rev. Douglas Baker, in Woodstock Colloquium *Forgiveness in Conflict Resolution: Reality and Utility—The Northern Ireland Experience*, 54.

41 Baker, in Woodstock Colloquium *Forgiveness in Conflict Resolution: Reality and Utility—The Northern Ireland Experience*, 54.

42 Shriver, *An Ethic for Enemies*, 8.

43 Cited in Joseph V. Montville, "Justice and the Burdens of History," in *Reconciliation, Justice, and Coexistence: Theory and Practice*, ed. Mohammed Abu-Nimer (Lanham, MD: Lexington Books, 2001), 121.

44 Montville, "Justice and the Burdens of History," 122.

45 Drew Christiansen, SJ, in Woodstock Colloquium *Forgiveness and Conflict Resolution: Reality and Utility*, 3-4.

46 Matt Wickenheiser, "Tewksbury Doctor Treated Kosovo's Neediest, Witnessed Its Most Ruthless." Black is also quoted as saying, "What you don't hear are three little words, 'I forgive you.' It's an absolutely unheard of concept."

47 Shriver, *Woodstock Report* (March 1996).

48 Shriver, *Woodstock Report* (March 1996).

49 Shriver, in Woodstock Colloquium *Forgiveness in Conflict Resolution: Reality and Utility—The Bosnian Experience*, 111.

50 Shriver, in Woodstock Colloquium *Forgiveness in Conflict Resolution: Reality and Utility—The Bosnian Experience*, 112.

51 Shriver, *An Ethic for Enemies*, 9.

52 Pope John Paul II, 2002 World Day of Peace Message "No Peace Without Justice, No Justice Without Forgiveness" (January 1, 2002), no. 9, http://www.vatican.va (accessed in October 2003).

53 Shriver, in Woodstock Colloquium *Forgiveness in Conflict Resolution: Reality and Utility—The Bosnian Experience*, 109.

54 Shriver, in interview with William Bole, Washington, DC, May 2002.

55 Shriver, interview.

56 Botcharova, in Woodstock Colloquium *Forgiveness in Conflict Resolution: Reality and Utility—The Bosnian Experience*, 89.

57 Cf. Shriver, *An Ethic for Enemies*, 108-112.

58 Quoted in Shriver, *An Ethic for Enemies*, 110.

59 Shriver, *An Ethic for Enemies*, 112.

60 Shriver, *An Ethic for Enemies*, 112.

CHAPTER 4

Political Forgiveness: Acts and Agents

Forgiveness has various agents and transactions, each raising distinct questions about forgiveness and its usefulness as a political tool.

At his presidential inauguration in February 1998, Kim Dae Jung of South Korea made a vow: "This new government will not practice the politics of retaliation."[1] Seated prominently were four former presidents, including General Chun Doo Hwan, who, in 1980, had arranged a court decision to sentence Kim to death. Donald W. Shriver Jr., who attended the inauguration, recalled later, "The embodiment of that statement was sitting behind him in the man who had tried very hard to kill him. . . . That, it seems to me, in all of its ambiguity, is what we're talking about. We're talking about the possibility, after a relationship has been deeply damaged, that it can be repaired."[2]

Kim, who later received the Nobel Peace Prize, did not use the word "forgiveness." Nevertheless, he conducted a transaction of forgiveness: a few words and a symbolic gesture that expressed forbearance from revenge, together with the commitment to repair relationships. The former dissident acted as a leader, representing many who had suffered persecution—but also as a victim himself. In that dual sense, he occupies a place in the chronicles of forgiveness alongside another former president, Nelson Mandela of South Africa, who similarly made his white jailer an honored guest at his own inauguration.

Other kinds of transactions, other agents of forgiveness, can be identified. Acts of acknowledgment and repentance have played a visible role in advancing the reconciliation process in a number of conflicts, most notably in Northern Ireland; and these have been enacted by a range of agents, from political representatives to civil-society mediators to ordinary people thrust onto the stage of forgiveness by virtue of victimization. Each of these agents and transactions raise distinct questions about forgiveness and its utility in politics and intergroup conflict resolution. They also point, in the end, to the ultimately conditional and inevitably ambiguous quality of forgiveness as it travels beyond the personal to the political.

This treatment of acts and agents begins with victims and personal or "prophetic" gestures, before turning to corporate or public agents as clearer illustrations of forgiveness as a political project. Those discussions open the way to an examination of the apology process, followed by an assessment of the strengths and weaknesses of individual and corporate agents. Finally, what are the social conditions that help give rise to these acts and agents? And what do the various strategies tell us about the finitude, or limitations and ambiguities, of forgiveness in politics?

VICTIMS AND PROPHETIC ACTS

The first agents of forgiveness are victims and sufferers, who are privileged interpreters in this journey of reconciliation. What does it mean to be a "privileged interpreter" in this way? To start with, victims are the ones who should decide whether the political crime against them or their loved ones merits forgiveness on the personal level. In other words, they should not be pressured to forgive the wrongdoer, out of some sense of social utility or responsibility. Second, their feelings and memories must be given special attention by the wider community, although the community's interest in values like justice or reconciliation goes beyond the preferences of any individual.

Sufferers are also teachers, especially in the service of political truth. Shriver makes this point in the context of Jews and their resistance to President Ronald Reagan's controversial visit to the German military cemetery at Bitburg in 1985:

> [Victims] can be agents for keeping a society reminded of past evils which a majority of its members easily forget because neither they nor their families and friends were touched intimately by those evils. Who are the more likely and trustworthy agents of such a service to the democratic public interest than just such a group? Theirs is an "epistemic privilege," for they are the authorities on what they have suffered.[3]

The inspiring examples of Kim, Mandela, and some other political leaders have brought the attention, yet many sufferers who take the leap of forgiveness come from the larger ranks of the people. Their most visible transactions have been what might be called prophetic acts of forgiveness—extending mercy to the wrongdoer without cause or conditions, thereby paying witness to reconciliation. These gestures might reflect what psychologist Olga Botcharova termed the "wisdom of suffering":[4] the insights of victims like the mother in Bosnia who glimpsed a different future for her and her oppressors (see Chapter 3 for the full account).

At times a solitary act of public forgiveness can serve as an occasion of transcendence in an otherwise brutal moment. Such was the witness of Gordon Wilson, a Methodist layman and legislator whose moment came on Remembrance Day, November 8, 1987. On that day, in honor of Britain's war dead, Wilson took part in a ceremony at the Enniskillen War Memorial with his daughter, Marie, a twenty-year-old nurse. In the midst of the morning observance, an Irish Republican Army bomb exploded, killing eleven people and injuring sixty-three. Wilson recalled later in a radio interview,

> We were both thrown forward, rubble and stones and whatever in and around and over us and under us. I was aware of a pain in my right shoulder. I shouted to Marie was she all right

and she said yes. She found my hand and said, "Is that your hand, Dad?" Now remember we were under six foot of rubble. I said, "Are you all right?" and she said yes, but she was shouting in between. Three or four times I asked her, and she always said yes, she was all right. When I asked her the fifth time, "Are you all right, Marie?" she said, "Daddy, I love you very much." Those were the last words she spoke to me.[5]

Marie Wilson died that night. Loyalist paramilitaries were intent on retaliation. But they were stopped in their bloody tracks by Gordon Wilson's simple words of forbearance and forgiveness: "I bear no ill will. I bear no grudge."[6] His gesture made a profound impression on both Protestants and Catholics in Northern Ireland and sent a message of hope to communities in other parts of the world. Though solitary, it was not a purely isolated event in the annals of forgiveness. "There have been many such words of forgiveness spoken by sufferers on both sides; their authenticity was unmistakable and their impact was real," says retired Cardinal Cahal B. Daly of Northern Ireland's Diocese of Armagh. "When the expression of sorrow and remorse, with manifest purpose of amendment, is accepted by the sufferer and responded to with sincere forgiveness, then the repentance becomes a true healing process in society as well as within individuals."[7]

Wilson's words of forgiveness echoed in the British Parliament and even in Queen Elizabeth II's Christmas Day address. Wilson went on to travel throughout Ireland, speaking of his tragic loss and the need for reconciliation. "He has become one of the great icons of grace," declares the Rev. Douglas Baker of the ecumenical Corrymeela Community:

Such icons are essential because the icons that we have grown up with glorify aggression and sectarianism; they depict men with guns, or combatants plunging swords through the hearts of their enemies. They are portrayed on gable walls, on banners, and in literature. They fuel violent attitudes in the minds of the young. But now there is emerging a significant group of people who are icons of peace and forgiveness. Because of them, many of us look at life differently.[8]

Another such witness grew out of the murder of Michael McGoldrick in 1996, a recent university graduate and young family man who was shot down by Protestant loyalist gunmen near Portadown "for no other reason than that he was a Catholic and an easy target,"[9] as Baker comments. In the wake of his murder, his parents made it known that they were praying for his killers and had forgiven them. They have continued to speak, at both Catholic and Protestant gatherings, about the need for political dialogue and an end to violence. In Baker's experience, the boundaries between Protestant and Catholic, unionist and nationalist, begin to fade in the light of prophetic forgiveness.

Prophetic Burdens

These acts of forgiveness, however, rest on the shoulders of people who are carrying an excruciating burden. The McGoldricks contemplated suicide, before their faith carried them through the ordeal of losing their son. Wilson's story is even more tragic. Six years after the death of his daughter Marie, he came to speak at Baker's church. "He stumbled through his address, frequently overcome with tears. His pain was crushing," Baker recalled at a forgiveness colloquium in 1997.[10] A couple of years later, Wilson's son died in a car crash; shortly after, Wilson himself died "with a broken heart"[11] at age sixty-seven, after a short illness. Almost a decade after losing his daughter, Wilson still struggled with the original act of forgiveness, with the pain and grief that lay behind his choice to forgive. His ordeal sheds a somber light on the "finitude" of forgiveness, to use the word Shriver applies to this discussion: the limitations and ambiguities of this whole endeavor of personal and social healing.

One problem is that personal acts of forgiveness can be overwhelmed by social strife—not surprising, given what we have learned from clinical psychology. Remember the "hothead factor" (explained in Chapter 1), which makes it hard for cooler heads to prevail, even when those heads are in the majority. As Everett L. Worthington Jr. relates from the findings of marital research (see Chapter 1), it can take many positive events to compensate for a single negative event. Yet prophetic acts of forgiveness have their own value and also often have the effect, however short-term, of encouraging forbearance.

Drew Christiansen, SJ, notes that early public forgiveness from families of victims, particularly in a funeral setting, is an important way to avert calls for revenge.[12] But here, too, the finitude of forgiveness must be considered. Such a plea may deter acts of retribution, but it can also come too soon, for both individuals and the community. That is why, in the United States, the few calls for forgiveness in the aftermath of September 11, 2001, seemed precipitous even to most peacemakers. "Grief and anger have to have their day, maybe their days," Shriver explained eight months after September 11.[13]

CORPORATE AGENTS AND THE FORGIVENESS PROCESS

Both Wilson and the McGoldricks granted forgiveness unilaterally, with no sign of repentance by perpetrators. That is part of the prophetic quality of personal forgiveness, against the political backdrop. Beyond personal witness are corporate acts (public or representative), which in many ways illuminate forgiveness as a social process with built-in components such as truth and the will to reconcile. Unlike prophetic acts, however, corporate forgiveness tends to have a distinct air of conditionality and reciprocity, sometimes beginning with a process of acknowledgment and repentance. A victim might feel moved to extend forgiveness to an offender, no questions asked; but in politics, forgiveness almost always means "having to say you're sorry," or at least having to acknowledge that there's something to be sorry for.

By definition, agents of corporate forgiveness act as representatives of a community, which may or may not agree with the representation. Kim Dae Jung and Nelson Mandela, without speaking directly of forgiveness, acted as corporate agents when they engaged in the complex and symbolic gestures of forbearance and reconciliation at their respective inaugurations.

The late King Hussein of Jordan acted as such an agent when he traveled to a border town where one of his soldiers had fired on Israeli schoolgirls who were on a class trip in 1997. Seven of the eighth graders were fatally shot. In a gesture that combined empathy with acknowledgment and the vision of future relationships, he visited the homes of the Israeli families and knelt before the parents, begging forgiveness. "I looked in his face and I saw that he was ashamed, and he had tears in his eyes, and he was honest," said the mother of a thirteen-year-old girl killed in the attack; the mother said she could see the truth in his eyes.[14]

Holocaust survivor and Nobel Peace laureate Elie Wiesel made a corporate gesture when he delivered an appeal to political leaders in Germany on the same day that German officials dedicated a vast site in Berlin for a Memorial to the Murdered Jews of Europe. On that January day in 2000, he held out the possibility of ultimate forgiveness, with conditions, including formally asking for forgiveness: "Ask the Jewish people to forgive Germany for what the Third Reich had done in Germany's name. . . . Do it, and the significance of this day will acquire a higher level. Do it, for we desperately want to have hope for this new century."[15]

In El Salvador, the Jesuit community acted as a corporate agent in calling for a process of forgiving those who had murdered six Jesuits, along with their housekeeper and her daughter, at the University of Central America. The Jesuit provincial, Fr. Jose Maria Tojeira, and his colleagues laid out conditions in an appeal to the legislature in the midst of a truth commission and in the wake of a sham trial of soldiers and officers believed responsible for the killings. Douglass W. Cassel Jr. was the American Bar Association's observer at the 1991 trial of (low-level) military personnel charged in the Jesuit massacre. He recalled later that the Jesuits did not simply say, "Forgive and forget," the preferred maxim of the Salvadoran military. Rather, Tojeira offered forgiveness with two provisos: "First, the truth must come out," Cassel related. "As long as the truth is hidden, Salvadoran society should not, and the victims' relatives should not, be asked to forgive those who continue to assert and to live a lie. . . . Secondly, there should be some form of acknowledgment of the truth and even repentance."[16] That story is not over, because the principal perpetrators who ordered the killings remain unrepentant.

The Irish Republican Army (IRA) acted corporately—and many would say belatedly—when it offered "our sincere apologies and condolences" to the families of civilians killed as a result of IRA violence since the late 1960s. In a statement marking the thirtieth anniversary of 1972's Bloody Friday, the IRA also expressed regret for fatalities among combatants in Protestant-Catholic hostilities over the years, saying, "We also acknowledge the grief and pain of their relatives." At this writing, it was hard to gauge the effects of this show of repentance, mired as it was in the politics of the moment, particularly arguments over terms of the 1998 Good Friday Agreement in Northern Ireland.[17]

All of the agents cited above were able to enter a process of corporate forgiveness on some personal ground, either as victims or, in the case of King Hussein, as leaders who bear some (distant) responsibility for the suffering. Often, though, leaders have neither suffered themselves nor perpetrated the political misdeeds that divide peoples and nations. Their roles and transactions illustrate further the complexities of political forgiveness and the standing of those who conduct the transactions. Consider two cases of repentance or acknowledgment, in Germany and Britain.

In December 1970, Chancellor Willy Brandt of West Germany visited the memorial to the Warsaw ghetto uprising of 1943. In what many saw as a spontaneous gesture, Brandt fell on his knees in front of the monument in a sign of repentance.[18] It was a historic event, of a piece with his more tangible steps toward restoring relationships with Poland and the international Jewish community. Still, his symbolic deed generated debate about whether one leader can repent on behalf of a nation, especially if that leader had no direct part in the crimes— Brandt had spent the Nazi era exiled in Scandinavia. Some say this act of repentance would have been more credible or profound if Brandt had taken any part in the Nazi regime.

While British Prime Minister Tony Blair did not actually repent on anyone's behalf, he did acknowledge British Protestant responsibility for past wrongs against Irish Catholics. Specifically, he acknowledged England's responsibility for the famines of the mid-nineteenth century and called for construction of a monument in Liverpool to honor victims. Blair certainly had no greater responsibility for the Irish Potato Famine or even Ireland's Bloody Sunday than Brandt had for the Nazi regime. This made Blair in that respect a distant agent of forgiveness, far removed from the events in both time and culpability, and so perhaps less convincing in the role of repenter.

Yet it should count for quite a lot that he acted as the leader of the United Kingdom in trying to resolve the Northern Ireland conflict; and in that capacity, he helped take the reconciliation process another step ahead with gestures of acknowledgment. "It is safe to say that Tony Blair played a big part in the success of the pro-peace referendum among Catholic voters in 1998," explains Joseph V. Montville of the Center for Strategic and International Studies, referring to the Good Friday Agreement ratified by voters that year. "But from a psychological point of view, there's so much more to acknowledge."[19] In other words, Blair's transactions came up short, and this may have dampened his effectiveness more than his status as a corporate agent with nothing to personally apologize for.

Corporate Apologies and Mutuality

As the Brandt and Blair gestures show, corporate acts of acknowledgment and repentance are critical to the process of social forgiveness. Apologies, in word, deed, or gesture, are often necessary conditions, if insufficient. Like forgiveness itself, corporate apologies are a process, in which three steps can be identified:

1. Acknowledging transgression
2. Feeling and expressing remorse, sorrow, and repentance for the wrongful act
3. Doing something to restore an injustice

Based on her experience in the Balkans, Olga Botcharova points out, "Reconciliation is impossible without the fulfillment of the repentance: the confession process as a public apology is the first step, as well as coming to terms about compensating the wronged. These are necessary conditions for reconciliation as well as forgiveness."[20]

As for the Irish, while it has been said that they neither forgive nor forget, Northern Ireland has paradoxically served as a showcase of corporate forgiveness, with its possibilities and limitations. The wide-ranging apology tendered by the IRA in July 2002 was but the most recent in a line of corporate gestures by parties to the violence in Northern Ireland as well as by leaders of the Protestant and Catholic communities. One early and illuminating exchange came in the 1990s from two agents of civil society: then-Archbishop of Canterbury George Carey, and now-retired Cardinal Daly of Northern Ireland.[21]

On March 18, 1994, Carey took the first step in a sermon at Christ Church Cathedral in Dublin: "As an English Churchman, I am aware of just how much we English need to ask forgiveness for our often brutal domination and crass insensitivity in the eight hundred years of history of our relationship with Ireland."[22] Then, on the same day, Daly offered his response in a sermon at Canterbury Cathedral: "I wish to ask forgiveness from the people of this land for the wrongs and hurts inflicted by Irish people upon the people of this country on many occasions during our shared history, and particularly in the past twenty-five years. I believe that this reciprocal recognition of the need to forgive and to be forgiven is a necessary condition" for the healing of political relationships.[23]

These mutual apologies clearly represented a commitment to repairing fractured relationships between the communities. The continuing exchange also highlighted the importance of seeking the truth about atrocities and recovering authentic memories. (Recall that truth and the commitment to reconcile are the first and last items of Shriver's definition of political forgiveness.) On November 26, 1994, speaking at Fitzroy Presbyterian Church in Belfast, Daly asked forgiveness for historic misdeeds by Catholics in Northern Ireland, recalling "atrocities which we now name by the place where they happened, such as Whitecross, Darkley, Shankill Road, Enniskillen."[24]

Both the archbishop and the cardinal seemed to recognize the pitfalls and limitations of such a process of mutual repentance and forgiveness. In his sermon, Carey cautioned that "it can be pointless and somewhat over-indulgent to wallow in confession to one another."[25] Daly agreed, noting that words like "reconciliation," "repentance," and "apology" are easily rendered trivial: "Repentance must go far beyond verbal formulae. Apology means much more than personal change. Communal change, political change are also required. Political relationships must be changed if forgiveness is to be politically effective and lead to conflict resolution."[26]

During one colloquium at Georgetown University, Daly also was quick to acknowledge that a plea for forgiveness is more powerful when expressed by someone who has committed or is otherwise implicated in violent deeds.[27] He pointed to Gusty Spence, a former Protestant loyalist paramilitary leader who, in announcing a ceasefire in October 1994, offered "the loved ones of all innocent victims over the past twenty-five years abject and true remorse."[28]

Who Shall Forgive? Who Shall Repent?

Even with these qualifications, the cardinal's account of mutual repentance and requests for forgiveness in Northern Ireland prompted some of the closest questioning during the dialogues on forgiveness sponsored by the Woodstock Theological Center. On the most basic level, who can apologize? Who can forgive? Who can speak for the community? What social and political conditions are necessary for a successful, mutual transaction of forgiveness? What does justice have to do with it? These questions have bearing on the efficacy of corporate forgiveness.

To continue with the example of Northern Ireland, the wave of official church apologies did not end with the Carey-Daly exchange. During a surge of provocative marches by Protestant unionists in summer 1996, twenty-five Presbyterian leaders asked God as well as Catholics to forgive the fact that Presbyterians "have been directly involved [in sectarian conflict] and that all of us, by association, have been tainted by this communal sin."[29] (The family of a Catholic who died in the rioting triggered by the marches had earlier expressed Christian forgiveness during the funeral.) In response, a lay Catholic organization accepted the Presbyterian offer of repentance and asked forgiveness for the wrongs inflicted by the Catholic community.

At the same time, the apologies by the archbishop and cardinal generated some hostility and resentment in the Protestant and Catholic communities. Negative reactions usually turned on the perception that both church leaders presumed to apologize on behalf of those communities. Carey, the Anglican archbishop, seemed particularly vulnerable on this point because he was viewed (perhaps inaccurately) as purporting to speak on behalf of Presbyterians, who are predominant among Protestants in Northern Ireland. For his part, Daly met with criticism for seeming to imply that Catholic misdeeds were equal to Protestant misdeeds, historically. (Likewise, the specter of "moral equivalency," or the fear of being accused of such, has reportedly kept some clergy in the Balkans from speaking out against violence.)

In the view of Gerard F. Powers, who directs the Office of International Justice and Peace of the United States Conference of Catholic Bishops, the apologies were not always well received because they imply a notion of social sin that is not widely shared or understood. In other words, Catholics and Protestants do not necessarily believe they share in the sins of the IRA and loyalist paramilitaries, respectively: "Even if the concept of social sin and collective responsibility were accepted and understood, Northern Ireland shows how corporate acts of forgiveness quickly get side-tracked by debates over who speaks for the community."[30] While he supports highly visible corporate acts of apology, Powers offers a mixed judgment about their efficacy:

> On the one hand, it seems to me that they're efficacious and that they're educative and hortatory . . . they try to bring people to look at history in a different way—that is, reinterpret history, get out of their one-sided sense of victimization. . . . But, on the other hand, this efficacy seems to be dimin-

ished a bit by the distance in time or moral responsibility of those who are asking forgiveness from the acts in question. In your [Daly's] case, asking forgiveness at Coventry for the Birmingham pub bombing, for example. Clearly you had no role in that bombing, but you ask forgiveness on behalf of the Catholic community.[31]

Cardinal Daly agrees in part with this assessment of such transactions of forgiveness:

> Their effectiveness is not dramatic, but I think it helps to gradually build up a climate of readiness for listening to what the other side is saying. . . . It is one of the things that I think helps to alleviate some of the mistrust and helps us to gradually reduce some of the myth-making on both sides. . . . I do think that anger can be countered only by a genuine offering of forgiveness, hoping to evoke a genuine spirit, a willingness to re-think some of the myths. . . .[32]

In essence, Daly saw a positive if limited role for vicarious apologies in the conflict-resolution process.

The Culpable

One message of the exchange between Carey and Daly is that the most powerful and potentially effective apologies on behalf of groups may come from those who share culpability for crimes and misdeeds. Powers points out that while the cardinal and archbishop seemed quite distanced from personal responsibility, the Presbyterian pastors were a bit closer, because their own church, to an extent, has sustained the sectarianism associated with the Loyal Orange Institution (the Protestant organization of unionists, based in Northern Ireland and more commonly known as "the Orange Order"). That connection, too, has its limitations. More meaningful, according to Powers, have been apologies by loyalist paramilitary leaders who have clear institutional responsibility for violent deeds.[33]

Even so, apologies by the culpable have their own pitfalls, especially if the acts of repentance ring hollow—that is, if they fail to include clear acknowledgment, genuine remorse, and a commitment to make restoration. In the case of the IRA, the apology was seen as late in coming, even if welcomed by some parties; but the questions surrounding the statement seemed to turn on the third condition of repentance: a commitment to make restoration. Protestant unionists charged that the IRA's act of repentance was unmatched by political deeds, such as fully honoring a ceasefire and disarmament plan put in place by the Good Friday Agreement.

Further, a forgiveness process shouldn't hinge altogether on repentance by such agents, partly because people who are truly responsible for wrongdoing seem less inclined to actually take responsibility. Simply put, it's usually easier to apologize for someone else's wrongdoing than to apologize for one's own misdeeds.

Besides, in conflicted contexts, both parties tend to view themselves as victims, not aggressors, and feel that if an apology is in order, it should be made to them, not by them. Anthony Cary, counselor of the British embassy, observes, "The greatest difficulty in Northern Ireland is that both communities feel sinned against. There's a great sort of self-righteousness and a feeling that they would be ready to offer forgiveness if other people would see their point of view, but very few people are willing to ask forgiveness, except, possibly, once removed."[34]

This should not be surprising, given the psychological profile of the perpetrator in social and political conflicts. "These folks are complex centers of subjectivity of their own . . . not comfortable with thinking of themselves as people in need of forgiveness. They are trained in many ways to think of themselves as exemplary people," notes John P. Langan, SJ, a social ethicist and professor of philosophy at Georgetown University.[35] These elements present drawbacks to any strategy of seeking to resolve tensions by encouraging public acts of apology by those with real culpability. (Langan continues his point by noting that perpetrators are often members of political, economic, and military elites, and that more attention should be given to bringing them into a process of forgiveness and reconciliation.[36])

That said, there should be no rush to generalize from these cases of corporate apology in Northern Ireland. To whatever degree the forces of unforgiveness may persist there, many people on both sides of the divide were ready for gestures of the kind made by religious leaders. A language of forgiveness had taken wing in the Catholic and Protestant communions.

The atmosphere of Northern Ireland was distinct from a setting such as the Balkans, where public acts of repentance could perhaps more easily backfire or fall on deaf ears. In the Bosnian context, religious leaders have pointed out that public acts of repentance are easily co-opted by the other side. Enemies have been quick to seize upon admissions of guilt as justifications for revenge, which undermines the search for peace. Citing these concerns, Powers also cautions that "public acts of repentance and apology can also exacerbate this collective guilt phenomenon that is so much a part of this sense of grievance [against adversaries], fueling more grievances."[37] In other words, apologizing and admitting mistakes can be dangerous to one's community, or simply futile, if one is living in the midst of brutal intergroup conflict.

It is fair to say that the status of agents of repentance and forgiveness—be they ecclesiastics or paramilitaries—has much to do with the success of such transactions. At the same time, various agents of forgiveness can advance an apology process by fulfilling the three main conditions: clear acknowledgment, sincere repentance, and steps toward restitution. These particular conditions, however, are not entirely independent of political context. The repentance process might very well contribute to a "climate of readiness," as seen by Daly, but it can also become another casualty in a very different climate of absolute rejection, as described by Powers.

ACTS AND AGENTS, INDIVIDUAL VS. CORPORATE: AN ASSESSMENT

Those seeking to apply themes of forgiveness to social conflicts usually start with an understanding that forgiveness is deeply personal, and it must remain so. That is why sufferers are considered the first agents of political forgiveness.

"No one else can perform it," insists Brian Lennon, SJ: "When someone says they forgive, we need to ask, is this person a victim? Of what? What wrong has been committed? By whom?" Part of the apprehension here is that partisans might use forgiveness as a tactical advantage against their enemies or opponents: "Failing to be specific about these issues can mean people use forgiveness as a weapon to claim a high moral ground or simply to put down their opponents, and in Northern Ireland we sometimes use forgiveness in this way."[38]

In the context of truth commissions, Neil J. Kritz of the United States Institute of Peace identifies a fairly broad consensus that it is up to individual victims to forgive what happened to them.[39] In conflicts where the wrongdoers and the wronged are often the same people or groups, one could also argue that forgiveness begins with victims' forgiving victims—but does not necessarily end there. While Daly obviously sees wider possibilities, even he acknowledges, "I think that we have to accept that forgiveness is very, very costing and very, very difficult. It's easier to forgive vicariously than to forgive personally the one responsible for the horrible wrong that has been suffered."[40]

Still, respect for the personal quality of forgiveness can lead toward, not away from, an appreciation of the role of forgiveness in politics. From a philosophical and theological perspective, Pope John Paul II pointed out in his 2002 World Day of Peace message that while forgiveness is highly personal, it is also deeply social, in that people are basically social beings, interconnected on many levels: "Consequently, *society too is absolutely in need of forgiveness*. Families, groups, societies, States and the international community itself need forgiveness in order to renew ties that have been sundered, go beyond sterile situations of mutual condemnation and overcome the temptation to discriminate against others without appeal."[41]

Personal acts do have political consequences. Forgiveness enters the public arena by way of individual as well as corporate transactions. Indeed, many believe that personal "prophetic" acts are often among the most effectual political gestures of forgiveness, as Powers explains:

Interestingly, the most socially and politically significant acts of forgiveness sometimes are those that are personal in nature. It is difficult to judge the impact of the Catholic family's offer of forgiveness and prayers for their persecutors after the violence of last summer. But these acts undoubtedly help calm public anger and, at a minimum, avoid fueling the cycle of violence. Even if they have no impact at all on the wider community, so many people in Northern Ireland have suffered personally during the past twenty-five years that individual healing is essential for broader communal healing.[42]

Publicly proclaimed in the setting of social conflict, these transactions are hardly apolitical. In many ways, the solitary gestures anticipate a wider constituency that will expand the possibilities of political forgiveness. (This anticipation itself is testimony to the social dimensions of forgiveness, compared with the individualism that infects most conventional notions.) Still, for forgiveness to become truly social, it must get over "the hump of the individual," as Shriver styles it.[43] In other words, forgiveness is personal, but it can be much more than that. It needs to find a "new home" (another of Shriver's images), a collection of acts and agents that turn forgiveness into a process of relationship building.

It's Called Leadership

Leadership is unavoidable in any social project of forgiveness. As the Daly-Powers conversation (described above) suggests, a number of factors should be considered in assessing when and whether leaders can forgive or repent on behalf of groups, regardless of whether the leaders have either suffered or perpetrated the misdeeds. However, if solitary gestures do anticipate a wider constituency, then leaders are the ones who will either act or fail to act in recognition of that possible or emerging constituency.

"We often hear that nobody can forgive or repent on behalf of others," Shriver says. "But we expect leaders to do things on our behalf . . . even things that a lot of us don't agree with."[44] Even so, leaders would be well advised not to get too far out in front of their populations, in any such process. Some, like James L. Connor, SJ, would stress that caution: "Necessarily, I think the leadership can only speak to the extent that the community as a whole or to some large measure is in agreement with the expression of sorrow."[45]

Others emphasize the importance of challenging constituencies to forge a process of intergroup repentance or forgiveness, as Shriver does. On the more pointed question of whether religious and political leaders can repent on behalf of constituents, he goes further: "My answer to that tends to be yes, and I have a name for it: *leadership.*"[46]

Leadership is what West German Chancellor Brandt provided when he fell to his knees at the Warsaw monument, as recounted earlier. At the time, Brandt faced a "statesmen's dilemma,"[47] remembers Brandon Grove, a career diplomat and international policymaker who knew Brandt during his days of duty with the U.S. State Department in Berlin. Grove believes that the chancellor's act was spontaneous but that, if he had considered it beforehand, he would have seen that he had two choices:

> First, he could have bowed his head for a few moments after placing a wreath, which is what was expected of him and would fully have met the requirements of protocol. Or, in acting as he felt, he could have dropped to his knees to make the stunning gesture for himself and Germany that he intended. That's what leaders do, and I will never forget the famous photograph. If not Brandt, then who could have done this? No one. He was providing compelling evidence of a change in Germany.[48]

Recall the criticism, cited earlier, that Brandt, having spent the war years in exile, was not qualified to repent for the Nazi crimes. Grove counters the argument: "Germany had only one chancellor, and only this one moment in Warsaw, and for him to have hesitated on the basis of such considerations, missing the opportunity, would have been wrong and out of character for him."[49]

In the politics of forgiveness, it matters whether one is a sufferer or a representative, and whether the acts are solitary or corporate. Nonetheless, a process-oriented view of forgiveness does not lend itself well to hard-and-fast judgments about the inherent value of one set of agents and acts versus the value of another set. For example, straightforward forgiveness by victims is not necessarily more conducive to conflict transformation than symbolic acts of acknowledgment or forbearance by political representatives.

Complementarity is key to this understanding of the forgivenss process. Unilateral, unconditional ("prophetic") acts of forgiveness by victims can open the door to corporate action, and corporate action can help build an atmosphere of forgiveness that encourages the prophetic acts. Still, distinctions are important. It must always be remembered that corporate agents normally do not have the privilege of sufferers, who alone can tell their oppressors, "I will no longer hold this against you. You are forgiven." Political leaders, as agents of forgiveness, inevitably engage in a process that is more conditional or ambiguous—reflecting the ambiguity of, say, a Tony Blair who symbolically acknowledges some group misdeeds but not others. What remains is the need for constant interplay between act and agent, corporate and individual, personal and political.

Arguably, for some years, such interplay has been seen in Northern Ireland. That these acts and agents are still waiting to win the day is testimony to the forces of unforgiveness. What can we learn about the potential benefits of a forgiveness strategy from that laboratory of conflict *and* resolution? Even before the 1998 Good Friday Agreement, the Rev. Kenneth Newell was able to realistically assess the impact by making four points in that context:

> (1) The profile of forgiveness is small but growing. (2) When forgiveness becomes center stage its impact is enormous. (3) A climate of forgiveness cannot spread unless we address the painful memories that have frozen people's emotions into mistrust. (4) The only soil in which the plant of forgiveness

can take root is that of contact between isolated persons, groups, and communities.[50]

Newell concluded, "Saying sorry to each other in Northern Ireland is hugely creative: it enables hurt people to move on. Although it is rare, it is growing. There will be no healing without it."[51]

Conditions of Forgiveness: Social and Political

If peace is more than the absence or avoidance of war—if it consists of positive elements such as human rights and development, as Christiansen articulates—then the same can be said of forgiveness. That is why Shriver calls human rights "the simple moral core of forgiveness in politics," the way of "protecting the next generation's right to live and work, to write and to read. . . ."[52]

And that is why agents of forgiveness go beyond individuals, whether they are victims or leaders, and why the transactions go beyond the gestures of these agents. Broadly put, society is a potential agent of forgiveness, and it can, through its structures, laws, and cultures, conduct transactions of forgiveness. This might take this text beyond the scope of forgiveness as a tool of conflict transformation. Still, the social, political, and economic infrastructures of forgiveness are worth noting.

As a practical matter, acts and gestures of forgiveness or repentance can lose any serious chance of efficacy if broader social and political initiatives are missing. In terms of Northern Ireland's politics, Powers observes, "Specific acts of forgiveness easily become victims of sectarian politics if they are not part of a wider effort to end violence, to address injustices even-handedly, to find a political solution that respects the rights and aspirations of both communities, to deal with the problem of paramilitary prisoners, and to deepen relationships of mutual trust."[53]

Forgiveness does not operate in a vacuum; it is highly dependent on social conditions and political circumstances. While the "soft" approach of forgiveness is often contrasted with the "hard" approach of politics and negotiation—which is fair enough—forgiveness also can find its openings through *realpolitik* engagement. With respect to Northern Ireland, R. Scott Appleby writes, "A cease-fire or a political settlement provides reconciliation groups space to blossom, as did the 1994 cease-fire. The cessation of violence granted these groups the opportunity to sustain their focus on the delicate task of building trust among representatives of the opposing parties."[54] This could be said about the 1998 Good Friday Agreement as well.

Likewise, political engagement can find its openings through acts and agents of forgiveness. Appleby points out that a "discourse of forgiveness" permeated the debate over ratification of the Good Friday Agreement and helped to channel popular sentiment into a political program of peace.[55]

As with many specific acts of forgiveness, broad measures of social and political change can signal the desire to repair fractured relationships between groups. This point highlights the importance of restitution to any scheme of forgiveness. Daly stresses that while expressions of repentance and forgiveness are important steps in the process of conflict resolution, they are not enough:

> They are not effective without cessation of the wrongs and the hurts of conflict, without, in short, the change of behavior and the full purpose of amendment which the Christian tradition has always held to be the defining condition of genuine repentance, and without the just changes of structures and institutions which are necessary for true reconciliation.[56]

MANY POSSIBILITIES, FEW GUARANTEES

This treatment of the agents and transactions of forgiveness is hardly exhaustive. Small-group dialogues, profiled in the next chapter, can be integral to any process of forgiveness that goes to the roots of memories and transgressions. Some specialists in conflict resolution have taken an interest in the symbolic power of practical deeds, as an instrument of forgiveness and reconciliation. Rabbi Marc Gopin has suggested that what he terms "unilateral gestures of aid" could serve as a form of conflict resolution in the Israeli-Palestinian conflict, where dialogue has been a non-starter and the cultures remain mired in a symbolism of offense and humiliation.[57] Such acts could create "cognitive dissonance" among those with a one-sided view of the enemy.

Such strategies are speculative, however, and Gopin is soberly aware of what would be involved in withstanding the forces of unforgiveness:

> It would take repeated and extensive gestures of Israelis work-ing in Arab and Palestinian villages to build good, permanent homes before it became clear that there were Israelis who understood the Palestinian demand for justice and were serious about their desire for reconciliation and co-existence. . . . It would take repeated Palestinian offers of condolences, visits, and gestures of comfort toward Israeli victims of bombs for it to sink in that not all Arabs wanted those bombs to go off.[58]

Although it is fair to speak of the forces of forgiveness versus the unforgiving forces, it is also useful to remember that the strategies of forgiveness are seldom a simple question of good and evil. In the strategic sphere, advocates of forgiveness have to understand that they are dealing with moral contingencies as much as with absolutes. It should be kept in mind that forgiveness in politics takes place *in politics*. The transactions may derive from transcendent values such as truth and empathy; but once transported to the political realm, they become subject to the uncertainties of that realm, the ambiguities of judgment and possibilities of miscalculation or unintended conse-quences. For that reason, agents of forgiveness can expect few "free rides" in the back-and-forth of political argument and policymaking.

Take, for example, the issue of sectarian schools, which have been widely accused of contributing to religious and ethnic divisions in places such as Northern Ireland and the former Yugoslavia. Many assume that abolishing sectarian schools would be a step toward rec-onciliation. Replacing them with multi-ethnic or ecumenical schools might understandably be seen as a way of promoting harmony and turning relationships "alongside" into relationships "with." In theory, such a restructuring measure could be understood as a transaction of forgiveness. Yet it could well have the opposite effect and indeed could be the wrong thing to do, even apart from possibly unintended consequences. "People could see that as a threat to their community and cohesion, another way of destroying their culture. And that's what they're fighting for in the first place—their culture and their identity," Powers notes.[59]

In other words, doing away with sectarian or single-ethnicity schools might rekindle resentments while distracting communities from more practical and politically sound measures. Such measures might include initiatives to bring together schoolchildren of different ethnic groups to promote crosscultural understanding. A more ambitious effort, short of creating new school systems, might be to forge common history texts as one way of combating "mytho-history" (the distorted memories of offense and injury that have fueled many conflicts) and instead establishing historical truth in post-conflict societies.

One lesson, in wider perspective, is that forgiveness is not above politics, not immune to the contingencies of conflict and strategy. "Not all aspects of this [forgiveness] process will be positive. Particular steps may misfire. That's part of the risk. The process will be open to contestability, the normal criticisms of social and political exchange. There will be benefits and drawbacks," explains John Langan.[60] In other words, agents of forgiveness will have to reckon with the finitude of forgiveness as a set of political strategies.

In (But Not Of)

Nevertheless, while *in* politics, forgiveness need not be entirely *of* politics. Agents and transactions of forgiveness typically operate in a somewhat different realm and proceed along another track of conflict resolution. Their most traveled route is civil society, which is key to the plausibility structure of forgiveness in (but not of) politics.

In their exchange of apologies, Daly and Carey acted as religious agents of civil society. For these and other civil agents, this role in the search for reconciliation is not entirely new. One thinks readily of Mahatma Gandhi, Martin Luther King Jr., and Desmond Tutu. These were protagonists of great struggles, but many other peacebuilders in civil society are working on another level, "from the middle," in the words of Douglas Johnston.[61] The cardinal and the archbishop entered the Northern Ireland process as activists or spokesmen for groups in conflict, in one sense; but they also acted as mediating parties. (Hence the accusations of "moral equivalence" leveled especially against Daly by some Catholics.) According to Johnston, whether official and in the open, or unofficial and behind the scenes, "these third-party intervenors are making their mark in the world of negotiation and conflict resolution."[62]

Virtually all of the agents mentioned in this chapter have staked out a place in, but not of, politics (or politics as usual). These include third parties and civil-society actors as well as statesmen like former presidents Kim Dae Jung and Nelson Mandela. Alongside people and leaders are also institutional mechanisms of forgiveness and reconciliation—projects, organizations, and official as well as semi-official bodies. These initiatives are aimed primarily at promoting forgiveness at either the broad atmospheric levels or among individuals and in small communities. The next chapter looks at examples of two such mechanisms: truth commissions and facilitated small groups.

NOTES

1   Quoted by Donald W. Shriver Jr., in Woodstock Colloquium *Forgiveness in Conflict Resolution: Reality and Utility—The Experiences of the Truth Commissions* (March 11, 1998) (Washington, DC: Woodstock Theological Center, n.d.), 100.

2   Shriver, in Woodstock Colloquium *Forgiveness in Conflict Resolution: Reality and Utility—The Experiences of Truth Commissions*, 100-101.

3   Shriver, *An Ethic for Enemies: Forgiveness in Politics* (New York, Oxford: Oxford University Press, 1995), 102.

4   Olga Botcharova, in Woodstock Colloquium *Forgiveness in Conflict Resolution: Reality and Utility* (December 9, 1996) (Washington, DC: Woodstock Theological Center, n.d.), 45.

5   Part of this account, including Gordon Wilson's remarks during the radio interview, is taken from "The Enniskillen Remembrance Day Massacre," http://www.iraatrocities. fsnet.co.uk/enniskillen.htm (accessed in January 2004).

6   "The Enniskillen Remembrance Day Massacre."

7   Cardinal Cahal B. Daly, in Woodstock Colloquium *Forgiveness in Conflict Resolution: Reality and Utility—The Northern Ireland Experience* (June 18, 1997) (Washington, DC: Woodstock Theological Center, n.d.), 8.

8   Rev. Douglas Baker, in Woodstock Colloquium *Forgiveness in Conflict Resolution: Reality and Utility—The Northern Ireland Experience*, 58-59.

9   Baker, in Woodstock Colloquium *Forgiveness in Conflict Resolution: Reality and Utility— The Northern Ireland Experience*, 59.

10 Baker, in Woodstock Colloquium *Forgiveness in Conflict Resolution: Reality and Utility— The Northern Ireland Experience*, 59.

11 Baker, in Woodstock Colloquium *Forgiveness in Conflict Resolution: Reality and Utility— The Northern Ireland Experience*, 59.

12 Cf. Drew Christiansen, SJ, in Woodstock Colloquium *Forgiveness in Conflict Resolution: Reality and Utility*, 67.

13 Shriver, interview with William Bole, Washington, DC, May 2002.

14 Barton Gellman, "Hussein, on His Knees, Begs Forgiveness for Massacre," *Washington Post*, March 17, 1997, A1.

15 William Bole, "Did They Say the 'F' Word?", *Our Sunday Visitor*, March 5, 2000, 12-13.

16 Douglass W. Cassel Jr., in Woodstock Colloquium *Forgiveness in Conflict Resolution: Reality and Utility—The Experiences of Truth Commissions*, 43; cf. 37-45.

17 Charles M. Sennott and Ted Oliver, "IRA Apologizes for Killing, Injuring Hundreds of Civilians," *Boston Globe*, July 17, 2002.

18 Shriver, *An Ethic for Enemies*, 91.

19 Joseph V. Montville, "Justice and the Burdens of History," in *Reconciliation, Justice, and Coexistence: Theory and Practice*, ed. Mohammed Abu-Nimer (Lanham, MD: Lexington Books, 2001), 125.

20 Botcharova, Woodstock Colloquium *Forgiveness in Conflict Resolution: Reality and Utility—The Bosnian Experience* (October 24, 1997) (Washington, DC: Woodstock Theological Center, n.d.), 94.

21 Cf. Daly, in Woodstock Colloquium *Forgiveness in Conflict Resolution: Reality and Utility—The Northern Ireland Experience*, 5-7.

22 Archbishop George Carey quoted by Daly, in Woodstock Colloquium *Forgiveness in Conflict Resolution: Reality and Utility—The Northern Ireland Experience*, 5.

23 Recounted by Daly, in Woodstock Colloquium *Forgiveness in Conflict Resolution: Reality and Utility—The Northern Ireland Experience*, 5-6.

24 Recounted by Daly, in Woodstock Colloquium *Forgiveness in Conflict Resolution: Reality and Utility—The Northern Ireland Experience*, 6.

25 Carey quoted by Daly, in Woodstock Colloquium *Forgiveness in Conflict Resolution: Reality and Utility—The Northern Ireland Experience*, 7.

26 Recounted by Daly, in Woodstock Colloquium *Forgiveness in Conflict Resolution: Reality and Utility—The Northern Ireland Experience*, 7.

27 Cf. Daly, in Woodstock Colloquium *Forgiveness in Conflict Resolution: Reality and Utility—The Northern Ireland Experience*, 6.

28 Daly, in Woodstock Colloquium *Forgiveness in Conflict Resolution: Reality and Utility— The Northern Ireland Experience*, 6-7.

29 Cited by Gerard F. Powers, in Woodstock Colloquium *Forgiveness in Conflict Resolution: Reality and Utility*, 63.

30 Powers, in Woodstock Colloquium *Forgiveness in Conflict Resolution: Reality and Utility*, 65.

31 Powers, in Woodstock Colloquium *Forgiveness in Conflict Resolution: Reality and Utility—The Northern Ireland Experience*, 34.

32 Daly, in Woodstock Colloquium *Forgiveness in Conflict Resolution: Reality and Utility— The Northern Ireland Experience*, 35.

33 Cf. Powers, in Woodstock Colloquium *Forgiveness in Conflict Resolution: Reality and Utility*, 65.

34   Anthony Cary, in Woodstock Colloquium *Forgiveness in Conflict Resolution: Reality and Utility—The Northern Ireland Experience*, 27.

35   John P. Langan, SJ, in Woodstock Colloquium *Forgiveness in Conflict Resolution: Reality and Utility—The Experiences of Truth Commissions*, 97.

36   Langan, in Woodstock Colloquium *Forgiveness in Conflict Resolution: Reality and Utility—The Experiences of Truth Commissions*, 97-98.

37   Powers, in Woodstock Colloquium *Forgiveness in Conflict Resolution: Reality and Utility—The Bosnian Experience*, 36.

38   Brian Lennon, SJ, in Woodstock Colloquium *Forgiveness in Conflict Resolution: Reality and Utility*, 56.

39   Cf. Neil J. Kritz, in Woodstock Colloquium *Forgiveness in Conflict Resolution: Reality and Utility—The Experiences of the Truth Commissions*, 68-69.

40   Daly, in Woodstock Colloquium *Forgiveness in Conflict Resolution: Reality and Utility—The Northern Ireland Experience*, 28-29.

41   Pope John Paul II, 2002 World Day of Peace Message "No Peace Without Justice, No Justice Without Forgiveness" (January 1, 2002), no. 9, http://www.vatican.va (accessed in October 2003).

42   Powers, in Woodstock Colloquium *Forgiveness in Conflict Resolution: Reality and Utility*, 65.

43   Shriver, interview.

44   Shriver's comment during meeting of Forgiveness Working Group, Woodstock Theological Center, December 2000.

45   James L. Connor, SJ, in Woodstock Colloquium *Forgiveness in Conflict Resolution: Reality and Utility—The Northern Ireland Experience*, 72.

46   Shriver, in Woodstock Colloquium *Forgiveness in Conflict Resolution: Reality and Utility—The Bosnian Experience*, 114.

47   Brandon Grove, letter to William Bole, May 27, 2002.

48   Grove, letter.

49   Grove, letter.

50   Rev. Kenneth Newell, in Woodstock Colloquium *Forgiveness in Conflict Resolution: Reality and Utility—The Northern Ireland Experience*, 56.

51   Newell, in Woodstock Colloquium *Forgiveness in Conflict Resolution: Reality and Utility—The Northern Ireland Experience*, 61.

52   Shriver, *An Ethic for Enemies*, 72.

53   Powers, in Woodstock Colloquium *Forgiveness in Conflict Resolution: Reality and Utility*, 66.

54   R. Scott Appleby, *The Ambivalence of the Sacred: Religion, Violence, and Reconciliation* (Lanham, MD: Rowman & Littlefield, 2000), 191.

55   Appleby, *The Ambivalence of the Sacred*, 238.

56   Daly, in Woodstock Colloquium *Forgiveness in Conflict Resolution: Reality and Utility—The Northern Ireland Experience*, 12.

57   Cf. Marc Gopin, *Between Eden and Armageddon: The Future of World Religions, Violence, and Peacemaking* (New York, Oxford: Oxford University Press, 2000), 186-187.

58   Gopin, *Between Eden and Armageddon*, 186-187.

59   Powers, telephone interview with William Bole, January 2003.

60   Powers, interview.

61   Douglas Johnston, "Introduction: Beyond Power Politics," in *Religion, the Missing Dimension of Statecraft*, ed. Douglas Johnston and Cynthia Sampson (New York, Oxford: Oxford University Press, 1995), 4.

62   Johnston, "Introduction: Beyond Power Politics," 4.

CHAPTER 5

Social Truth and Personal Healing: Projects of Forgiveness

Truth commissions and facilitated small groups represent
two concrete manifestations of alternative diplomatic or
Track II thinking—two initiatives of political forgiveness.

T hey are, in some clear ways, creatures of the state—official bodies vested with political and often juridical authority. Yet they also depart from diplomacy as usual by working with the tools of forgiveness, symbolizing a society's desire to eventually repair relationships. These are *truth commissions*, which have helped provide transitional justice in a growing number of post-conflict nations.

Less visibly, other people cross the most contentious lines of ethnicity and belief, with help from experienced practitioners of conflict resolution. They come together quietly in local communities to voice grievances, share pain, and acknowledge their faults or the faults of their groups. These *facilitated small groups* have become part of the broad landscape of political forgiveness.

Truth commissions and facilitated small-group reconciliation are responses to the characteristic conflicts of the post–Cold War period, conflicts often arising from clashes of group identity rather than strictly political or ideological rivalry. These initiatives also respond to the limitations of purely military and diplomatic approaches to solving these conflicts.

In the 1990s, violent clashes of cultures and groups prompted a serious look at strategies of forgiveness that might seem counterintuitive in such unforgiving places. Some have concluded that the possible benefits of a forgiveness-based approach are "worth all the efforts and risks since no military or diplomatic solutions have succeeded in bringing true peace among people."[1] This is, if you will, forgiveness by default, the negative cause of interest in applying the concept. Perhaps in places like Rwanda and Burundi, forgiveness is "just another word for nothing left to lose" (with apologies to Janis Joplin).

More positively, the post–Cold War realities have also generated interest in a two-track theory of international conflict resolution. Track I is the realm of "nation-state negotiations and the interactions of official diplomats," as articulated by Douglas Johnston[2] and modeled in *Politics Among Nations*, the landmark 1948 study by Hans Morgenthau.[3] Track II is the terrain of civil society, mediating institutions, and non-governmental organizations and is characteristically where forgiveness makes its entrance as a political possibility. "Although there are situations where one track or the other will clearly represent the preferred course, conflict prevention or resolution does not have to be a single track process," writes Johnston. "In the mounting disorder of the 'new world order' . . . practitioners will need to use every approach available to them, including synergistic combinations of tracks I and II."[4]

In its broader spirit, Track II conflict resolution is not only defined by the people and institutions at work on that level; but it also involves different strategies and outlooks. The approach gives great credence to the kinds of initiatives—aimed at building trust and relationships—that can easily get slighted in a purely Track I or *realpolitik*[5] mindset. This chapter focuses on truth commissions and facilitated small-group reconciliation as two concrete manifestations of Track II thinking—two initiatives of political forgiveness.

In fairly obvious ways, truth commissions are connected to channels of government (Track I). They are, for one thing, official bodies that investigate atrocities of the past. They are often conceived in the context of settlements to violent conflicts and transitions from periods of massive social injustice and wholesale abuse of human rights. At the same time, these institutions rest on the plausibility structure of civil society (Track II). They generally include agents of civil society, domestic and international, and pursue objectives beyond the known orbit of official diplomacy (in the very search for social truth and long-term reconciliation). In South Africa, retired archbishop and Nobel Peace laureate Desmond Tutu clearly thought of the country's Truth and Reconciliation Commission as a Track II undertaking. (The archbishop himself was an embodiment of civil society in his role as chairman of the commission.) He viewed the commission as a decisive break with conventional politics and diplomacy, going further to speak of it in theological terms: "For most of us [commission members], what we were being asked to undertake was profoundly religious and spiritual, and consequently spiritual resources were appropriately brought to bear on our task."[6] Truth commissions are indeed a "synergistic combination" of Track I and II resources.

Similarly, small-group dynamics highlight a deficit of normal strategic relations and conventional notions of national security. "In today's world of ethnic strife and high-technology weaponry, orthodox concepts of security based on competition of armaments will no longer be adequate. Increasingly, security will become a function of the strength and durability of national and international relationships," Johnston explains, adding, "The challenge is to reach beyond the state-centric focus of the power-politics model to accommodate nongovernmental interactions at the subnational and individual levels."[7] Non-governmental actors perform a distinct role in building and changing these relationships through dialogue and conflict prevention and transformation.[8] At the interpersonal and local levels, facilitated small groups offer one such form of intervention.

This chapter turns first to truth commissions, beginning with a brief overview, before looking in particular at questions surrounding political amnesty as a strategy of social forgiveness. A discussion of the (debatable) role of truth commissions in effecting personal healing follows, bringing into view the broad priorities of truth commissions.

The second part of this chapter discusses and evaluates the small groups. What role do they play in the overall movement of reconciliation? How might they help to reverse the cycle of revenge?

After a side look at the efficacy of dialogue in general as an approach to intergroup reconciliation, the chapter ends with thoughts on connecting the two tracks of conflict resolution.

SOCIETIES IN SEARCH OF TRUTH

The talk of forgiveness in international relations would sound more unlikely than it does (to some) were it not for the experiences of truth commissions. The tribunals have given high visibility to an agenda of social truth and eventual reconciliation that often falls outside the conventional confines of diplomacy as well as the usual capacities of political parties in fractious societies. These bodies have emerged in approximately two dozen countries, including South Africa, Uganda, Nigeria, Sri Lanka, Argentina, Chile, and El Salvador. A number of other nations—as diverse as Indonesia, Colombia, and Bosnia—recently considered or assembled their own commissions.[9]

As John P. Langan, SJ, a Georgetown University social ethicist, points out,

> On the one side, one can think about truth commissions as a certain way of realizing or incarnating a cluster of values—forgiveness, reconciliation, truth, justice, freedom—a lot of good things to which we're all deeply committed. As a certain way of giving this cluster an institutional form and a political reality, they are enormously attractive, and they become almost a first best because they give talented and committed people an opportunity to work on some of the fundamental problems and tensions in their society.[10]

Calls for a truth commission typically arise in a social environment that mirrors the emotional state of individuals in shock. Neil J. Kritz, who directs the Rule of Law Program of the United States Institute of Peace, pointed to a consensus in human psychology that individuals emerging from severe trauma need to develop mechanisms that allow them to come to terms with a troubled past: "A

nation emerging from massive repression, abuse, and trauma, if it's
going to proceed forward in a healthy fashion, rather than simply
closing the door on that past, similarly needs to find appropriate ways
to reconcile itself with the pain it has experienced."[11]

Some legal and social mechanisms are focused on perpetrators—prosecution, for example. Among these approaches, some
emphasize holding a small number of criminal trials for political
crimes committed by senior officials—an approach that can break
down the process of collective blame and guilt. Other approaches
adopt non-criminal sanctions, such as barring officials from ever
holding public office again. (Both mechanisms were put to use in
Central and Eastern Europe after the collapse of communism.) There
are also victim-focused mechanisms, which employ measures such as
compensation for victims and relatives, individual counseling, and
ceremonies that in various ways recognize their pain; by way of
example, Kritz points to re-burials that continued in Rwanda years
after the genocide there.

In Kritz's analysis, truth commissions fall in the middle,
between perpetrator-focused and victim-focused mechanisms.
Venturing a definition, he suggests that "a truth commission, to state
it simply, is an institution through which a country attempts to establish an official reckoning, an official history and accounting of past
abuses that have been perpetrated."[12]

The South Africa Experience

Kritz's definition is a fitting description of South Africa's Truth and
Reconciliation Commission, appointed by Nelson Mandela in 1995
and headed by Tutu. The example set by that commission is no small
part of what has made truth commissions a reasonable international
proposition, lending greater plausibility to forgiveness as a tool of conflict resolution. What started out as a political compromise (between
the white minority regime and the ascending black leadership) "virtually defined the transition and put the country in a different place than
it would have been without it," according to truth-commission chron-
icler Priscilla Hayner.[13]

Tutu also looks back on it with awe: "Instead of the horrendous bloodbath that so many had feared and so many others had predicted, here were these amazing South Africans, black and white together, crafting a relatively peaceful changeover and transfer of power."[14] The South African commission arose as the alternative to extensive criminal trials of human-rights abusers—which, apart from other concerns, might have been logistically impossible in an ill-prepared judicial system. It became a way to balance diverse values, including justice, accountability, stability, and reconciliation. The archbishop's comment, quoted partly in the second chapter, bears repeating in full: "We could very well have had justice, retributive justice, and had a South Africa lying in ashes—a truly Pyrrhic victory if ever there was one."[15]

The commission, or a quasi-independent committee within it, had the power to grant amnesties to those who made a full disclosure of political crimes committed during the apartheid era. The burden was placed on perpetrators, who had to come forward and apply for amnesty; approximately seven thousand did so. Applicants were not obliged to express any remorse or ask for forgiveness.[16] This amnesty arrangement provoked widespread debate in the international community, throwing light on the compromises almost inherent in the establishment of truth commissions. Continuing with Langan's line of analysis (cited in the previous subsection), truth commissions may also represent a "second-best remedy in a deficit situation."[17] In the case of amnesties, such measures are "usually part of a package to end the conflict," as explained by John Carr, director of the Department of Social Development and World Peace of the United States Conference of Catholic Bishops, referring to South Africa in particular: "These aren't perfect situations."[18] (Indeed, as Tutu was said to remark, amnesty is not for nice people. Recipients of amnesty do not deserve it, and they are not rewarded by it. The granting of it is for the sake of society.[19])

Furthermore, as already indicated, truth commissions usually arise in some sort of juridical vacuum, in which judicial institutions and the rule of law are lacking. South Africa's experience may also illustrate some limitations of truth commissions, such as the extent to which they can promote individual healing and interpersonal forgiveness, as distinct from societal reconciliation.

Broadly stated, how do these commissions connect the values of truth and reconciliation to requirements of justice and punishment? Though often seen in opposition, these values and requirements can open doors to forgiveness, as Donald W. Shriver Jr. has suggested.[20] What are the connections between the social and personal dynamics addressed by truth commissions? Should these institutions seek to facilitate healing on an individual level, or should they focus more on building atmospheres of social forgiveness?

Participants in dialogues on forgiveness and international politics have generally seen the truth commission as a potentially effective institution of political forgiveness in the aftermath of harsh ethnic, religious, and political conflict. For one thing, as Kritz has observed, the commissions permit a "cathartic public airing of the evil and pain which has been inflicted, resulting in an official record of the truth."[21] This is part and parcel of a "paradigmatic shift" (as noted in Chapter 3), in which negotiators or mediators no longer believe that bringing up past atrocities, in itself, poses obstacles to peace.[22]

The commissions do, however, remain experimental. One question concerns whether truth commissions have in fact carried out or made possible the minimum requirements of justice and restoration, crucial to genuine reconciliation. On that count, there appears to be strong and wide sentiment against blanket amnesties (like that offered in Chile) that can prevent truth from emerging and can undermine the justice dimension of forgiveness: "There cannot be an amnesty which precludes any possibility of investigation, of revealing truth, or of arriving at a verdict."[23] In addition, doubts remain about whether the catharsis of public airing will necessarily promote healing and forgiveness at the personal and interpersonal levels.

Amnesty = Forgiveness?

The question of amnesty opens the door to issues of justice, punishment, repentance, and indeed the whole conditionality of forgiveness in international conflict resolution. It is easy to equate amnesty with societal forgiveness, and in some cases it may advance the cause of eventual reconciliation. Amnesty, however, could just as easily become a roadblock to essential elements of forgiveness, such as truth and reckoning. Particularly questionable in the context of grave social wrongs are blanket amnesties, which "undermine the possibility of social truth and social justice, not to speak of forgiveness."[24] For one thing, blanket amnesties leave truth commissions with little leverage in probing political crimes and eliciting admissions of guilt from perpetrators.

Similarly suspect are amnesties granted in effect by perpetrators to themselves, as happened in Chile. Douglass W. Cassel Jr., an international human-rights lawyer, comments, "*Auto-amnistías*, self-amnesties, don't count. If you want to have any kind of social amnesty, it must be one which is adopted democratically by the appropriate organ, usually the legislature, of a democratic society. Even in those cases the rights of the victims must be respected."[25] A separate question concerns the validity of sweeping amnesties, under international law. Cassel argues that South Africa did not have the legal power to grant even a conditional amnesty for what could be classified as crimes against humanity. That is likely a minority view, but his argument highlights a tension between amnesty and provisions for international human rights and the common good: "We cannot give individual countries, any more than we could give individual victims, the right to waive justice when the interests of the world community are at stake as they were, for example, most obviously in the case of the Holocaust. Could we have allowed Germany to pardon all the Nuremberg defendants?"[26]

South Africa and Chile offer contrasting lessons about political amnesty and its breadth, in the context of truth-seeking efforts. The choice faced by the former was characterized starkly in Tutu's book *No Future Without Forgiveness*, in the chapter titled "Nuremberg or National Amnesia? A Third Way."[27] Widespread criminal trials of those who committed atrocities during apartheid's reign in South Africa represented the Nuremberg model, in the archbishop's assessment. Amnesia reflected an inclination to "let bygones be bygones" and leave the past alone (as if such a brutal past would just lie down and be quiet). The third way was a limited or individualized amnesty, granted to specific applicants in exchange for a full disclosure of political crimes. Disclosing such crimes, through testimony by perpetrators as well as victims, was critical to the success of the Truth and Reconciliation Commission.

As for letting bygones be bygones, one example Tutu had in mind was Chile. The regime of General Augusto Pinochet essentially gave itself amnesty in agreeing to transfer power from the military to a civilian government, which greatly hampered the effectiveness of Chile's truth commission. In his book, Tutu comments, "It has been important in the whole debate over impunity to point out that General Pinochet and his officers and government forgave themselves, they alone knew what precisely they had done; they were the accused, the prosecution, and the judges in their own case."[28] The amnesty law in Chile covered crimes committed between 1973, when Pinochet took power in a military overthrow of the democratically elected Salvador Allende government, and 1978—a five-year period of "the most systematic and scarring crimes committed during the dictatorship."[29]

Both Chile and South Africa employed amnesty to help surmount the colossal task of leaving behind one era of glaring injustice and beginning a new political order. So did El Salvador (in sweeping fashion, after its 1980-1992 civil war) and other countries. However, Shriver expresses a fairly wide sentiment: "Conditional amnesty in South Africa contrasts radically with unconditional amnesty in El Salvador" (or in Chile, for that matter); "societies have no right to accord to themselves unconditional amnesty."[30] One particular point of contrast has to do with the ability of victims to pursue claims, in civil courts, against human rights violators. Kritz relates that in cases where countries have enacted sweeping amnesties, individual victims have often been unable to make their case in court, because perpetrators do not willingly cooperate. Victims "can't get at the evidence. They can't do anything. They can't actually act on those rights [to pursue civil claims] if the state simply waves its wand and cleans everyone's slate."[31]

How do the parameters of amnesty affect the ultimate success or failure of truth commissions? One likely impact can be seen in the role of perpetrators in the truth-seeking process. A limited amnesty has tended to induce testimony and confessions more readily than have general amnesties. In South Africa, perpetrators who sought amnesty cooperated with the Truth and Reconciliation Commission, under pain of prosecution, as Hayner has described: "This is strikingly different from what we have seen in Latin America, including Chile and El Salvador, where cooperation from the armed forces was only provided confidentially and quietly. While in Latin America there was little formal cooperation between the perpetrators and the truth commissions, in South Africa that has been central to the truth that's coming out."[32]

General amnesty can dampen the very hope of genuine social reconciliation. It is often pointed out that victims, taking part in the process of truth commissions, are willing to extend forgiveness for the crimes against them. They can't forgive, however, without knowing whom to forgive—without knowing the truth. To the extent that general amnesty discourages a tone of repentance, it too gets in the way of forgiveness by victims, according to Juan Laval, counsel to the Central Bank of Chile and an investigator for the Chilean commission.[33]

Living with Amnesty

This does not mean that general amnesty or the likelihood of general amnesty renders a truth commission useless. In Chile, for example, the final report of the truth commission led political parties to acknowledge the facts described in the report—though the military rejected the findings outright. The final report also supplied courts with evidence that made it possible to prosecute a small number of perpetrators whose crimes were not covered by the amnesty law. (In addition, President Patricio Aylwin interpreted that law in a way that allowed investigations, though not prosecutions, of those covered by the general amnesty.)

Because of the built-in impediments to a full accounting of crimes, the commission in Chile also devoted much of its effort to designing policies aimed at providing reparations, such as a widows' pension and educational grants. "Though insignificant compared to the losses suffered by the victims and their families, those measures helped, to some extent, to relieve their pain and to provide an income—which had been absent for years—for the household," Laval recalls.[34] A similar reparation program in South Africa wound up being far less ambitious than originally proposed, and most of those who even qualified had yet to receive compensation at this writing.

Even under compromised conditions, the truth commission in Chile altered the debate over the past—the reality and extent of disappearances and political executions. Still, Laval concludes that the Chilean commission could not lead the country to reconciliation: "No reconciliation will ever be achieved without forgiveness on the part of the victims and their relatives and repentance on the part of the aggressor."[35]

In El Salvador, the amnesty law came after the findings and recommendations of a truth commission there. The commission did not endorse the plan, but neither did it call for criminal prosecutions, knowing that the cases could not be processed given the sorry state of the Salvadoran judiciary. Within great constraints, the commission decided to name names. It recommended the immediate removal from office of those responsible for human rights violations. Within four months, senior military officials resigned. The amnesty law was in all likelihood a *quid pro quo* move by President Alfredo Cristiani in response to the resignations. In the commission's final report, the military was linked to the overwhelming majority of allegations of massacres, tortures, disappearances, and other crimes (95 percent of 22,000 cases analyzed). To ensure justice in the future, if not the past, the commission recommended a series of judicial reforms, many of which were adopted by the Salvadoran legislature. It also called for reparations, although very few victims and their families received any compensation.[36]

But while limited, individual amnesty is far preferable to absolute measures, it is not in itself a formula for success or universal popularity. In South Africa, the amnesty program left a bitter taste in the mouths of many victims, and not simply because of any widespread desire for vengeance. "They understand the political realities [that produced amnesty] but they are not settled about the idea that their relative's killers are admitting to crimes and walking away free,"[37] Hayner explained at the time. Still, she believes limited amnesty was the best choice, partly because the new South Africa lacked the resources to successfully prosecute many human rights abusers.[38]

Another reason for the dismay in South Africa as well as in the international arena is that the granting of amnesty did not require any remorse or a statement of apology. In his book *The Ambivalence of the Sacred*, R. Scott Appleby gives weight to complaints that the lack of such stipulation created a "structural weakness" in the commission. As a result, many (he says most) perpetrators "refused to acknowledge their guilt and ask for or accept forgiveness" from those offering it.[39] In Appleby's rendering, this refusal undermined the commission's ultimate goal: genuine reconciliation. Nevertheless, he concludes, the panel "contributed positively" to building a democratic culture in the new South Africa by evoking the deepest, most reconciling values of its people.[40]

Other close observers were more understanding. Referring to the lack of a provision linking remorse to amnesty, Hayner said at the time, "This has rankled many, but it is based on the idea that if you require contrition, then you can never trust it when you hear it."[41] Tutu himself was initially discouraged because the legislation creating the truth commission did not include repentance among the conditions. He came to feel, however, that the omission was wise: "most applicants have in fact expressed at least some remorse and asked for forgiveness from their victims. Whether their requests have stemmed from genuine contrition is obviously a moot point."[42] (Contradicting the latter point, some observers say relatively few applicants, including the two thousand whose cases involved public hearings, sought forgiveness.[43])

Rwanda dealt with the question of remorse differently, through a special law passed in the aftermath of the genocide there in 1994. Rwanda focused its energies on criminal justice proceedings rather than on a truth commission, in order to put an end to impunity in the nation's bloody strife. Partly in response to the South Africa experience, Rwanda required that perpetrators not only acknowledge what they did, but also apologize to victims. Even this process did not deliver amnesty (which was not provided for in the law); it only gave the perpetrators a lesser penalty and swifter consideration. Whether these processes must elicit a sense of remorse, individually or socially, remains an open question among supporters of truth commissions.[44]

Partly at stake in these questions of amnesty is the conditional quality of social forgiveness, or the interaction between forgiveness and justice. One legitimate condition of political forgiveness is punishment, which, if not required, is at least compatible with a forgiving social arrangement. Here, the difference between social and personal dynamics is instructive: "It may be the right of individuals to forgo the punishment due to somebody who has deeply harmed them. But societies can ill afford that kind of justice or forgiveness because societies do need justice; they need to uphold the law."[45] At the same time, according to Shriver, "bringing to light the guilt of this and that perpetrator . . . is a version of punishment."[46] That latter view of truth and punishment reflects the thinking in South Africa. There, the truth commission held that simply being identified as a perpetrator is a form of punishment, with or without a requirement of remorse.[47]

Personal Healing: A Task of Truth Commissions?

The cathartic public airing of evil and pain is undoubtedly an attribute of truth commissions. Applied to individual dynamics, the commissions can contribute to individual healing by giving victims a chance to come forward and tell their stories. The often heard comment from victims—about their willingness to forgive if only given the truth—is one indication of the interpersonal potential. At the same time, truth commissions have notable limitations as agents of interpersonal forgiveness and healing.

Some question as naive the assumption that individual healing and personal catharsis necessarily result from letting victims tell their stories (a notion stated explicitly in the formation of a number of truth commissions). "That will be true for some people," says Hayner:

However, for many [victims] it also reawakens trauma. Some people can walk out feeling quite upset and re-traumatized. There may be psychologists on a truth commission's staff, but certainly they are not in a position to provide extensive counseling to these individuals. Consequently, many people may feel worse than they did before. They had learned to suppress their pain. Perhaps it had been a decade since the event took place; coming forward and talking about it reawakens that pain.[48]

In short, there are limits to social truth's ability to foster personal healing. These limits lead to an important question about the purposes and possibilities of truth commissions. To what extent do they facilitate personal—as distinct from collective—reconciliation? Should they seek to bring individuals in contact with each other? Or should they focus on a broader societal message?

Hayner and others who have studied the issue closely argue that it is important to distinguish between the goals of national and individual reconciliation. In some ways, national reconciliation is viewed as a more realistic goal, because political actors are often inclined to move ahead with political business once grievances have been fully aired and fairly dealt with, along with other hard truths. In that sense, truth commissions are better equipped to help bring about national reconciliation, according to Hayner: "But individual reconciliation is a much longer and more painful process; individuals need much more than just being told what the truth is, or having the opportunity to tell their own truth."[49]

In this light, there is a general sense that states and even civil society cannot force the process of personal forgiveness, or forgive on behalf of specific victims. Early in their deliberations, members of the South African truth commission tended to expect victims to forgive when they told their story at special victims' hearings. In one case related by Hayner, Tutu asked a victim,

"Now that you've told your story, are you willing to forgive?" And this victim, an older woman, said, "Archbishop Tutu, I respect your commission very much. I think you are doing very important work. But you cannot forgive for me, and I am not ready to forgive." I think that the commission learned over time that forgiveness is a very individual and personal process.[50]

Along that line, most practitioners warn against putting pressure on victims to forgive or to do so prematurely.[51] Such heavy-handedness can violate the status of victims and sufferers as privileged interpreters in the journey of reconciliation, as discussed in Chapter 4. It can also undermine the important understanding that forgiveness is a social healing process that requires time.

The South Africa experience, successful in many ways, is sobering on the point of promoting personal healing, or at least public perceptions of it. One opinion survey taken in the latter stage of the process found that only 17 percent of South Africans expected the Truth and Reconciliation Commission to make people more willing to forgive. Twenty-four percent expected people to feel angrier, and 23 percent indicated that the commission would cause pain.[52] All this highlights the need for follow-up activities, especially counseling, social services, and reparations programs. Hayner points to the example of victims' support organizations that arose in South Africa and some other countries in response to truth commissions: "That process can be more powerful for victims in the long run than the truth commission itself."[53]

Tutu himself articulates the belief that truth commissions can reasonably provide therapeutic services to victims. The South Africa commission (dubbed the "Kleenex® commission" because Tutu always kept a box of tissues handy for when victims or their surviving loved ones broke down and cried) would have done so, he says in his book, if it had received adequate funding and the proper mandate from government. Putting the matter more delicately than does Hayner, the archbishop points to "critics" who were upset that the commission was unable to provide long-term counseling and support, and he says "it is possible" that some victims "went away more traumatized than before." Regarding reparations, he leaves no doubt about his "distress at the fact that successful amnesty applicants walked free immediately, while victims had still not received final reparations nearly a year after the report" of the truth commission.[54]

The Core Task: Promoting Atmospheres of Forgiveness

With an eye on the question of individual healing, many practitioners and observers have cautioned against expecting too much from truth commissions, which normally run for a couple of years. At the same time, they have suggested that, if designed properly in suitable circumstances, these institutions could help spark a larger process of accountability and transition to long-term peace. The other side of the limitation regarding personal healing and forgiveness is that truth commissions can and should promote a broader societal message of reconciliation.

"What a truth commission can arguably do best is the broad sweep, the patterns of abuses, the broad issues of history, of both what has happened in that particular society and how these things happened,"[55] Kritz emphasizes. "A commission may examine the detail of structures within a military, for example, which may result in recommendations regarding particular units which are a source of problems and should be reformed in the future. But the big picture is going to be the main focus."[56] (Ironically, the Truth and Reconciliation Commission in South Africa came under some criticism for paying too little attention to the big picture, while delving into the details of atrocities that some believed had been adequately documented. Apparently South Africa was determined not to repeat the mistake made by Chile's commission, which was justly criticized for refusing to name names.)

As Kritz has underscored, truth commissions need to "facilitate a degree of national consensus and closure regarding the facts of a troubled history."[57] In practice, the commissions have made it harder for entire societies to avoid coming to terms with their pasts and their evils (harder perhaps than would criminal trials, which assign responsibility to individual perpetrators). The principal goal is "getting society to exercise some level of introspection and really do some soul-searching."[58]

Many practitioners would settle on that goal as a bottom-line value of truth commissions, together with another value articulated by Hayner in her book *Unspeakable Truths*. For her, truth commissions represent one answer to the question of what to do with a "recent history full of victims, perpetrators, secretly buried bodies, pervasive fear, and official denial." In choosing to remember the past, rather than burying it, "a country will be in a stronger position to build a more stable future, less likely to be threatened with tensions and conflict emerging from the shadows of a mysterious past."[59]

In sum, the evidence suggests that truth commissions can contribute to building a public process of forgiveness in post-conflict societies. That process must include efforts to uncover painful truths and a willingness to forgo revenge as requisite steps toward envisioning a new political future. The *raison d'etre* of truth commissions is to make the past present, so to speak, and to privilege the excruciating memories of a people on the long path to reconciliation. In addition, through a truth commission the political community chooses forbearance over revenge and signals at least a desire to eventually repair relationships.

At the same time, questions remain about whether these commissions can adequately serve the goals of justice, which may include restitution and reparations. Those questions concern the ability of such tribunals to help usher in a new political future. Further, the commissions do seem, almost inevitably, to come up short when it comes to facilitating personal healing and reconciliation. That shortcoming, however, sheds light on the commissions' wider role in fostering atmospheres of forgiveness and offsetting the ever-threatening "hothead factor" in extremely polarized societies.

IN SEARCH OF PERSONAL HEALING: SMALL-GROUP RECONCILIATION

As truth commissions focus on the larger societal picture, the question of personal healing and forgiveness remains. Indeed, the limited reach of truth commissions points to a need for smaller groups that address individual and interpersonal dynamics of reconciliation. This broad project reflects a fresher understanding of security, based less on armaments and more on relationship building (including relationships at the sub-national and individual levels, as identified by Johnston at the start of this chapter).

The Center for Strategic and International Studies (CSIS) in Washington, D.C., has undertaken such an effort involving members of various religious communities (namely, Catholic, Orthodox, Muslim, and Jewish) in the former Yugoslavia. In the basic CSIS seminar, participants have an opportunity to express their grievances, which allows members of other ethnic and religious groups to see the harm done by their groups to their enemies. Inevitably, these memories trace the path by which the victim of aggression becomes the aggressor, and the aggressor becomes the victim, fueling the cycle of revenge. The dialogues invariably turn into a "walk through history," which "has led to some surprisingly open acknowledgments of the collective transgressions of one's own people," reports Johnston, who led the team that launched the seminars after the 1992-1995 war in Bosnia.[60]

In this and other ways, CSIS's seminars parallel the larger dynamics of political forgiveness (as conceived in Shriver's definition), beginning with truth and the recovery of authentic memories. Another critical step in the seminars is getting participants to re-humanize the enemy, which brings empathy into play. The possibility of forgiveness arises from "identifying with the very basic human needs of the enemy and understanding the fears behind them, while still respecting my own suffering," as psychologist and group facilitator Olga Botcharova explained at a Woodstock colloquium.[61]

At a certain point, these dynamics effect a turn toward the future, which makes possible the mending of fractured human relationships. In Shriver's terms, this marks a "collective turning from the past that neither ignores past evil nor excuses it, that neither over-looks justice nor reduces justice to revenge, that insists on the humanity of enemies even in their commission of dehumanizing deeds. . . ."[62] The turn from the past is what brings into operation all four components of forgiveness in Shriver's definition: truth, forbear-ance, empathy, and the commitment to repair relationships. (In the kindred understanding of renowned educator and peace practitioner Landrum Bolling, as described by Botcharova, forgiveness means "giv-ing up a desperate desire to change the past."[63]) In turning toward the future, one challenge is to "develop another 'I,' different from the one that was destroyed" or victimized, as Botcharova has explained.[64] Another challenge for both the individual and society is to accept the fact that retribution or retributive justice will not bring satisfaction and healing to victims.

Notice how, in this process of forgiveness, people might advance through the stages without ever saying or hearing the word "forgiveness." Indeed, CSIS's facilitators are rather cautious in their use of the word. Yet when the time is ripe, the concept of forgiveness is introduced in the workshops—with the goal of healing the victim, not of reforming the aggressor. Johnston explains, "Its purpose is to enable victims to let go of their hatred, their desire for revenge, and any need to change the past. With the act of forgiving, one does not forget the past, but rather elects to enter the present and the future by consciously breaking the cycle of revenge. In this context, the justice one seeks takes on a restorative, rather than a retributive, character."[65]

A central objective of small-group reconciliation is to help erase the psychology of "victimhood," which feeds the ongoing cycle of ret-ribution. As presented in Chapter 1, the stages of victimhood include injury and shock, realization of loss, suppression of grief and fears, anger, desire for justice and revenge, creation of myths, and, finally, the act of "justified" aggression. Botcharova, as a conflict-resolution trainer, has also outlined the stages through which the "closed circle of victimhood/aggression" is broken: mourning and expressing grief, confronting fears and accommodating loss, re-humanizing the enemy, choosing to forgive, establishing justice, and rewriting history and solving problems jointly. A summary of these stages to reverse the cycle follows.

1. MOURNING; EXPRESSING GRIEF. "To allow oneself to feel the pain in full instead of trying to get away from it is the first challenge for the victim. . . . Screaming, complaining, talking with friends, with a priest or psychologist, or praying to God—any expressions of those emotions of which we are usually frightened should be encouraged to make ourselves free from pain. The more we make ourselves release these emotions, the less power they will have over us in the future. Mourning is the process of saying goodbye to the past and expressing respect towards the suffering."[66]

2. CONFRONTING FEARS; ACCOMMODATING LOSS. "To get out of darkness we need to know specifically what we are frightened of. Even identifying and naming those fears, in spite of our own resistance to doing so, may become the first step in accepting what has happened to us."[67]

3. RE-HUMANIZING THE ENEMY; "WHY THEM?" "The efforts of our soul to find peace are often blocked by continuous questioning of ourselves—'Why me?' Failure to find an answer to this question may help us to reframe it: 'Why me?' is gradually transformed into 'Why them?' . . . Thinking of the enemy's motives . . . evokes a certain understanding of similarity to our human nature. Thus, our mind comes to separate the act of aggression from the human being who performed it. . . . Then the enemy should be perceived as a sinner disconnected from his/her spiritual center rather than as a creature of insane evil. 'Why them? Why did they do that to us? Why did they have to?' . . . When we find ourselves looking at things from another dimension, we begin to feel a kind of empathy toward the aggressor, who is not able to achieve a similar understanding and stays within the power of his own fears."[68]

4. CHOOSING TO FORGIVE; COMMITING; TAKING RISKS. "The first signs of forgiveness, hardly realized at the beginning, may develop into a kind of tranquility where we feel more and more united with our own souls and with everything and everybody in the universe. The deep inner transformation intensifies the healing process and culminates in full forgiveness. . . . [This] is a primary need of the victim in the healing process. It requires, however, not only conscious and free choice but tremendous commitment as well. One may forgive but the perpetrator may choose to ignore it or even strike again—because of his or her own fears. If we have to forgive our brother seventy-seven times, as Christ said, how many times then do we need to forgive our enemy? Commitment to forgiveness and taking risks is usually motivated by a personal need for complete healing and inspired by the initial success in achieving new inner freedom."[69]

5. ESTABLISHING JUSTICE. "No reconciliation will ever be completed without justice and paying tribute to our memory. . . . For the person who forgave, justice targets the future. Its aim is reintegration of the relationship between former victims and aggressors in a new, safe surrounding designed and built by both sides. It is achieved only with the realization of the spiritual unity of us all. . . . An important shift in the concept of justice is that a former victim healed from his victimhood through forgiveness can and should be given a principal role in establishing justice. He is equipped with the wisdom of suffering that provides a unique clear spiritual perspective in solving the most complicated problems. What is more important, he is guided by love."[70]

6. REWRITING HISTORY; PROBLEM SOLVING JOINTLY. "Building a secure future means listening to each other's grievances and accepting responsibility for the past, 'rewriting' history together. . . . In intra-group conflict, it should be symbolized by a public apology from the aggressor. Then the road is open to negotiating solutions that will require appropriate changes in

the socio-political environment. Only after we are able to forgive are we healed and capable of engaging in practical problem
solving with the other party. Even if reconciliation does not take
place (depending on numerous factors, the principal ones being
confronting the perpetrator and establishing justice), forgiveness empowers us to proceed with life as happier and stronger
persons and becomes the inspiration to search creatively for
solutions in the future."[71]

Does the general project of small-group reconciliation hold out
promise for bringing individuals to forgiveness and shared responsibility for the future? Some will question the adaptability of therapeutic methods to civil disputes in societies unaccustomed to such intervention. "There is too much Western therapy" in the approach articulated by Botcharova, argued George Irani, of the United States
Institute of Peace, in a Woodstock colloquium.[72] Drew Christiansen,
SJ, responded, "It is not therapy in the pejorative, self-centered sense.
This is a real healing process that has public dimensions."[73]
(Christiansen added that one question, however, concerns how to
effectively "integrate the public justice questions and public repentance into this process."[74])

Others who are comfortable with the small-group reconciliation
approach will nonetheless warn against possible distortions, a temptation to pursue forgiveness with a blunt or overly programmatic
hand. Botcharova herself cautions that, with the concept of forgiveness spreading beyond the spiritual and personal spheres,

> there is a danger of a simplified approach: a tendency to
> "overuse" it, to impose it on the sides in conflict while ignor-
> ing its subtle, delicate, and truly intimate spiritual nature.
> Sometimes even the slightest suspicion on the part of a victim
> that he might be pressed to forgive may provoke an outburst
> of resistance. The victim may feel humiliated and abused
> again (this time, probably, by "outsiders of good will"). . . . My
> concern is not to formalize forgiveness, not to try and turn it
> into a tool or practical model to utilize, though the temptation

is great, but to see it rather in its gentle, spiritual, and, in a way, mysterious nature.[75]

Other questions might arise from the difficulty of verifying the success of such a "mysterious" process. Botcharova acknowledges that her interpretation "offers no familiar instruments to measure and no estimated quick results; thus it may provoke much skepticism and nonacceptance from some respected political scientists."[76] Still, her experience with ethnic conflicts in the Balkans has led her to conclude that those who are dedicated to resolving intergroup conflict should look upon forgiveness as a strategically important concept, despite its subtle and unpredictable ways.

Notwithstanding her caution about "outsiders of good will" who might tell people to forgive, Botcharova points to the role of third-party facilitators in creating a "safe environment for the 'enemies' to listen to each other, to develop initial trust, and to begin inner healing through sharing personal experiences."[77] A critical part of success, along that line, is diversity of staff. For example, the Center's conflict-resolution team in Bosnia included an American, a Russian, a Pole, and a Dutchman (part of the point being to avoid the perception that Americans were telling other people what to do). In addition to conflict-resolution skills, members contributed expertise in theology, psychology, socio-anthropology, intercultural communications, and political analysis. Another ingredient of success is continued local support to reinforce the conflict-resolution training, especially among leaders and local facilitators.[78]

The Limits of Dialogue: Alternatives and Variations

The peacemaking potential of facilitated small-group reconciliation would be difficult to assess without a broader look at intergroup dialogue as a tool of conflict resolution. While that stretches beyond this treatment, it is worth relating that some practitioners and theorists have begun to stress the limitations of facilitated dialogue in this field.

One such challenge has come from Rabbi Marc Gopin, who has participated in conflict-resolution initiatives in the Middle East. Part of his concern is that the dialogues are usually carried out among elites, which fosters the delusion that there can be "peace without people." To an extent, he refers to the official Middle East peace process and its failure to bring along communities across that divide.

However, he also critiques the kinds of dialogue workshops that are a staple of Track II intervention in intergroup conflicts.[79] "The culture surrounding the efficacy of the dialogue workshop assumes that direct verbal dialogue is a path to deep change within people," he writes in his book *Between Eden and Armageddon*, adding that one root of this assumption is a "culture that values rhetoric and debate."[80] Gopin also suggests that in the throes of extreme intergroup conflict, dialogue may already represent a major concession that parties are unwilling to make, because it involves an explicit recognition of the other. As one alternative, he says that unilateral, symbolic acts and gestures may carry greater resonance in certain cultures, especially religious communities.

One of his models is Maha Gosananda, Buddhism's patriarch in Cambodia, who led peace marches across all of that tragically wounded land. On those pilgrimages, "the monks dip flowers in buckets of water and sprinkle the water on the shops and homes as they walk,"[81] gestures that resonate deeply and somewhat mysteriously among Cambodians. Many observers, like Gopin, believe Gosananda's gestures have contributed to healing and reconciliation in Cambodia, but they also feel he has taken a premature step by calling for forgiveness of Khmer Rouge members.[82]

The practical import of Gopin's critique is twofold. First, much can be done short of dialogue, especially when it comes to conflict in traditional, religious societies. Second, even when people are ready for an authentic dialogue, there are some whose talents and interests dispose them better toward the kinds of symbolic gestures undertaken by Gosananda.

Beyond Gopin's critique, some sponsors and funders have recently grown skeptical of the conventional dialogue method, especially in the Middle East, where this approach has a longer history than in most other places. "One concern is that it could be a flash in the pan," notes David Smock of the United States Institute of Peace, referring to programs such as Seeds of Peace, which brought together Israeli and Palestinian youth. He explains that the breakthroughs often take place in isolated settings where dialogue partners are removed from their everyday world of conflict, and that these breakthroughs can quickly evaporate when participants return to the usual pressures of those settings.[83]

What bearing do these perspectives have on the project of facilitated small-group reconciliation?

Some architects of this particular approach say the key is a certain kind of dialogue that centers on telling personal stories of loss, in the framework of conflict resolution. Joseph V. Montville, of the Center for Strategic and International Studies (CSIS), argues that the approach is "practically always successful in beginning a healing process if the third party facilitators are psychologically sensitive. The safe environment within which individuals can present grievances permits each side to gradually educate the other in the dimensions of loss felt by the other."[84] Turning to the example of truth and reconciliation commissions, Montville points to observations that during hearings held by the South African commission, "storytelling usually had a cathartic effect on the victim telling the story"[85] (though others have questioned the personal cathartic effects of that commission, as discussed in the first part of this chapter). "But in the private confines of the small, facilitated workshop, storytelling also penetrates the defenses of the other side that has stoutly resisted the broadside accusations" by members of other ethnic groups.[86] Montville says that he has seen this happen in several such groups.

On that point, the extent of the difference between the storytelling technique employed by CSIS and the conventional dialogue workshop may be less than clear. Smock, who directs the Religion and Policymaking Initiative of the United States Institute of Peace, notes that storytelling has become standard in the latter settings, too. Nonetheless, his program at the peace institute has supported the CSIS seminars. He points out that these seminars have shown promise in part because they are "more process-oriented," involving extensive follow-up among participants (many of whom attend several work-shops) and their communities.[87]

Perhaps the bottom line here is that practitioners and peace-builders should not assume that a storytelling technique is enough to produce a successful dialogue encounter. Yet this component as well as others, including repeated encounters and intensive follow-up, may advance healing and reconciliation at the personal and grassroots levels.

⌒

Although truth commissions are usually official bodies, both commissions and facilitated small groups illustrate the pathways of Track II intervention or alternative conflict resolution in fractious societies. Both aim to build trust and relationships—truth commis-sions at the social level, and small groups at the individual and inter-personal levels.

Still, these actors and aims do not exist in a realm apart from the Track I realm of official diplomacy. As Johnston has explained, con-flict prevention or resolution may at times call for "synergistic combi-nations" of the two tracks: "Using the two tracks in combination can sometimes reduce, if not eliminate, the limits to what can be achieved when using only one in isolation."[88]

Where are the critical connection points between these two tracks of official and unofficial diplomacy? Where is the intercross between forgiveness and *realpolitik* engagement? These are fairly new questions in the discussion of forgiveness and conflict resolution. What is certain is that the actors in both realms need to be more attentive to the existence and strategies of each other. Christiansen asserts, "I still think ears need to be tuned and sensibilities refined between the people who are doing Track II diplomacy, who are largely working with this business of forgiveness, and the people doing Track I and [for example] the Dayton [peace] process," which led to an agreement to end the Bosnian conflicts:[89]

> I don't think that politicians and diplomats are hearing the religious community or social scientists yet. . . . They are

showing more acceptance of the fact that the Track II people are there. . . . They even talk of the need for Track II people in this new world of slender diplomatic means and major, complex problems which need to be addressed, but it seems to me that Track II has to be engaged still more fully.[90]

By their very design, truth commissions—official bodies that work with the tools of forgiveness—offer a potentially powerful connection between the two tracks of diplomacy and conflict transformation. In an enlarged notion of security, which includes the building of trust and relationships at all levels of society, facilitated small groups provide another clear link.

As Chapter 8 explores further, the spin-off activities of small groups facilitated by the Center for Strategic and International Studies in the former Yugoslavia have led some participants straight into the political and diplomatic spheres—even though these groups are composed mostly along (ecumenically) religious lines, which are not the usual conduits of *realpolitik* engagement. The next few chapters delve into the prospective roles of these faith communities in helping to remold forgiveness into a project of political import.

NOTES

1   Olga Botcharova, in Woodstock Colloquium *Forgiveness and Conflict Resolution: Reality and Utility* (June 18, 1997) (Washington, DC: Woodstock Theological Center, n.d.), 38.

2   Douglas Johnston, "Looking Ahead: Toward a New Paradigm," in *Religion, the Missing Dimension of Statecraft*, ed. Douglas Johnston and Cynthia Sampson (New York, Oxford: Oxford University Press, 1995), 326.

3   Cited in Johnston, "Looking Ahead: Toward a New Paradigm," 326.

4   Johnston, "Looking Ahead: Toward a New Paradigm," 327.

5   *Realpolitik* is defined as "a diplomatic policy based on the aggressive pursuit of national interests without regard for ethical or philosophical considerations," in *Webster's II New College Dictionary* (Boston and New York: Houghton Mifflin Company, 1995).

6   Desmond Mpilo Tutu, *No Future Without Forgiveness* (New York: Doubleday, 1999), 82.

7   Johnston, "Looking Ahead: Toward a New Paradigm," 333.

8   Cf. Johnston, "Looking Ahead: Toward a New Paradigm," 333.

9   Cf. Priscilla B. Hayner, *Unspeakable Truths: Confronting State Terror and Atrocity* (New York, London: Routledge, 2001), 14.

10   John P. Langan, SJ, in Woodstock Colloquium *Forgiveness in Conflict Resolution: Reality and Utility—The Experiences of Truth Commissions* (March 11, 1998) (Washington, DC: Woodstock Theological Center, n.d.), 98.

11   Neil J. Kritz, in Woodstock Colloquium *Forgiveness in Conflict Resolution: Reality and Utility—The Experiences of the Truth Commissions*, 5.

12   Kritz, in Woodstock Colloquium *Forgiveness in Conflict Resolution: Reality and Utility— The Experiences of the Truth Commissions*, 7.

13   Hayner, in Woodstock Colloquium *Forgiveness and Conflict Resolution: Reality and Utility—The Experiences of Truth Commissions*, 59.

14   Tutu, *No Future Without Forgiveness*, 10.

15   Tutu, *No Future Without Forgiveness*, 23.

16   Tutu, *No Future Without Forgiveness*, 49.

17   Langan, in Woodstock Colloquium *Forgiveness in Conflict Resolution: Reality and Utility—The Experiences of the Truth Commissions*, 99.

18   John Carr, in Woodstock Colloquium *Forgiveness and Conflict Resolution: Reality and Utility—The Experiences of Truth Commissions*, 74-75.

19   Donald Shriver Jr., interview with William Bole, Washington, DC, May 2000.

20   Cf. Shriver, in Woodstock Colloquium *Forgiveness in Conflict Resolution: Reality and Utility—The Experiences of the Truth Commissions*, 102.

21   Kritz, in Woodstock Colloquium *Forgiveness in Conflict Resolution: Reality and Utility— The Experiences of the Truth Commissions*, 8.

22   Cf. Kritz, in Woodstock Colloquium *Forgiveness in Conflict Resolution: Reality and Utility—The Experiences of the Truth Commissions*, 5.

23   Douglass W. Cassel Jr., in Woodstock Colloquium *Forgiveness in Conflict Resolution: Reality and Utility—The Experiences of the Truth Commissions*, 85.

24   Shriver, in Woodstock Colloquium *Forgiveness and Conflict Resolution: Reality and Utility—The Experiences of Truth Commissions*, 102.

25   Cassel, in Woodstock Colloquium *Forgiveness and Conflict Resolution: Reality and Utility—The Experiences of Truth Commissions*, 71.

26   Cassel, in Woodstock Colloquium *Forgiveness and Conflict Resolution: Reality and Utility—The Experiences of Truth Commissions*, 72.

27   Tutu, *No Future Without Forgiveness*, 27-30.

28   Tutu, *No Future Without Forgiveness*, 27-30.

29   Juan Laval, in Woodstock Colloquium *Forgiveness and Conflict Resolution: Reality and Utility—The Experiences of Truth Commissions*, 21.

30   Shriver, in Woodstock Colloquium *Forgiveness and Conflict Resolution: Reality and Utility—The Experiences of Truth Commissions*, 104.

31   Kritz, in Woodstock Colloquium *Forgiveness and Conflict Resolution: Reality and Utility—The Experiences of Truth Commissions*, 76.

32   Hayner, in Woodstock Colloquium *Forgiveness and Conflict Resolution: Reality and Utility—The Experiences of Truth Commissions*, 58.

33   Laval, in Woodstock Colloquium *Forgiveness and Conflict Resolution: Reality and Utility—The Experiences of Truth Commissions*, 25.

34   Laval, in Woodstock Colloquium *Forgiveness and Conflict Resolution: Reality and Utility—The Experiences of Truth Commissions*, 23.

35   Laval, in Woodstock Colloquium *Forgiveness and Conflict Resolution: Reality and Utility—The Experiences of Truth Commissions*, 24.

36   Cf. Cassel, in Woodstock Colloquium *Forgiveness and Conflict Resolution: Reality and Utility—The Experiences of Truth Commissions*, 41-44.

37 Hayner, in Woodstock Colloquium *Forgiveness and Conflict Resolution: Reality and Utility—The Experiences of Truth Commissions*, 72.

38 Cf. Hayner, in Woodstock Colloquium *Forgiveness and Conflict Resolution: Reality and Utility—The Experiences of Truth Commissions*, 72.

39 R. Scott Appleby, *The Ambivalence of the Sacred: Religion, Violence, and Reconciliation* (Lanham, MD: Rowman & Littlefield, 2000), 235.

40 Cf. Appleby, *The Ambivalence of the Sacred*, 200-201.

41 Hayner, in Woodstock Colloquium *Forgiveness and Conflict Resolution: Reality and Utility—The Experiences of Truth Commissions*, 60.

42 Tutu, *No Future Without Forgiveness*, 50.

43 Kritz, letter to William Bole, December 7, 2000.

44 Cf. Kritz, in Woodstock Colloquium *Forgiveness and Conflict Resolution: Reality and Utility—The Experiences of Truth Commissions*, 11-12.

45 Shriver, in Woodstock Colloquium *Forgiveness and Conflict Resolution: Reality and Utility—The Experiences of Truth Commissions*, 103-104.

46 Shriver, in Woodstock Colloquium *Forgiveness and Conflict Resolution: Reality and Utility—The Experiences of Truth Commissions*, 102.

47 Cf. Hayner, in Woodstock Colloquium *Forgiveness and Conflict Resolution: Reality and Utility—The Experiences of Truth Commissions*, 73.

48 Hayner, in Woodstock Colloquium *Forgiveness and Conflict Resolution: Reality and Utility—The Experiences of Truth Commissions*, 35.

49 Hayner, in Woodstock Colloquium *Forgiveness and Conflict Resolution: Reality and Utility—The Experiences of Truth Commissions*, 63.

50 Hayner, in Woodstock Colloquium *Forgiveness and Conflict Resolution: Reality and Utility—The Experiences of Truth Commissions*, 61.

51 Cf. Hayner, in Woodstock Colloquium *Forgiveness and Conflict Resolution: Reality and Utility—The Experiences of Truth Commissions*, 35-36.

52 Cf. Hayner, in Woodstock Colloquium *Forgiveness and Conflict Resolution: Reality and Utility—The Experiences of Truth Commissions*, 63.

53 Hayner, in Woodstock Colloquium *Forgiveness and Conflict Resolution: Reality and Utility—The Experiences of Truth Commissions*, 36.

54 Tutu, *No Future Without Forgiveness*, 233.

55 Kritz, in Woodstock Colloquium *Forgiveness and Conflict Resolution: Reality and Utility—The Experiences of Truth Commissions*, 69.

56 Kritz, in Woodstock Colloquium *Forgiveness and Conflict Resolution: Reality and Utility—The Experiences of Truth Commissions*, 69.

57 Kritz, in Woodstock Colloquium *Forgiveness and Conflict Resolution: Reality and Utility—The Experiences of Truth Commissions*, 9.

58 Kritz, in Woodstock Colloquium *Forgiveness and Conflict Resolution: Reality and Utility—The Experiences of Truth Commissions*, 91.

59 Hayner, *Unspeakable Truths*, 254.

60 Johnston, in Woodstock Colloquium *Forgiveness in Conflict Resolution: Reality and Utility—The Bosnian Experience* (October 24, 1997) (Washington, DC: Woodstock Theological Center, n.d.), 82.

61 Olga Botcharova, in Woodstock Colloquium *Forgiveness in Conflict Resolution: Reality and Utility—The Bosnian Experience*, 93.

62 Shriver, *An Ethic for Enemies*, 9.

63 Cited by Botcharova, in Woodstock Colloquium *Forgiveness and Conflict Resolution: Reality and Utility—The Bosnian Experience*, 92.

64 Botcharova, in Woodstock Colloquium *Forgiveness and Conflict Resolution: Reality and Utility*, 44.

65 Johnston, in Woodstock Colloquium *Forgiveness and Conflict Resolution: Reality and Utility—The Bosnian Experience*, 82.

66 Botcharova, in Woodstock Colloquium *Forgiveness in Conflict Resolution: Reality and Utility*, 45.

67 Botcharova, in Woodstock Colloquium *Forgiveness in Conflict Resolution: Reality and Utility*, 46.

68 Botcharova, in Woodstock Colloquium *Forgiveness in Conflict Resolution: Reality and Utility*, 46-47.

69 Botcharova, in Woodstock Colloquium *Forgiveness in Conflict Resolution: Reality and Utility*, 47.

70 Botcharova, in Woodstock Colloquium *Forgiveness in Conflict Resolution: Reality and Utility*, 48.

71 Botcharova, in Woodstock Colloquium *Forgiveness in Conflict Resolution: Reality and Utility*, 48-49.

72 George Irani, in Woodstock Colloquium *Forgiveness in Conflict Resolution: Reality and Utility—The Bosnian Experience*, 98.

73 Drew Christiansen, SJ, in Woodstock Colloquium *Forgiveness in Conflict Resolution: Reality and Utility—The Bosnian Experience*, 105.

74 Christiansen, in Woodstock Colloquium *Forgiveness and Conflict Resolution: Reality and Utility—The Bosnian Experience*, 105.

75 Botcharova, in Woodstock Colloquium *Forgiveness in Conflict Resolution: Reality and Utility*, 38.

76 Botcharova, in Woodstock Colloquium *Forgiveness in Conflict Resolution: Reality and Utility*, 38.

77 Botcharova, in Woodstock Colloquium *Forgiveness in Conflict Resolution: Reality and Utility*, 38.

78 Cf. Johnston, in Woodstock Colloquium *Forgiveness and Conflict Resolution: Reality and Utility—The Bosnian Experience*, 85.

79 Marc Gopin, interview with William Bole, Concord, MA, February 2001.

80 Gopin, *Between Eden and Armageddon: The Future of World Religions, Violence, and Peacemaking* (New York, Oxford: Oxford University Press, 2000), 43.

81 Gopin, *Between Eden and Armageddon*, 44.

82 Cf. Gopin, *Between Eden and Armageddon*, 42-48.

83 David Smock, interview with William Bole, Washington, DC, March 2001.

84 Joseph V. Montville, "Justice and the Burdens of History," in *Reconciliation, Justice, and Coexistence: Theory and Practice*, ed. Mohammed Abu-Nimer (Lanham, MD: Lexington Books, 2001), 122.

85 Montville, "Justice and the Burdens of History," 122.

86 Montville, "Justice and the Burdens of History," 122.

87 Smock, interview.

88 Johnston, "Looking Ahead: Toward a New Paradigm," 327.

89 Christiansen, in Woodstock Colloquium *Forgiveness in Conflict Resolution: Reality and Utility—The Bosnian Experience*, 105.

90 Christiansen, in Woodstock Colloquium *Forgiveness and Conflict Resolution: Reality and Utility—The Bosnian Experience*, 106.

CHAPTER 6

Religious Communities: "Compromised But Capable"

*While often implicated in sectarian conflict,
many religious communities are helping to build a
"new home" for forgiveness in the public arena.*

I ncreasingly, and especially since the passing of the Cold War, religion has raised its not-always-peaceable voice in a range of violent intergroup conflicts around the world. According to a wide perception, religion—whether that means people, institutions, or doctrines—has more often than not been part of the problem, not the solution, in these conflicts. In the view of many, organized religion was an agent of antagonism, a force of unforgiveness, even before crews of hijackers, presumed to be acting in the name of Islam, slaughtered thousands of innocents on September 11, 2001. This is roughly the face of religious faith seen by Warren Zimmerman, who has commented that while serving as U.S. ambassador to Yugoslavia, "I formed a degree of skepticism about the churches . . . because I felt they were a significant part of the problem. They were abetting and pushing forward the nationalism which created all the trouble."[1]

But another side of religion and conflict has attracted far less notice. It is reflected in a comment by Belgium's foreign minister Louis Michel regarding the St. Egidio Community, a lay Catholic organization based in Rome that performs charitable works worldwide. "Their activity is conducted with discretion; they cannot rely on aircraft or threats of an embargo. Dialogue, trust, and the use of reason are their strengths," said Michel, who was part of a blue-ribbon panel that gave

UNESCO's 2000 peace award to St. Egidio. In 1992, the community mediated an end to the Mozambique civil war, a mission of diplomatic mercy that, by some accounts, saved hundreds of thousands of lives. Since then it has intervened, with less dramatic results, in places such as Algeria and the former Yugoslavia.

The award offered signs that religious peacebuilding has not disappeared from the geopolitical radar. UNESCO's redoubtable chair, Henry Kissinger—former U.S. Secretary of State and arguably the avatar of political realism, or *realpolitik*—made a point of saying that the panel chose to honor St. Egidio "in a period when many countries around the world are experiencing ethnic, religious and other conflicts."[2]

In the work of conflict transformation, religion has been said to be capable rather than committed (R. Scott Appleby)—or compromised but capable (Douglas Johnston).[3] If that is generally so, what are the "capabilities" of religious actors, and how can they become less compromised and more committed? More to the point, what role can religions play in illuminating a geopolitical process of forgiveness that transcends the exclusively spiritual and personal realms? Donald W. Shriver Jr. has spoken of the need to give forgiveness "a new home" in the political sphere. That phrasing might invite the thought of religion as the traditional home of forgiveness, though personal piety and interpersonal relationships would come closer to that mark. That said, the pressing question concerns what religious communities can do to put forgiveness on a squarely social plane, along the continuum of conditions examined throughout this book. In other words, how are religious communities contributing to the search for truth, forbearance, empathy, and the will to reconcile (the components of Shriver's definition of forgiveness)?

Organized programs of conflict resolution are one piece of this picture of religion and political forgiveness, but not yet a very considerable part. As Appleby, who teaches history at the University of Notre Dame, remarked at a Woodstock Theologican Center forum in 2002, "the people who are committed to nonviolence and just peacebuilding of course are woefully under-recorded, often under-organized, not staffed, and not funded."⁴ Putting the issue in a broader framework, religions do contribute to the forgiveness process by promoting the *conditions* of peacebuilding, which include justice, human rights, and social development. While much broader than conflict resolution as such, advocacy of this kind has sometimes led to religious actors' playing mediating roles. For example, noting the leadership of African Catholic clergy and bishops in movements against dictatorship, historian and religious studies scholar Philip Jenkins relates that the Church has been in demand as an "honest broker in countries that did not even have a Christian majority."⁵

As a potent system of motivation and values, religion operates through a multiplicity of agents, personal and institutional. As mentioned at the start of Chapter 4, South Korea's former president Kim Dae Jung acted, in a sense, as a religious as well as political agent when he engaged in acts of forgiveness after triumphing over his authoritarian enemies. When Kim was awarded the Nobel Peace Prize in 2000, the *National Catholic Reporter* noted the scant attention paid to his deep personal faith—he happens to be Catholic.⁶

Yet Kim made no secret of his belief that religion—as both a spiritual and institutional force—had been pivotal to South Korea's political transformation as well as his own peacemaking passion. Further, another political institutional actor, South Africa's Truth and Reconciliation Commission—though an official body of reckoning—embodied religious meanings and motivations. Jenkins, who teaches at Pennsylvania State University, calls the commission "an innovative attempt to apply Christian ideas of repentance and forgiveness to national secular politics, rather than just individual relationships."⁷

This chapter, as well as the next two, looks specifically at religious agents as religious agents: that is, people and projects acting in the organized realm of religious conflict transformation. As in previous chapters, certain assumptions operate in these pages (more explicitly so in the next chapter). Most basic and theological, perhaps, is an assumption that self-transcendence is at the core of what it means to be religiously, and indeed humanly, authentic. That is, human beings may be hard-wired to reach out to others, to be social. This constitutes progress in the fullest sense; but there is also the reality of decline, of failing to move beyond one's perceptions, horizons, and interests, including the distorted memories or "mytho-history" of one's group, and this comes close to what theologians call "sin." In the grip of extreme nationalism, in which symbols of religious faith are co-opted for jingoistic purposes, this lack of human transcendence might also be cast in theological terms as "idolatry."[8]

In practical terms, these chapters draw upon lessons from the field, especially from the Balkans. Different kinds of religious actors have contributed to a process of forgiveness in that region, as well as to the forces of unforgiveness. These include religious leaders and institutions from among the ethnic communities in conflict, some of whom have played what has been called, in other regional contexts, an "insider-partial" role in seeking to mediate and transform the conflicts. The next chapter turns to other actors, including peacebuilding organizations from outside the region, which have played third-party or "outsider-neutral" roles.

SKEPTICISM AND ITS LIMITS

It is fair to say that most experts in international relations are somewhat skeptical of religion's potential to transform societal conflicts on any serious scale. "The assumption, conventional by now, is that religious faith commitment, or sense of identification with a faith community, fosters division, hatred, and violence," writes Raymond G. Helmick, SJ, who teaches international conflict resolution at Boston College and has mediated in a number of disputes around the world.[9]

Much of this suspicion is grounded in post–Cold War conflicts that have implicated religion, but it seems also to have philosophical and cultural underpinnings as well as historical roots. At a conference organized in 1995 by DACOR (Diplomatic and Consular Officers Retired), Douglas Johnston offered a sobering assessment of the reception given to religion among diplomats and others concerned with Track I or official diplomatic efforts: "Based on our seven-year examination, our conclusion was that within the Foreign Service generally, a combination of dogmatic secularism and economic deter-minism had created a learned repugnance to contending intellectually with anything that is religious or spiritual in nature."[10] He was refer-ring to his project at the Center for Strategic and International Studies that produced the path-setting book *Religion, the Missing Dimension of Statecraft*. Among several factors noted by Johnston was the assump-tion, dating to eighteenth-century Enlightenment ideas, that religion would become a declining influence in the affairs of state, as well as the realist school and its fixation on maximizing power.[11]

Rev. J. Bryan Hehir, an expert on ethics and international rela-tions, has traced these sentiments further back to the 1648 Peace of Westphalia, the treaty that ended thirty years of religious warfare in Europe. The product of Westphalia, Hehir suggested at the 1995 DACOR conference, was a "rather determined decision . . . in the study and discipline of international politics to radically separate reli-gion from politics."[12] In Hehir's interpretation, the Westphalian legacy produced a strongly secular conception of the world: "The argument is that religion can only be more trouble than help, if you introduce it into world affairs and, therefore, it is better to keep it separate."[13] In a casual survey, Hehir turned up barely a mention of religion in the stan-dard texts on international relations, which gave—at least before the terrorist attacks of September 11, 2001—an impression of internation-al politics as being devoid of religious content. "If we continue to think about religion as purely private, not having public implications, we continually end up with bad briefings and mistaken expectations."[14] That is arguably what we did "end up with" in the late 1990s, after two decades of flawed thinking about religion and international relations.

Islamic fundamentalism, springing especially from the Middle East, has since occupied a vast portion of the anxiety over religion's ill effects on geopolitical stability. Nevertheless, there has been a sort of ecumenism about religion's contributions to civil conflict, especially since the demise of bipolar world politics and new challenges to cul-tural identity posed by globalization. Indeed, in the first half-decade after the Cold War's end, the war in Bosnia helped generate many of the impressions about religion's role in deadly violence, and Islamic forces were by some accounts the least of the religious problem there, especially in the early years. The Bosnian war became, to cite one influential opinion, a prime exhibit in Samuel P. Huntington's thesis of a "clash of civilizations," namely between Orthodoxy and Catholicism as well as Islam.[15]

Near the end of the 1990s, exposure to that conflict and others left Francis Terry MacNamara, a retired ambassador who served as an election monitor in Bosnia, wondering if "secularization ultimately may be more promising than the reinforcement of religion, because religion has become a symbol of extreme nationalism."[16] Likewise, international law specialist William Stuebner, of the United States Institute of Peace, observes,

> On the Serb side and the Croat side, the worst people I had to deal with were the ones who took on the most religious trappings. I'm not talking about the clergy, but the actual criminals, the guys with the guns in their hands. . . . And so . . . Do you secularize and go back to brotherhood and unity or do you really strengthen these religious communities . . . so that they can take a leadership role for change . . . ?[17]

The Secularization Question

Many in the official diplomatic community have raised these questions, rooted in the long and troubled history of religion and political or international conflict. Should secularization be encouraged as the better path to international peace and stability? Wouldn't it be better to highlight universal values rather than lend credence to sectarian beliefs and institutions?

In wondering whether secularization might be preferable, MacNamara remembers women in Bosnia wearing fashionable, Western-style clothes in Muslim areas, which he saw as an encouraging sign of secularization. Responding to the same question at a forgiveness colloquium, Stuebner remarked, "As a Christian myself, the thing I resented more than anything else was that the cross had become a symbol of hatred."[18]

MacNamara's and Stuebner's were minority voices at this colloquium on forgiveness and the Bosnian experience—but not coincidentally, theirs were also the voices representing the official track of international diplomacy. Drew Christiansen, SJ, summarized without endorsing the sentiments heard during the gathering sponsored by the Woodstock Theological Center:

> There were some dissenting voices saying that we should not focus on the religious communities as the foci for the forgiveness process and that we need instead to take a secularized approach to the question of creating an environment where the values to which we all adhere can be upheld and transmitted, that we should build up secular institutions. I think [the proposal] that an international ethic is all that you need is another dissenting voice. It says that international humanitarian standards are what you need to apply and religion is not the way to proceed.[19]

During that dialogue, counterpoints were of course voiced, mostly from within the Bosnian context—where secularization had already been practiced quite sweepingly, and where religion was hardly working from a position of strength. Beyond any one regional context, it is fair to ask: Is the question of whether to secularize a timely and important question, or does it echo the battles fought in the last ideological war?

What has gradually surfaced in these conversations is a more textured version of the secularization thesis that seems to lurk behind many of the discussions. In the scholarly world, sociologist Jose Casanova has shed light on this foundational assumption by dividing the secularization thesis into three distinct theories.[20]

First, as Casanova explained at a March 2001 forum, secularization is a theory of "differentiation" between the religious and secular orders. In other words, this theory describes how the secular spheres—of politics, economics, science, culture, and so forth—were emancipated from ecclesiastical control and religious doctrine. Casanova suggests that this is the core of the secularization thesis—

a suggestion that has proven to be right on the mark. The historic process of differentiation, including separation of church and state, is "mainly completed throughout the Western world."[21]

Second, the secularization theory holds that progressive "marginalization" is the pathetic fate of religion in the modern world, as religious belief and practice become a mainly private affair. This piece of the secularization theory is questionable, according to Casanova. In fact, he argues that recent decades have seen a trend toward the "deprivatization" of religion in much of the world, as religion has crashed the outdoor party of secular modernity. He points to the rise of such disparate movements as the religious right in America, liberation theology in Latin America, and Islamic fundamentalism in many lands.[22]

Third, the theory says that secularization brings a drastic decline in personal religious belief and private practice. This proves true in Western Europe, where the number of people who take part in formal religious activities such as worship fluctuates between 5 and 10 percent of the population. Many analysts have seen Europe as the norm, while etching out a theory of "exceptionalism," notably for the United States and India. Casanova, however, turns the argument around: "Today, I am more and more convinced that Europe is the exception to the rule, that the rest of the world is much more religious, that there is a unique historical explanation for the process of secularization in Europe that is not being reproduced elsewhere, not in Hindu civilization, not in Islam, not in Buddhism," he said, alluding in part to Europe's religious wars.

Thus, the thought of encouraging broad secularization as a way to resolve intergroup conflicts that implicate religion is problematic at best, and probably unrealistic. With the right strategies and circumstances, one can see the possible benefit of encouraging a "differentiation of the realms" in a place like Sudan, where the surpassing dominance of one religion, Islam, has contributed to violent ethnic and regional conflict. However, encouraging the "marginalization" of religion in public or personal life might run against social realities while turning away potential partners in peacebuilding. During the 1997 Woodstock colloquium on Bosnia, William Vendley, of the

World Conference of Religions for Peace, argued that if the international community fails to cultivate religious forces, "it leaves these groups open to even more mischief instead of unfolding their extraordinary possibility."[23]

Likewise, the promotion of a purely international ethic, as opposed to grappling with distinctive religious values and traditions, can be impractical or unproductive in many cultural settings. One pitfall has to do with some of the very religious forces that are helping to "de-privatize" religion on the world stage. These religious movements are often reacting furiously to what they see as a universal ethic, whether globalization or liberal modernity in general. As important as universal commitments are to international consensus, these "may not be a sufficient common denominator for people who are defining their religiosity in opposition to universal, secular values," writes Rabbi Marc Gopin.[24] Those who seek to promote an international ethic must also be keenly aware of the understandable longing for cultural boundaries in an increasingly interlocked world.

Irreducible Complexity

If the skeptical view is correct, then religion is primarily a destructive rather than civilizing force in international affairs—it is primarily a cause of conflict, rather than a symptom (let alone a solution). However, this more likely reflects what R. Scott Appleby refers to as one of the two most common mistakes about religion and international affairs. The first is to characterize religion as "inherently intolerant, violent, extremist, and deadly."[25] The other mistake is to say that when religious agents commit violence, they are not really acting as religious agents but instead are motivated or manipulated by secular ideological agents, according to Appleby. So in explaining such violence, some will say, "That's not Islam, that's not Judaism, that's not Christianity." This fails to explain, in Appleby's analysis, why some would do such things in the name of Islam, Christianity, or Judaism.[26]

Such are the usual polarities in these debates; but some analysts have identified an irreducible complexity in religion's role in international affairs. It is often extremely difficult to isolate the religious factor even in those conflicts deemed "religious," like that in Northern Ireland. It can be even harder to determine the weight of religious factors compared to other cultural, ethnic, political, and economic causes of conflict.

A number of promising strategies today involve an understanding that religion can be both corrosive and constructive, both a symptom and a cause of conflict (as well as a solution). In his work as head of the Washington-based International Center for Religion and Diplomacy, Johnston has tried to engage Christian and Muslim religious leaders ecumenically in Sudan with a goal of taking religion (in this case, the second-class status of non-Muslims under Islamic law) "off the table" of that civil conflict. The idea is to allow religious and secular leaders to focus on other causes—which Johnston has argued are usually more consequential than religious factors per se: "The political, economic, and security dimensions of most social confrontations usually outweigh the religious, even when the conflict is superficially about religion."[27]

Such a thesis would have to be tested region by region. For example, some analysts have found that the war in Bosnia confirmed Johnston's observation, as Gerard F. Powers wrote at the war's end: "Religious and cultural factors clearly are present in the war. But the explanatory value of these factors is limited."[28] Among other points, Powers, who directs the Office of International Justice and Peace of the United States Conference of Catholic Bishops, noted that religious leaders themselves did not define the conflict in religious terms, that most political and military leaders did not act out of religious motivations, and that the wider populations exhibited low levels of religious affiliation. At the same time, many of the people and leaders clung to Muslim, Catholic, or Orthodox cultural identities—and so, by the "insane logic of ethnic cleansing, their life might depend on whether they are Muslim atheists, Orthodox atheists, or Catholic atheists," writes Powers. "At this point, religious identity has lost its religious meaning; religion has been reduced to little more than an artifact, another way of describing cultural, ethnic, or national differences."[29]

It is no mystery that, as Stuebner observed earlier in this chapter, the worst people who took on the most religious trappings during the war were "the guys with the guns in their hands." This largely secular bunch commandeered the symbols of religion, which is why the thought of Orthodox soldiers wearing crosses while raping Muslim women will remain a ghastly image of that conflict. These religious trappings led an astute observer such as Henry Kissinger to declare that it was a "religious war," not an ethnic war, "since all the groups are of the same ethnic stock"—that is, Slavs.[30] If that is true, then we have to chew on the paradox of a religious war "fought largely by irreligious people," as religion scholar Paul Mojzes has described it.[31]

In the Balkans and other conflict-torn regions, some have noted a further paradox: that religious causes of conflict can be a function of religion's weakness, not its strength. In other words, in some regions it is actually a lack of solid religious identity—and education—that facilitates ethnic hatred. Vendley has gone so far as to say, "It's not too much religion. It's too little religion," explaining that, when weakened, religious communities "too easily get taken over by nationalism."[32] He has worked extensively in the Balkans, where religion and its institutions were too "enfeebled" by decades of communism to resist the extreme ethnic-nationalist impulses behind the wars in Bosnia, Kosovo, and Croatia. Weakness of religion usually includes a lack of religious literacy, and other analysts have pointed out that religious extremists often find their most willing audiences among those with, at best, a superficial understanding of their religious doctrines and traditions.[33]

Vendley's explanation is probably a good match with ethno-religious conflicts (as in the Balkans), which involve the unhappy pairing of strong nationalism and weak religion. These ethnic, territorial, and nationalist conflicts recruit religion to "sacralize the killing," as Appleby puts it.[34] However, the term "enfeeblement" has far less explanatory power when it comes to conflicts connected to fundamentalism, which involve strong expressions of religion such as the varieties of Islamic extremism. For the most part, in such conflicts the extremists are "fighting for religion," Appleby notes.[35] The multi-dimensional reality is that both too little religion and too much religion have contributed to conflicts—but from both could come resources and agents able to transform conflicts.

RELIGIOUS COMMUNITIES IN THE BALKANS

. . . and the Forces of Unforgiveness

Cynical (and secular) manipulation of religious symbols aside, how did religious actors comport themselves in the midst of the former Yugoslavia's conflicts? Analysts such as Appleby point to religion's "generally bleak record in the Bosnian war."[36] For the specific purpose of this text, the question is this: how far did these actors take us toward—or away from—the conditions of social forgiveness? To what extent did they transcend the conflict by, for example, contributing to a truthful rendering of its causes or exhibiting empathy toward other ethnic groups?

There is no question that religious leaders, as well as religion as a belief system, often failed to transcend the intergroup rivalries in that region. Not only did religion fail to act in its transcendent role, but often it was itself transcended or absorbed by ethnic and national identity conflict. One typical explanation is the high degree of correlation between religion and ethnicity in the region: that is, typically speaking, "Serb" is a synonym for "Orthodox," and "Croat" a synonym for "Catholic." As Chapter 1 described, Vendley makes this point in another context, the corrosion of religious civil society, saying that this correlation between religion and ethnicity "allowed a co-option of religious symbols by a national program. Consequently, there has been an extreme nationalization of religious symbols and a consequent loss of credibility."[37] He added, during a colloquium on the Bosnian experience, "If, for example, one of the religious communities fervently held forth publicly about the importance of some project to social reconstruction, it would be seen through the lenses of extraordinary suffering, animosity, and suspicion by other communities."[38]

This failure to resist extreme nationalism, and the unwitting or purposeful stoking of it, goes to the heart of religion's immanence (or lack of transcendence) in the Balkans conflict. Powers, who worked on interfaith peace initiatives in Bosnia as a representative of the Catholic bishops of the United States, concludes that, to the extent religious institutions had a role in this conflict, "it has been in supporting and legitimating various kinds of nationalism."[39] Surveying the major religious communities, Powers argues that the Catholic Church supported a weak form of ethno-nationalism and that Muslim religious leaders struck a similar pose with regard to an Islamic state in Bosnia, while many Serbian Orthodox leaders subscribed to a strong form of nationalism. Even when supporting legitimate expressions of nationalism, according to Powers, religious leaders often "played into the hands of the political extremists," and their identification with nationalist aspirations "diverted them from finding ways to bridge the ethnic-nationalist chasms in the Balkans."[40]

In an analysis focusing on the Catholic and Orthodox churches, David Steele raises the question of whether religious leadership drew the connection between religion and ethnic identity, or whether, instead, political leadership promulgated the misuse of church traditions for this purpose. His answer, though not direct, suggests that religious as well as political leaders forged these links: "Some leaders within both Christian churches fostered a social/political infrastructure that was both nationalistic and intolerant."[41] He points to the Serbian Orthodox Church, noting among other examples that Serbian Orthodox priests and bishops literally blessed weapons and paramilitary units deployed in the most brutal ethnic cleansing. As a facilitator of fifty interfaith dialogues in the former Yugoslavia (as of February 2004), Steele has tried to interest the Orthodox hierarchy in those initiatives.[42] Such dialogues, while no guarantee of harmony, can be seen as signaling a desire to transcend ethno-religious divisions.

Not being a strictly national church, the Roman Catholic Church probably experienced fewer nationalist pressures in the Balkans. And by most accounts, Catholic leaders did not contribute to nationalistic ideology as self-consciously as did some Orthodox leaders. Still, Steele goes into some detail about wartime Catholic sins in this regard, noting that the Croatian Catholic Church had pressed for the exclusive use of the Croatian alphabet in its society and had given "almost unconditional support" to the nationalist government that came to power in 1990.[43] (Of course, the previous government had been communist.) Steele points especially at the Franciscans of Herzegovina, whom he describes as the "staunchest supporters of this militant nationalist agenda."[44] He reports that portraits of World War II–era Croatian fascist leader Ante Pavelic hung in the homes of local Franciscans during the war in Bosnia.[45]

As clear marks of non-transcendence, one could name many occasions when religious leaders turned away from a search for truth and expressions of empathy. For one thing, religious leaders often could not agree even on the facts or the nature of the conflict, even when they came together for fledgling interreligious efforts. Powers observed at the time, "The religious dimension to the conflict has been exacerbated by the diametrically opposed views of the Orthodox, on the one hand, and the Catholics and Muslims, on the other, of the causes of the conflict and the meaning of self-determination."[46] More to the point, one of the most frequent failures of religious actors in the Balkans conflict has been either to downplay or to condemn, in vague terms, abuses of human rights by members of their respective ethnic or national groups.

This attitude often took the form of outright denial, notably among Serbian Orthodox leaders in Bosnia and Herzegovina. Steele notes that the bishops of that church denied that Serbian militias had raped thousands of Muslim women and placed them and others in concentration camps, despite careful documentation by human rights groups.[47] On the Catholic side, while advocating for the rights of their people, the Croatian bishops turned a deaf ear to legitimate concerns of the Serb minority, which contributed to a "major escalation" of Serbian fears that they were under threat, in Steele's analysis. For example, the Catholic Church generally ignored pleas to condemn Croatian war crimes against the Serbs during World War II.[48] Both churches, even while officially opposing the war in Bosnia-

Herzegovina, tended to focus attention on the suffering of their own peoples. In so doing, they passed up clear opportunities to voice empathy for members of other groups.

. . . and the Forces of Forgiveness

Particularly during the war, many religious actors contributed to a general atmosphere of unforgiveness in Bosnia, often indirectly and sometimes unwittingly. At the same time, key leaders and unknown numbers among the laity and local leadership helped to pave some of the groundwork for a process of social forgiveness, offering crucial gestures of forbearance along with signs of a desire to repair relationships. At the end of the war, Powers noted that while they sometimes exacerbated divisions, "many religious figures have taken positive, even heroic, steps to minimize the conflict and have remained lonely voices for moderation and tolerance amidst the extremism that surrounds them."[49]

A hero among hierarchs was Bishop Franjo Komarica, of the Bosnian Catholic diocese of Banja Luka, the largest city in Bosnia's Serb republic. The vast majority of Croatian Catholics had to flee the diocese because of ethnic cleansing during the 1992-1995 war, and relatively few have been able to return to Serb-controlled areas since the 1995 Dayton Peace accords—a reality that constitutes, among other humanitarian problems, a great obstacle to future reconciliation. Komarica himself staged several hunger strikes in protest of ethnic cleansing and spent most of 1995 under house arrest, yet this experience seemed only to solidify his insistence on forbearance and rebuilding relationships. Even while in house arrest, he continued to organize interfaith religious services and opened his home to war refugees of all backgrounds. He coordinated wartime relief efforts with the mufti of Banja Luka, Hadzi Ibrahim Efendi Halilovic. Together with two lay peace workers—one Catholic, the other Orthodox—the bishop and mufti received the 1996 annual peace award of Pax Christi International, a Catholic peace organization.[50]

In expressing the value of forbearance, Komarica went so far as to call on the faithful to turn the other cheek: to "avoid using weapons, even for self-defense, to be prepared to suffer injustice rather than impose it on others, to love their neighbors and forgive their enemies,"[51] as Steele summarizes. (Cardinal Vinko Puljic of Sarajevo gave a resounding echo of such forbearance following the destruction of Catholic and Muslim religious sites there in summer 1996: "In the name of the Sarajevo diocese . . . we once again raise . . . the moral teaching that no crime against Catholic shrines can justify crimes against the shrines of others."[52])

At the time of Komarica's visit to Washington, D.C., Diane Paul of Human Rights Watch/Helsinki remarked that the bishop "has never uttered a word against the Serb people"[53]—but that does not mean that he had issued no challenges to their religious and political leaders. "We are ready for forgiveness and reconciliation, but we also expect from the other side that they also extend their hand," he declared in Washington. "I hope we are not expecting the impossible."[54]

While recognizing the work of Komarica, many observers had even higher praise for the Bosnian Francisans. Not to be confused with some of their extreme fellow friars in Herzegovina, these good Franciscans demonstrated "the most open and tolerant stance among all the religious communities in Bosnia-Herzegovina," Steele writes.[55] Most impressive among them was Fr. Ivo Markovic, who headed the Sarajevo-based interreligious organization Face to Face. He consistently challenged religious leaders to separate themselves from nationalistic expressions and opportunistic political leaders, leading many of his fellow priests to brand him a traitor to the Croatian cause.[56]

These transactions of forgiveness or acts of social transcendence were not entirely isolated during the conflict. Early in the war, leaders of the Islamic, Serbian Orthodox, and Catholic communities declared "emphatically" that it was not a religious war—perhaps a minimal statement, but a sign of their desire to move beyond the inflamed religious rhetoric of that moment. Further, they stated that the "characterization of this tragic conflict as a religious war and the misuse of all religious symbols used with the aim to further hatred, must be proscribed and is condemned."[57] As Powers points out, many religious leaders also issued blanket calls for people to stay in or return to their homes, even as minorities—actions that, in his view, directly challenged nationalist politicians who encouraged "voluntary 'ethnic cleansing.'"[58] To this day, refugee return is a crucial question of reconciliation, a prerequisite of turning relationships "alongside" into relationships "with."

From the Serbian Orthodox Church came what Steele calls "a few alternative voices" of reconciliation.[59] These voices include Bishop Hrizostom of Bihac-Petrovac in Bosnia-Herzegovina, who called for a "separation of religion and nationalism" and supported interfaith peace efforts, among other measures aimed at reconciliation. He was one of several Orthodox clerics who called on Serbs to admit that their people, including their military and police, had committed wrongs against other groups.[60] The complexity of this association of religion and nationalist aspiration is reflected in the statements and actions of many religious leaders. For example, Steele points out that as late as 1996, Cardinal Franjo Kuharic' of Zagreb (who died on March 11, 2002, at 82) proclaimed support for the Croatian state and that this stance translated into support for nationalist symbols. In this connection, Steele mentions that the Croatian Catholic Church pushed for exclusive use of the Croatian alphabet in that country.[61] But as Powers relates, Kuharic' also became known for his frequent admonition: "If the opponent burns my house, I will guard his. If he demolishes my church, I will protect his. And if he kills my father, I will safeguard the life of his father."[62] This is forbearance with a vengeance.

One problem in cataloguing religious transactions of social forgiveness is that many go undetected by international radar. This creates what Christiansen considers an "un-level playing field" in the analysis of religion's role in conflict resolution, in that such initiatives are often left undocumented.[63] His comments shed light on his view (related at the end of Chapter 5) regarding the failure of Track I or official personnel to adequately engage religious and other agents of Track II intervention.

In particular, Christiansen, who traveled to Bosnia several times to assess the religious response, questions the work of U.S. State Department representatives during the region's conflict. With some notable exceptions—including official efforts to reopen churches damaged or destroyed in the conflict—diplomats remained inattentive to diplomatic openings provided by religious actors, in his assessment. He points, for example, to critical help provided by Catholic Relief Services and Caritas Croatia in helping to launch organized Muslim relief efforts, as well as organizing formal training in conflict resolution, conducted with Catholic priests by the Diocese of Djakovo, which includes Eastern Slavonia.[64] (For the most part, these initiatives remain undocumented.)

At issue here is the frequent failure to discern critical connection points between Track I and Track II intervention, in particular the "inability of State Department people to take advantage" of Track II initiatives.[65]

◦———

It would be simplistic to say that religious leaderships in Kosovo learned all of the lessons from the war in Bosnia. Yet one may fairly say that these leaderships showed a greater awareness of the need to both avoid entanglements with nationalistic causes and positively pursue efforts toward peace and tolerance through interfaith channels.

Religious leaders in Kosovo began meeting before the eruption of all-out war there, though not before the rise of the Kosovo Liberation Army. They were quick to organize new structures of inter-religious cooperation in the wake of NATO's bombing campaign (with help from Bosnian religious leaders, as will be related in the next chapter's profile of the World Conference of Religions for Peace). Serbian Orthodox leaders in Kosovo, who had been even more nationalistic than their counterparts in Bosnia, by some indications, began altering their attitudes after the war in Bosnia. The church's leadership reached deep into its tradition and began to warn against "ethnophyletism,"[66] a chauvinist nationalistic heresy condemned by the church in the nineteenth century. In November 1998, Orthodox bishops issued a statement pleading for Serbs and Albanians to coexist in friendship, though it regressed into blaming Albanian separatists alone for bloodshed in Kosovo. Some church leaders criticized secularists for abusing the symbols of Serbian Orthodoxy for nation-alistic purposes. The Decani Monastery in Kosovo granted aid and refuge to a few hundred Albanians displaced by the conflict.[67]

The "Semantics of Fault" and Other Assets

The Balkans experience throws light on the ambiguity of religious com-munal life in its interactions with cultures caught in extreme conflict. This ambiguity is rooted in the phenomenon of religion, resting as it does on the power of the sacred as interpreted by imperfect human beings and communities. (In truth, the same could be said of all human constructs and institutions, limited and ambiguous, afflicted with an imperfection that theologians call sin.[68]) Following the insight of the great religious interpreter Rudolph Otto, R. Scott Appleby points out that the core of the religious phenomenon, the experience of the holy or sacred, is "pre-moral." It does not come with a clear guide to which interpretations are good and which are bad.[69] Awareness of this ambi-guity is crucial to realistically appraising religion's role, neither exagger-ating nor dismissing its peacebuilding potential.

During conversations facilitated by the Woodstock Theological Center, career diplomat Warren Zimmerman shared his skepticism about a "Statement of Shared Moral Commitment" adopted by church leaders in Bosnia-Herzegovina. He asked how "seriously and how energetically" its principles could be "carried out by people . . . who have not really subscribed very faithfully" to those principles in the past.[70] "A capacity for complexity is a prerequisite for answering your question," Vendley replied:

> There is a high irony quotient, a sense of dialectic, in the way religious communities operate. Religious communities, when they're functioning well, are very alert to their overwhelming propensity to get it wrong. They all have a semantics of fault, which is why forgiveness is a term that is cognate to religious communities. When they don't get it right, they twist that language, but the extraordinary thing is that even then the

language continues to function normatively for those communities. . . . we've always found that holding the community to its own commitments is the smart way to go. . . . The trick, I think, is not to be totally surprised that those human beings, too, get it fouled up.[71]

What assets do religious communities bring to the task of transforming conflicts and building a culture of forgiveness? The remarks by Vendley suggest one asset: their teachings, including a propensity to acknowledge wrongdoing, at least in theory or in the realm of personal piety. In separating out the roles of transnational religious actors, Bryan Hehir points to three major resources that they bring to world politics: ideas, institutions, and communities (the institutions having more to do with leadership and communities with people on the ground).[72] Note that in the Balkans—a context of "weak religion"— some religious leaders were able to bring these assets to bear on the conflicts. This suggests that even weak or "enfeebled" religion can, to some degree, transcend strong nationalism or ideology.

In leveraging their religious assets, religious leaders such as Komarica and Hrizostom played an "insider-partial" role, in that they came from the communities of conflict. John Paul Lederach, of Eastern Mennonite University, has developed this role terminology, applied by Appleby in his book *The Ambivalence of the Sacred.* Based on his work in peacebuilding, Lederach finds that the deepest experiences in reconciliation involve teams of people who, as individuals, "were seen as close to one side or the other but who as a team themselves had built transparency and trust."[73] Both he and Appleby point to the leading role religious insiders have played in mediating an end to some violent conflicts, notably in Nicaragua, where both the Moravian Church and Cardinal Miguel Obando y Bravo—hardly neutral actors in that nation's conflicts—intervened as peacebuilders and reconcilers. The Moravian Church, although representing indigenous people of the Atlantic Coast, mediated successfully between armed indigenous groups and the left-wing Sandinista government in the late 1980s. Obando y Bravo, though known for his ties to the anti-Sandinista resistance movement, had a strong hand in the national reconciliation process that bore fruit in 1990.[74]

Nonetheless, insider-partial peacemakers often need the assistance of outsider-neutral actors, including those who helped the Moravian Church to facilitate peace talks. In the Balkans, religious leaders themselves, even if willing, were not entirely able to come together on their own. Referring to third-party neutral settings, Powers recalls,

> These were the only times, the only opportunity they had to dialogue or yell at their counterparts because nobody was meeting during the war. You needed an outside group like the U.S. Institute of Peace or the World Conference on Religion and Peace [now World Conference of Religions for Peace] or the Appeal of Conscience Foundation. You needed an outside group to bring these folks together because they couldn't do it on their own. If any one of them initiated it, the others would be suspicious. And you also needed to have it on neutral territory.

In that vein, the next chapter highlights intellectual, spiritual, and institutional assets contributed by religious communities through the work of outsider-neutral organizations, primarily during the long recovery stage in Bosnia.

NOTES

1   Warren Zimmerman, in Woodstock Colloquium *Forgiveness in Conflict Resolution: Reality and Utility—The Bosnian Experience* (October 24, 1997) (Washington, DC: Woodstock Theological Center, n.d.), 19.

2   Catholic News Service, "UNESCO Panel Gives Peace Prize to Sant'Egidio Community," February 2, 2001.

3   R. Scott Appleby, *The Ambivalence of the Sacred: Religion, Violence, and Reconciliation* (Lanham, MD: Rowman & Littlefield, 2000), 281; Douglas Johnston, in Woodstock Colloquium *Forgiveness in Conflict Resolution: Reality and Utility—The Bosnian Experience*, 80.

4   Appleby, in Woodstock Theological Center Forum "Being Radically Religious in Public Life" (March 14, 2002), *Woodstock Report* (June 2002), http://www.georgetown.edu/centers/woodstock/report/r-fea70b.htm (accessed January 2004).

5   Philip Jenkins, *The Next Christendom: The Coming of Global Christianity* (New York, Oxford: Oxford University Press, 2002), 149.

6   *National Catholic Reporter*, editorial, "The Catholic Content of President Kim's Nobel Prize," October 27, 2000, http://natcath.org/NCR_Online/archives2/2000d/102700/102700p.htm (accessed February 2004).

7   Jenkins, *The Next Christendom*, 148.

8   Donald Shriver Jr. added the terms "sin" and "idolatry": Shriver, interview with William Bole, Washington, DC, May 2002.

9   Raymond G. Helmick, SJ, "Does Religion Fuel or Heal in Conflicts," 82, in *Forgiveness and Reconciliation: Religion, Public Policy, and Conflict Transformation*, ed. Raymond G. Helmick and Rodney L. Petersen (Philadelphia: The Templeton Foundation Press, 2001).

10   Douglas Johnston, cited in Robert T. Hennemeyer, Martin Van Heuven, Ralph Stuart Smith, and Thomas M. F. Timberman, *Religion in World Affairs: The Findings of a Conference Organized by the DACOR Bacon House Foundation* (Washington, DC: DACOR Bacon House Foundation, 1995), 64.

11   Johnston, cited in Hennemeyer et al., *Religion in World Affairs*, 64.

12   J. Bryan Hehir, cited in Hennemeyer et al., *Religion in World Affairs*, 13

13   Hehir, cited in Hennemeyer et al., *Religion in World Affairs*, 13.

14   Hehir, cited in Hennemeyer et al., *Religion in World Affairs*, 14.

15   Cf. Samuel P. Huntington, *The Clash of Civilizations and the Remaking of World Order* (New York: Simon and Schuster, 1999).

16   Francis Terry MacNamara, in Woodstock Colloquium *Forgiveness in Conflict Resolution: Reality and Utility—The Bosnian Experience*, 45.

17   William Stuebner, in Woodstock Colloquium *Forgiveness in Conflict Resolution: Reality and Utility—The Bosnian Experience*, 50. MacNamara's and Stuebner's assessments came during the Woodstock Theological Center colloquium on forgiveness in Bosnia in autumn 1997, with bloodshed from the hostilities in Bosnia still vividly in the international backdrop.

18   Stuebner, in Woodstock Colloquium *Forgiveness in Conflict Resolution: Reality and Utility—The Bosnian Experience*, 50.

19   Drew Christiansen, SJ, in Woodstock Colloquium *Forgiveness in Conflict Resolution: Reality and Utility—The Bosnian Experience*, 108.

20   Cf. Jose Casanova, *Public Religions in the Modern World* (Chicago: University of Chicago Press, 1994).

21   Casanova, in Woodstock Theological Center Forum "Religion and Public Life: A New Alliance?" (February 7, 2001), *Woodstock Report* (March 2001), http://www.georgetown.edu/centers/woodstock/report/r-fea65a.htm (accessed in January 2004).

22   Casanova, *Woodstock Report* (March 2001).

23   William Vendley, in Woodstock Colloquium *Forgiveness and Conflict Resolution: Reality and Utility—The Bosnian Experience*, 20.

24   Marc Gopin, *Between Eden and Armageddon: The Future of World Religions, Violence, and Peacemaking* (New York, Oxford: Oxford University Press, 2000), 199.

25   Appleby, *Woodstock Report* (June 2002).

26   Appleby, *Woodstock Report* (June 2002).

27   Douglas Johnston, "Review of the Findings," in *Religion, the Missing Dimension of Statecraft*, ed. Douglas Johnston and Cynthia Sampson (New York, Oxford: Oxford University Press, 1995), 263.

28 Gerard F. Powers, "Religion, Conflict and Prospects for Peace in Bosnia, Croatia, and Yugoslavia," in *Religion and the War in Bosnia*, ed. Paul Mojzes (Atlanta: Scholars Press, 1998), 223.

29 Powers, "Religion, Conflict and Prospects for Peace in Bosnia, Croatia, and Yugoslavia," 223.

30 Mojzes, quoted in Powers, "Religion, Conflict and Prospects for Peace in Bosnia, Croatia and Yugoslavia," 223.

31 Mojzes, quoted in Powers, "Religion, Conflict and Prospects for Peace in Bosnia, Croatia and Yugoslavia," 223.

32 William Vendley, telephone interview with William Bole, July 2001.

33 Vendley, interview.

34 Appleby, *Woodstock Report* (June 2002).

35 Appleby, *Woodstock Report* (June 2002).

36 Appleby, *The Ambivalence of the Sacred*, 76.

37 Vendley, in Woodstock Colloquium *Forgiveness in Conflict Resolution: Reality and Utility—The Bosnian Experience*, 10.

38 Vendley, in Woodstock Colloquium *Forgiveness in Conflict Resolution: Reality and Utility—The Bosnian Experience*, 10.

39 Powers, "Religion, Conflict and Prospects for Peace in Bosnia, Croatia, and Yugoslavia," 238.

40 Powers, "Religion, Conflict and Prospects for Peace in Bosnia, Croatia, and Yugoslavia," 245.

41 David Steele, "Christianity in Bosnia-Herzegovina and Kosovo: From Ethnic Captive to Reconciling Agent," in *Faith-Based Diplomacy: Trumping Realpolitik*, ed. Douglas Johnston (Oxford, New York: Oxford University Press, 2003), 132.

42 Steele, telephone interview with William Bole, June 2001

43 Steele, "Christianity in Bosnia-Herzegovina and Kosovo: From Ethnic Captive to Reconciling Agent," 139.

44 Steele, "Christianity in Bosnia-Herzegovina and Kosovo: From Ethnic Captive to Reconciling Agent," 141.

45 Steele, "Christianity in Bosnia-Herzegovina and Kosovo: From Ethnic Captive to Reconciling Agent," 141.

46 Powers, "Religion, Conflict and Prospects for Peace in Bosnia, Croatia, and Yugoslavia," 239.

47 Steele, "Christianity in Bosnia-Herzegovina and Kosovo: From Ethnic Captive to Reconciling Agent," 132.

48 Steele, "Christianity in Bosnia-Herzegovina and Kosovo: From Ethnic Captive to Reconciling Agent," 139.

49 Powers, "Religion, Conflict and Prospects for Peace in Bosnia, Croatia, and Yugoslavia," 245.

50 Catholic News Service, "Pax Christi Peace Award Given to Four from Former Yugoslavia," November 26, 1996.

51 Steele, "Christianity in Bosnia-Herzegovina and Kosovo: From Ethnic Captive to Reconciling Agent," 143.

52 Catholic News Service, "Bosnian Clergy Continue to Appeal for Peace, International Aid," August 1, 1996.

53 Jennifer Reed, "Bishop Says Despite Atrocities, Bosnians Want to Coexist in Peace," Catholic News Service, June 12, 1996.

54 Reed, "Bishop Says Despite Atrocities, Bosnians Want to Coexist in Peace."

55   Steele, "Christianity in Bosnia-Herzegovina and Kosovo: From Ethnic Captive to Reconciling Agent," 143.
56   Steele, interview. Markovic is also cited by Steele in "Christianity in Bosnia-Herzegovina and Kosovo: From Ethnic Captive to Reconciling Agent," 144.
57   Cited by Powers, "Religion, Conflict and Prospects for Peace in Bosnia, Croatia, and Yugoslavia," 218-219.
58   Powers, "Religion, Conflict and Prospects for Peace in Bosnia, Croatia, and Yugoslavia," 244.
59   Steele, "Christianity in Bosnia-Herzegovina and Kosovo: From Ethnic Captive to Reconciling Agent," 136.
60   Steele, "Christianity in Bosnia-Herzegovina and Kosovo: From Ethnic Captive to Reconciling Agent," 136-137.
61   Steele, "Christianity in Bosnia-Herzegovina and Kosovo: From Ethnic Captive to Reconciling Agent," 138-139.
62   Powers, "Religion, Conflict and Prospects for Peace in Bosnia, Croatia, and Yugoslavia," 231.
63   Drew Christiansen, SJ, interview with William Bole, January 2003.
64   Christiansen, interview.
65   Christiansen, interview.
66   Steele, "Christianity in Bosnia-Herzegovina and Kosovo: From Ethnic Captive to Reconciling Agent," 149-150.
67   Christiansen, interview.
68   Caveat offered in Shriver, interview.
69   Appleby, *Woodstock Report* (June 2002).
70   Zimmerman, in Woodstock Colloquium *Forgiveness in Conflict Resolution: Reality and Utility—The Bosnian Experience*, 18.
71   Vendley, in Woodstock Colloquium *Forgiveness in Conflict Resolution: Reality and Utility—The Bosnian Experience*, 18-19.
72   Hehir, cited in Hennemeyer et al., *Religion in World Affairs*, 16.
73   John Paul Lederach, "Five Qualities of Practice in Support of Reconciliation Processes," 195-196, in *Forgiveness and Reconciliation: Religion, Public Policy, and Conflict Transformation*, ed. Raymond G. Helmick and Rodney L. Petersen (Philadelphia: The Templeton Foundation Press, 2001).
74   Cf. Appleby, *The Ambivalence of the Sacred*, 219-220, for discussion of the insider-partial concept as well as the case of Nicaragua.

CHAPTER 7

Religious Intervention:
The "Outsider-Neutral" Parties

Faith-based organizations are mining the peacebuilding
assets of religion, crafting models of intervention aimed at
nurturing atmospheres of forgiveness as well as
healing at the interpersonal level.

How do religious institutions draw on their peacemaking
assets in promoting truth, forbearance, empathy, and the
quest for reconciliation in societies scarred by conflict? All
of these elements of forgiveness require human beings and communities to extend themselves beyond their immediate perceptions and
interests—beyond previously known horizons.

To borrow from the terminology of the late Jesuit theologian
Bernard Lonergan, these are steps beyond the world of immediacy, "a
world quite apart from questions and answers,"[1] in which parties to
intractable conflict find it hard to examine or correct their mythological pictures of history. How do religious people and whole communities make this leap collectively onto the public stage of conflict transformation, into what Lonergan calls "the world mediated by meaning
and motivated by value,"[2] a world in which they can more readily critique their perceptions of social reality? How can they break out of religious ghettoes that have often served to obscure their assets as reconcilers? Can they move us any closer to finding a "new home" of forgiveness in the push and pull of international politics?

The following profiles aim to throw light on these questions
through the programs and strategies of two "outsider-neutral," or

third-party, organizations: the World Conference of Religions for Peace (WCRP), headquartered in New York, and the Washington, D.C.–based Center for Strategic and International Studies (CSIS). These profiles underscore the variety of strategies needed for mining the peacemaking resources of faith, with a view toward finding political space for forgiveness.

MINING RELIGIOUS ASSETS: WORLD CONFERENCE OF RELIGIONS FOR PEACE (WCRP)

Founded in 1970 and active in some of the world's most troubled places, the WCRP aims to help religious communities discern their peacebuilding assets and use these as a fresh mode of entry into the public square. The organization seeks to identify moral or intellectual as well as institutional assets (to harken back to the categories used by Rev. J. Bryan Hehir in the previous chapter).

Bearing on the moral and intellectual assets is William Vendley's assertion, at the end of the last chapter, that practically all religions have a "semantics of fault" as well as of restitution. In more technical terms, they are all experts in pathology and soteriology. *Pathology* gives an account of what has gone wrong, while *soteriology* (referring in Christianity to the mystery of salvation) asks the question of what should be done about it, according to Vendley, a theologian by training.[3] Alongside moral assets, like the semantics of fault, are institutional assets, which are routinely taken for granted, even in places like the post-communist former Yugoslavia. Counted among these are various levels of leadership, aid societies, publishing houses, and links to religious bodies of other regions, not to mention the simple but awesome fact of regular access to the faithful through worship and other rituals.[4]

The WCRP encourages religious communities to re-inventory these assets, to reconsider themselves from the perspective of peacemaking, in Vendley's terms.[5] For example, membership in a communion that ranges across borders becomes an opportunity to extend the lessons of one region to another. More locally, a funeral becomes a setting in which the cleric can begin to help people work through the stages of grief and anger (one piece of advice being offered to clergy in those settings).

These and other resources are processed through the structures of a religious community with a view toward helping the community to become a public actor. This presents a new challenge for religions: to stretch beyond their sectarian modes of discourse and develop a public language. Sectarian, or primary, language is what secures the identity of a religious community through a unique narrative, in Vendley's understanding. While it is crucial to a community's moral orientation, sectarian language is limited to a circle of believers who share that same language. In other words, it is not the language of multi-religious cooperation—rather, public language is. Not simply secular, public language is the way in which religious communities express their "moral concerns" or "shared care," rooted in ultimate concern, to each other and to a pluralistic society.[6]

Moving religions to this public language becomes the "modest mission" of WCRP. In the framework of multi-religious dialogue, a methodological key is to leave aside religious doctrines or truth claims, which belong to first-order discourse. The challenge in shifting the focus to what Vendley also terms "moral cares" is to transpose these cares from one mode of discourse to another, from a sectarian to a public expression of ultimate concern. Discussing cares rather than doctrines is thus conceived as central to the task of building what Vendley refers to as "scalable, sustainable, multi-religious infra-structures" towards the end of peacebuilding.[7]

Vendley gleans many of these thoughts from Bernard Lonergan's notion of "differentiations of consciousness,"[8] an intricate theory of knowledge that involves different modes of reasoning and different realms of meaning. Basically, this theory leads to an understanding that religious peacebuilding is a work of translation: in this case, a transposition of sectarian modes into public modes of discussion. That this is not really a translation from the religious into the secular is worth emphasizing. The public mode of conversation is religious as well, in the sense that the parties (religious peacebuilders) are aiming for the higher ground of ultimate concern, which is religion, stripped to its bare essence.[9]

Reaching the shared realm of concerns or cares is the deeper project of the WCRP, and the organization's experience in Bosnia-Herzegovina indicates how formidable this "modest mission" can be. Even in the diligently diplomatic wording of the public communiques of the WCRP, religion was "deeply implicated" in the 1992-1995 war in Bosnia.[10] Though hemmed in by their horizons, religious actors had only one realistic way to re-emerge peacefully and constructively in the public square: through cooperation with other faiths. As Vendley remarked at the time, "the credibility loss is so substantive and pervasive that the only way the religious leaders can regain credibility in the civil sphere is to stand together. This is where they are incontestably seen as not simply promoting their own community's nationalist agenda."[11]

Multi-Religious Collaboration: Speaking in Public

In its first public communique from Bosnia-Herzegovina beginning in December 1996, the WCRP stated cautiously that "regardless of whether" religion was co-opted by political forces during the war, religious identity in Bosnia-Herzegovina was powerful enough to make it a necessary point of engagement in any reconstruction.[12] That engagement took a visible step forward in autumn 1996, when the principal leaders of the Islamic, Jewish, Roman Catholic, and Serbian Orthodox communities met for what the WCRP described as their first encounter since the end of the war. (During the war, the Appeal of Conscience Foundation, led by Rabbi Arthur Schneier, had sponsored a number of interreligious initiatives involving the region's religious leaders and third parties, including now-Cardinal Theodore McCarrick of Washington, D.C.). At that session facilitated by the WCRP, these leaders developed a "provisional document" that outlined the goals of multi-religious collaboration and agreed to lay the groundwork for an interreligious council.[13]

With progress slowed in part by violence directed at religious communities in Sarajevo and Mostar, it took time to negotiate the language of a durable document and to pass it through formal ecclesiastical channels. Seven months after the initial meeting, on June 7, 1997, the principal religious leaders unveiled the "Statement of Shared Moral Commitment" at a ceremony carried on national television. While recognizing that their traditions "differ from each other," the leaders affirmed common values, namely human dignity and human "value" as a gift from God, which could serve as a foundation of "free common living" and collaboration in Bosnia-Herzegovina. The statement, published widely in newspapers, condemned violence and violations of human rights, including those based on ethnicity and religion, acts of revenge, the spreading of hate by mass media, and obstruction of the free right of return. In issuing the statement, the leaders also launched the Inter-Religious Council.[14]

A quick offshoot of the statement was the coordination of two bilateral meetings involving Orthodox and Roman Catholic bishops, in which the church leaders issued mutual apologies for the harm done to each other by their respective communities. The "approximate impact" of the statement, in Vendley's terms, was that the religious leaders were able to "positively demonstrate a profound commitment to common living based on moral principles that could be anchored in all three civilizational religious heritages."[15] In what he describes as an "ameliorative" effect, he says that these ecclesiastical leaders were able to undo some of the political damage caused by them or their subordinates. These religious communities "had been plagued, in fact they had been drug [sic] into virulent nationalist ambitions based on ethnic identities, and therefore religion was drug in [sic]. And so minimally, this was a distancing of religion from that and trying to point it in another direction."[16] (Other observers, noting the efforts at peacebuilding related in the previous chapter, would clarify that some but certainly not all of the region's religious actors were dragged into the nationalist conflicts.)

That statement illustrates Vendley's point about the public quality of interreligious conversation, which is central to the WCRP's overall strategy. He emphasizes that, notwithstanding a couple of references to God, the statement was dominantly framed as a public document:

That means that the four religious leaders who promulgated it were functioning appropriately as public actors, not simply as sectarian advocates. That's a genre, a *genus literarium*, a public document stated in public terms about the public salience of religion in terms of its value to the common areas of congruence, its value to the common good. That is extremely significant in terms of religions' learning how to become most secure in their identities, and yet public actors in the way they comport themselves in the public arena. They can still function sectarianly among their believers, and they should. That's how the traditions are passed on. But can they become public actors? If so, what are, if you will, the requirements of publicness?[17]

Beyond Words

The "Statement of Shared Moral Commitment" served as the foundation of the WCRP's work in the Balkans. In the second phase of its project there, the organization sought to make the statement "fully operational" in the religious communities through the Inter-Religious Council. Facilitators brought together critical segments of these communities, from scholars and youth to local clergy, for a series of ecumenical gatherings. For instance, at a seminar on religious freedom and human rights, theologians of the four communities issued a declaration condemning "the manipulation of faith by all nationalistic politics." They also spoke the language of forgiveness, calling for forgiveness as well as repentance and guarantees of human rights. In addition to these meetings, senior religious leaders made several trips outside the region, carrying messages about the nature of the conflict in Bosnia-Herzegovina.[18]

In its most recent phase, the WCRP project has sought to cultivate other assets of religious institutions, including their roles as agents of civil society and their cross-border connections to sister communions.

A legal task force set up by the Inter-Religious Council is advocating a reform of legal codes, held over from the Marxist era, that have in essence defined civil society. As part of that lobbying, the task force is seeking to restore the rights of religious groups as independent social actors and is pressing for the return or restitution of property confiscated during the war. This work is consistent with the "Statement of Shared Moral Commitment," which sought a public voice for faith groups. In different ways, both have addressed the requisite conditions of religious action for the civil good. These conditions must arise within the religious communities themselves (hence the interreligious dialogue) but also, often, through reform of sociopolitical structures that affect civil society (hence the legal task force). The push for legal reform also highlights the relationship between the unofficial realm of Track II conflict resolution and the official Track I intervention. In short, it offers a glimpse into how civil society or Track II agents depend on progress in the official realm of politics and statecraft.

Crossing borders, the broader WCRP project also clearly shows the international assets of religious communities, particularly in a period of crisis. In the wake of Kosovo's war, for top religious leaders to initiate a process of reconciliation was viewed as politically impossible. They had to be sensitive to perceptions by their people; and, in such aggrieved circumstances, families traumatized by violence might well have looked upon their leaders as "shaking hands with the religious [leader] of a community that raped our daughter," as Vendley recalls.[19] It was politically impossible, though, for those leaders to travel to Amman, Jordan, in November 1999 for the WCRP's seventh world assembly. There, they caucused with religious leaders from eight other states in southeastern Europe, yielding a wide-ranging statement that wove together themes of forgiveness, acknowledgment, truth, and justice.

Three months later, the Kosovar leaders (Orthodox, Roman Catholic, and Muslim) surfaced in the safe setting of Sarajevo for a meeting with their counterparts in Bosnia-Herzegovina. "Those [Kosovar] religious leaders couldn't yet meet in Kuzco, so you have a brilliant situation where, if you will, students of collaboration in their own acute period of crisis in Bosnia become the teachers of collaboration in their neighbors' crisis," Vendley explains.[20] Shepherded by the Bosnians, the Kosovars—in Sarajevo—issued their own "Statement of Shared Moral Commitment," moved ostensibly by the "slow and inefficient implementation" of the Kosovo peace plan.[21] Two months after that, in April 2000, leaders of the Inter-Religious Council of Bosnia-Herzegovina paid a visit to Pristina, helping to safely launch the Inter-Religious Council of Kosovo.

These ecclesiastical steps forward illustrate a distinct piece of the WCRP strategy and its conception of religious assets. The strategy rests on the simple recognition that religious communities have counterparts outside of their national boundaries, in areas of intense conflict. Internationally, these communities have "useful leverage in bolstering, strengthening the credibility of a particular religious community, both symbolically and substantively as a peacemaker in conflict."[22] This asset throws light on the roles of third parties like the WCRP as well as religious counterparts, as seen through Vendley's early peacebuilding in Bosnia: "I was very careful to always go via international cousins when I was approaching the religious leadership in the region for the first time," he notes, referring to such ecclesiastical "back doors" as the Vatican and the Moscow Patriarch.[23] "All of that is constructive exploitation of the fact that the infrastructure of religion is international, [which is] a way to leverage national capacity for being further mobilized and further equipped in conflict transformation."[24]

Questions About "Big Interfaith Initiatives"

Do high-level interfaith statements of the kind promoted by the WCRP make a direct and solid contribution to peacebuilding in the throes or aftermath of violent conflict? Opinions are mixed, even among some with a stake in this strategy. For one thing, questions center on the extent to which the interreligious statements in the Balkans have truly represented a meeting of the minds.

As a participant in similar initiatives, Gerard F. Powers, of the United States Conference of Catholic Bishops, observes that religious leaders in the Balkans were not able to agree on much other than sweeping principles of human dignity, justice, and religious freedom:

"There was very little agreement because everybody saw [the conflict and suffering] from their own perspective, and there was little agreement on controversial policy questions, such as: Should we lift the arms embargo or not?"[25] He adds in an interview, "There was a lot of agreement that religion shouldn't be used, manipulated by nationalist leaders for their own ends. Such statements were important but they really masked a situation of great disagreement."[26]

Powers did see a "modest value" in having religious leaders say loudly and clearly that, for example, the war in Bosnia was not a religious war. The Inter-Religious Council leaders carried that message during their trips to Brussels, Tokyo, and the United States. That was considered a reality check at a moment when many analysts either exaggerated the religious character of the conflict or naively thought it could be allayed somewhat with clarifications from spiritual leaders. Nevertheless, Powers argues, "It is a mistake to look at these big interfaith initiatives as the solution to reconciliation or the main way to do reconciliation. In fact, a lot of it is necessary background music."[27] In this reading, even the hierarchies themselves attached a fairly low priority to these statements and initiatives, amid all the post-war challenges.

Today, does the "Statement of Shared Moral Commitment" stand merely as an echo of useful background music? On the contrary—at the time it was signed, many specialists saw it as unique and promising, because it was linked to the creation of an institution, the Inter-Religious Council of Bosnia-Herzegovina. Vendley is quick to cite the more recent signs of vigor by that Council, especially the legal task force and the ecclesiastical intervention in Kosovo, to counter some perceptions that the council has been slow to surface in the peacemaking mix. Still, he is equally quick to acknowledge that the work has not been a straight line of progress in a region where societal decline has been a far more familiar force over the past decade. In such a sensitive undertaking,

> you're making advances on some fronts and then something flashes and then it cools and you've got three or four things

cooking, and then there are little setbacks and so forth. . . . Unfortunately, there are many saboteurs of collaboration because every community has a spectrum in it. And really, if you go to the Middle East, it's the same thing. You've got to continually look over your shoulder for your own right wing that's ready to gun you down, basically.[28]

These questions connect with other concerns about working exclusively with senior religious leaders. When Powers speaks of high-profile initiatives as background music, the religious foreground, in his view, is where religious leaders, local pastors, and counselors help people to deal with the death and destruction on a spiritual level. David Steele, of the Center for Strategic and International Studies (CSIS), who coordinated interfaith seminars, sees high-level religious leaders as often raising high barriers to reconciliation work. "The tops of the hierarchy are always looking over their shoulder at what the reaction of their institution is going to be. There's always that sense that they have to be protecting the institution," says Steele. "You don't have as much of that when you're dealing with lay people and sometimes the clergy."[29] With fewer ecclesiastical encumbrances, the CSIS has been able to pass its reconciliation work on to local institutions and partners, which are now carrying out the dialogues, for the most part. In most instances, these local institutions began as outgrowths of the seminars.

Yet when it comes to hierarchies' looking over their shoulders, is this a trifling worry on their part? Does it mean they represent a futile avenue to reconciliation? As one who recommends a pastoral approach but who works at the leadership level, Powers points out that top religious leaders have different and larger roles and responsibilities than the laity and local leaders:

> It would be a mistake to just say that the religious leaders are these scared, cowering, indifferent bureaucrats who aren't willing to do anything to take risks for peace. They just have to take into account a lot of things that the local folks don't. And how something is received [by constituencies] is not just playing

politics. It's part of your job to calculate . . . whether you're going to be totally misunderstood and misused.[30]

A minimal view might hold that collaboration among hierarchies is one of many requisites of reconciliation in post-conflict societies, as Powers puts it: "Obviously, you have to do about one hundred different things to move the reconciliation process forward, and big interfaith initiatives at the leadership level is just one of the hundred moves you need to be making."[31]

For its part, the WCRP is highly resistant to any characterizations of top-down approaches—as opposed to bottom-up approaches—to faith-based reconciliation. A key element of the WCRP's methodology is to respect religious communities as they are constituted, to work within the already existing structures, and to tap the labors already invested in themselves. That perspective leads Vendley to reject what he labels a false antithesis between the grassroots and leadership: "We look at the community as an organic entity. That community has leadership structures. It has recognized competence, sometimes 'portfolio-ed,' sometimes not. It has local communal structures. It has a variety of grassroots manifestations. All of those can be inventoried in terms of what is their particular comparative advantage to addressing an existing problem."[32]

There is, nonetheless, a real difference between bottom and top in any community, and the WCRP says it is as interested in the bottom as any other third-party actor. Yet Vendley adds, "We sometimes can get to the bottom more efficiently by going to the tree that the religious communities have grown for themselves and that's following their own representative structures."[33] Indeed, some experts, including Rabbi Marc Gopin, have found barriers to grassroots dialogue when religious authorities fail to send the right signals to the faithful, to describe the matter negatively.[34] Put another way, have the WCRP-facilitated activities of senior faith leaders in the former Yugoslavia played no role in fostering an atmosphere for dialogue among laity and lower-level clergy? While Steele is not sure of the extent to which hierarchical atmospheres have paved the way for his work, he readily acknowledges other advantages of working within those structures.[35] The broad public value of high-profile peace pronouncements is no small part of that conciliatory advantage.

From that view, high-profile ecclesiastical initiatives offer benefits analogous to those of truth and reconciliation commissions. They help to encourage atmospheres of forgiveness and could counter the "hothead factor" that often allows minorities of violent extremists to maintain the status quo of unforgiveness. The WCRP initiative in particular helps to build a climate for reconciliation by translating sectarian language and doctrines into a public language of justice, peace, and forgiveness. However, like truth commissions, high-level religious interventions aren't especially well positioned to bring about healing and reconciliation at the interpersonal level. There remains a pressing need for encounters that can deepen the healing and transform relationships in local communities.

MINING RELIGIOUS ASSETS: CENTER FOR STRATEGIC AND INTERNATIONAL STUDIES (CSIS)

The CSIS initiative seeks to draw on religious assets, especially communal and spiritual resources, through a process of facilitated small-group reconciliation. By reflecting theologically on their experiences, participants move along stages of conflict recovery that parallel a process of forgiveness.

For example, as related in Chapter 5, one challenging step in this process involves helping victims to move beyond the question "Why me?" This is an unanswerable question—no one deserves to be a victim, as psychologist and conflict-resolution trainer Olga Botcharova points out—and it fuels the psychology of victimhood. Instead, participants are encouraged to ask, "Why them?" The question is asked no longer (or not simply) in anger but also in truth as well as empathy: "Why did *they* do this to us?"

During a seminar held in Sarajevo—during the siege of that city—a Muslim imam began asking why the Serbs were "doing that" to them. Steele, a United Church of Christ minister who directs the CSIS religion and conflict-resolution program in the former

Yugoslavia, recalls that the imam thought his way back through history and found periods when the tables had been reversed, which led him to observe that Serbs were acting out of fear and the need for survival. The imam's conclusion was that Muslims in the region shared the same needs and motives. As Steele related in a United States Institute of Peace workshop, "Here was a man who was able to do that, putting himself in the shoes of the other, so to speak, and identifying their need by asking the question: Why are they doing this to us?"[36]

This was no small cognitive leap. In essence, the man was stretching beyond his own horizon of feelings, perceptions, and interests, or those of his own ethnic and religious group, his "world of immediacy." He was venturing into the mediated world of interpretation and judgment that leads a person to ask, "Is this really so?" This imam was able to identify with the needs of others and thus to re-humanize them, by pursuing questions about truth rather than mytho-history. What brought him to this level of intellectual transcendence, which made it possible for him to connect with other members of the facilitated small group, including Serbian Orthodox Christians?

A paradox is that the imam made his leap with the aid of religious faith, which has also prevented others from taking the leap. In these pages we have seen how religion can serve to sustain nationalistic ideologies and intergroup suspicion. At the same time, religious faith is arguably about self-transcendence, or breaking beyond the confines of the narrow self and its intellectual, moral, and spiritual presumptions. So, from this perspective, "religion is what opens the door to going beyond my gang, my group, my identity. It's the opening of one's whole mind, getting beyond all that," according to James L. Connor, SJ, former director of the Woodstock Theological Center at Georgetown University in Washington, D.C.

In reaching as far as he did, that imam drew on his own resources of faith at a seminar that included theological reflection upon experiences of victimization, as Steele describes: "His moving description of the way God opened his eyes, despite the terrible struggle of his own people for survival, was in itself a powerful creator of trust and solidarity. It was also a good illustration of theology's ability to broaden one's understanding of needs or interests to the level of common or at least compatible [needs and interests]."[37]

Seminar facilitators can point to other examples when spiritual reflection has led individuals and groups toward greater truth, empathy, forbearance, and will to reconcile. Since 1995, CSIS has held several dozen of these interfaith seminars in Yugoslavia, Croatia, Bosnia-Herzegovina, and Kosovo. Most of the seminars bring together members of different faiths, usually lay people from ethnic groups in conflict with each other. (Some sessions focusing on "identity formation" have involved only one community.) All of the seminars aim to build a wider sense of community by helping people to work through their grief together. Along the way, the seminars have produced core groups—which carry on the work—and a string of related peace-building initiatives.

This approach has less to do with immediate problems and more with long-term relationships. One key turn in this process came early, when facilitators realized that Western approaches to conflict resolution were falling short in the context of war or post-war trauma. The seminars began with the intent of solving problems and developing skills, the traditional approaches, but organizers concluded that such training was often a stretch for people who had deeper needs and psychological wounds. This was especially true for ethnically and religiously mixed seminar groups that needed to get past suspicions and narrow perceptions before attacking problems together. As a result, CSIS came away from the second seminar, in Sarajevo, with "a deep conviction that something needed to radically change in our approach" to intergroup reconciliation, as Steele recalled.[38] This was a turn away from the problem-solving method and toward a focus on building relationships and trust.

Broadly speaking, through such seminars, participants relate and reflect upon their experiences, often in a spiritual light, as a way of forging community among them. Participants begin by expressing grief and grievance, along with their fears of the future, through the *modus operandi* of storytelling. "There is more to this process than just sharing with one another. At the very heart of it is a sharing of the trauma with God," Steele points out.[39] In addition to contemporary theories of grief and trauma, the Scriptures common to Christian, Muslim, and Jewish traditions have served as a facilitating force in these dialogues and reflections.

In particular, the seminars draw upon the motif of laments in the Hebrew Scriptures, or Old Testament. Referring to the lamentation tradition, Steele writes, "Its method of handling grievance is to ritualize the expression of complaint within a community framework in a way that ensures that the victim is heard and that limits any vindictive response."[40] Elsewhere, Steele points to the psalms and the prophets in noting that the purpose of such ritualizing in ancient Israel was to "offer up to God all injury and hurt so that God could heal the pain and God could bring justice."[41]

This same method of lament creates a bridge between the voicing of grievances and the acknowledgment of wrongdoing by oneself and one's group. The prophet Jeremiah, for example, identified the suffering of the Jews but also asked his people to examine themselves and their society, as well as to remember the pervasive reality of God's forgiveness, as Steele explains:

> I find that people from war-ravaged societies identify with the losses suffered by the Jewish exiles of Jeremiah's time— the loss of country, language, Temple, all of the normal identity markers of their society. Yet they were challenged to examine the condition of their own hearts and the actions of their own ethnic group as a part of the healing process that God would perform in their midst.[42]

In other words, this weaving of grief and apology is brought about by theological reflection (which is Steele's catchall term for reflection upon experiences touching on themes ranging from acknowledgment to justice). For example, Serbs in one seminar "opened up to a profound exchange about Serbian responsibility for the war in Bosnia after discussing how the lament motif in its final stage of development, as found in the Old Testament prophets, specifically incorporates the confession of sin into the grief process."[43]

Could this bridge between grievance and acknowledgment serve as a guide for others coping with the experience of grave moral wrong? To cite no small example, Donald W. Shriver Jr. points out that grief and anger were at the forefront of America's response to the terror of September 11, 2001—and rightly so. But he adds the question: Is there room in this response for a reflection on American responsibility, an accounting of wrongs it has committed, particularly in the Islamic world? Can such reflections be incorporated into the nation's ongoing process of grief?

The Role of Acknowledgment

The previous section described how the World Conference of Religions for Peace aims to shift the language, among religious dialogue participants, from doctrines to "moral cares." Such a linguistic shift is one clear way of translating religious faith into a social process, a progression also seen in the CSIS's method of theological reflection. Through the prism of biblical and theological tradition, a more secular language of acknowledgment arises and becomes a centerpiece of these dialogues. It also becomes one of the "most explosive" elements of the CSIS seminar process, in Steele's explanation: emerging suddenly as a challenge to group perceptions and distorted memories.[44]

In one Serb-Croat seminar, participants were in theory submitting to the task of acknowledging wrongs committed by their group; but the dynamic was reversed as a Croatian man went on the attack. As Steele describes, the man began recalling a horrible atrocity committed by Serbs during the war, in which soldiers pulled people out of a hospital in Vukovar and staged a mass execution in a field nearby:

> As he was talking about it, he was getting more and more agitated, more angry. Finally, one Serb who had been a soldier during the war, a layperson, simply spoke up and said: "That happened. I know it happened. And it was wrong." And there was silence at that point. And what happened was, even though this Croat was turning the whole thing around, attacking the other group rather than his own group, this

Serb man was sensitive and courageous enough to recognize that this needed an acknowledgment that it was a terrible crime. And that was enough, at least at that moment, to satisfy this Croat.[45]

At another Serb-Croat seminar, participants were asked to compose a list of wrongful acts committed by their respective groups. That led to an outbreak of acknowledgment acrimony when one side, the Serbs, failed to acknowledge nearly as much as the Croats, according to Steele:

> And the Croats were extremely offended by that because they felt like they had really been harmed the most, and yet when it came to acknowledging things, they felt that the Serbs were glossing over all kinds of things and not nearly being so honest. And that's the dynamic that became very explosive, extremely explosive in fact within that seminar. It was towards the end of the second day, and the conflict was carried over into suppertime. And even after supper, certain people were going at it, with some Croats just demanding that there be an acknowledgment by the Serbs of the terrible things that had been done. And in this case, the Serbs resisted doing that, and the resistance would kind of grow as they were confronted by angry Croats.[46]

One key part of the immediate background of that seminar was the shifting strategic positions of the local Serbian/Orthodox and Croatian/Catholic communities. The Serbs, who had fled to that area of Croatia when it was under Serbian control, were suddenly vulnerable. The area was reverting to Croatian control, so they felt extremely anxious, knowing in some cases that they were living in homes not their own. That part of the learning curve helped CSIS organizers to realize the difficulty of moving people to acknowledgment in such insecure surroundings.

That said, Steele believes the acknowledgment process, though volatile, is necessary:

What people are constantly looking for is acknowledgment of those things that have terribly injured their own community. I hear person after person recounting how they expect an apology from the other side regarding X-Y-Z, particularly a grievance that they have in mind. And I think people need to do that, but I think also that different communities need to be helped in order to do that.[47]

That is partly why the CSIS dialogues take the initial step of acknowledging each other's suffering, which opens the door to a fuller acknowledgment of wrongdoing. One illustration occurred at a seminar in Kosovo, where ethnic Albanians recollected their suffering during the ethnic cleansing and bombing campaigns of 1999. One of the Serbs responded, "If these things are true, then they're terrible and should be absolutely condemned."[48] Though the response was qualified by the word "if," Steele recalls, "you could tell by the expression on his face, by the tone of voice that this was registering in a way that it had never registered before. He was suddenly taking in the scope of what happened during the ethnic cleansing, as he heard these real life stories."[49]

Acknowledgment as a theme has filtered into other efforts at dealing with extreme conflict. In the Israeli-Palestinian conflict, some practitioners of Track II mediation and dialogue have recently pointed to acknowledgment of suffering—through symbolic gestures especially—as one hope of easing the divide between populations, not just politicians. At a workshop held just as the second *intifada* was breaking out, Israeli and Palestinian participants were divided on a particular question of which should come first—an acceptance of co-existence (Israelis) or a discussion of justice and truth (Palestinians). What each side saw as absolutely necessary, though, was an acknowledgment of suffering and humiliation: "What I have discovered from that session and my experience is that acknowledgment is the best bet towards reconciliation," said Elham Atashi of George Mason University, who related the exchange during a United States Institute of Peace workshop.[50]

Likewise, some regard acknowledgment as the best handle on a process of forgiveness—or even, in some ways of looking at it, as preferable to encouraging explicit acts of forgiveness. "I've put the least emphasis on forgiveness, the greatest emphasis on acknowledgment, and ideally contrition, on the part of the perpetrator," explains Joseph V. Montville, a former career diplomat who defined the Track II concept and later directed the Preventive Diplomacy Program at CSIS:

> Contrition and remorse are actions that, if they're credible to the victims, starts the victims on the process of believing that they can exist safely and securely and think about a future for themselves and their children. If the acknowledgment and contrition are persuasive, the victim or victim's group might formally forgive the perpetrators and the nation that hurt them more likely or just as often. But more likely they'll quietly manifest a form of forgiveness by their acts of re-engaging with their perpetrators in a positive way, without any formal indication of forgiveness or formal ceremony. And that's good enough for me.[51]

Some cautionary arguments, however, must be voiced in regard to acknowledgment as key to any reconciliation strategy. Especially in the Balkans, concerns about collective apologies—that these gestures might perpetuate the collective-guilt syndrome as well as encourage retaliation by enemies—could apply to acknowledgments as well. One mitigating factor, though, might have to do with the low-profile nature of the process undertaken by CSIS, involving mostly lay people and local leaders in small-group encounters. The worries about distorting apologies and acknowledgments, and thereby turning them into a vehicle of collective accusation, would probably gravitate more toward public statements made by religious leaders in the midst of searing social conflict. Even then, the greatest risk would involve unilateral statements of apology, not the mutual statements characteristic of interreligious collaboration. Still, the strategy itself—of seeking to avoid instigating collective guilt at all costs—is likely to spark honest disagreement, as revealed in remarks by Steele: "I have some problems with that idea [i.e., the collective-guilt concerns] in that I think there is collective responsibility, but it's very common there for people not to accept it."[52] Practitioners who work in the Balkans are not of one mind about how to balance the social psychological need for public acknowledgment with the threat that it will spin into the region's violent cycles of collective retribution.

⌒──

The strategy of centering mostly on lay people, together with some local and middle-level clergy, harmonizes with a growing recognition that peacemakers must attempt to bring along people and communities, not just political elites. With Hehir's identification of religious resources—ideas, institutions, and communities—in mind, this recognition would place the CSIS project squarely in the communal role. In these local encounters, shared experiences of suffering lead to an exchange of acknowledgment. (Notwithstanding Montville's understandable separation of acknowledgment from forgiveness, such acknowledgment contributes to a process of forgiveness, notably in the service of truth telling and empathy.) In addition to the communal resources, religious ideas or teachings—intellectual assets—are clearly operative in the use of Old Testament laments and in recourse to spiritual or theological reflection.

When it comes to dialogue and action within religious communities, Steele says he often finds greater openness among the laity than with religious leaders. He also often finds greater freedom of initiative, most dramatically displayed in one instance involving a Serbian academic who is a lay Orthodox Church member. After one seminar, he and Steele had initiated a back-channel of communication between Belgrade and the State Department that continued through NATO's bombing campaign. Steele says diplomats later told him that the back channel contributed to shortening the war.[53]

Though he sees a tendency of religious leaders to "isolate themselves behind their theological language," Steele acknowledges that facilitating the voices of ecclesiastical leaders can also deliver greater impact symbolically in seeking to stem intergroup hostilities.[54] In other words, by tapping these religious structures, peacemakers can help build the broader atmospheres of forgiveness while perhaps making possible a more immediate impact on events. As we have seen, the WCRP represents one such experiment in leveraging the peacebuilding assets of religious institutions.

CSIS, WCRP, AND THE
PROCESS OF FORGIVENESS

The World Conference of Religions for Peace and the Center for Strategic and International Studies may tap different religious assets and resources. But a look at the larger picture places them in a similar position in international conflict transformation, in that both pursue long-term efforts at building trust and relationships across communal fault lines. In obvious ways, their strategies in the Balkans contrast with the Track I approach of seeking to resolve conflict through mediation between political leaders and others directly linked to policymaking. At the same time, these strategies contrast strongly with styles of Track II intervention that focus on high-level mediation aimed at solving immediate problems of conflict. The latter style shows in much of the peace work of the pacifist Quakers, as well as by the St. Egidio Community, most remarkably in its mediation of an end to Mozambique's civil war. (It should be noted that a huge part of this success was St. Egidio's awareness of its own limitations and its hand-in-glove work with Track I negotiators, who worked out practical points of settlement and transition.)

When it comes to religious organizations, a number of conflict-transformation experts have recently placed greater hope in the long-term approach, which is typified in many ways by the low-key, grass-roots work of Mennonite peacebuilders. "While high profile mediation interventions by organizations like St. Egidio capture public attention and on occasion prove productive, faith-based organizations are more likely to have long-term impact by nurturing local capabilities in zones of conflict," argues David Smock, who directs the religion and peace-making program of the United States Institute of Peace.[55] In that vein,

Smock points both to the WCRP's efforts to institutionalize interfaith collaboration and dialogue in conflict-prone countries, and to the dialogue and training seminars run by the CSIS. The United States Institute of Peace has assisted in both efforts.

The two approaches are, of course, complementary and overlapping in many cases. The argument here is that the lower-profile strategy—which often goes undetected by international political radar—is crucial to encouraging a process of forgiveness. That is especially the case if forgiveness is to be viewed as a social undertaking that transforms attitudes among wider populations in the long run.

CSIS and the "Choice to Forgive"

In different ways, the WCRP and CSIS strategies illustrate how religious initiatives can put forgiveness in secular or public view.

In the CSIS seminars, forgiveness enters explicitly into the design of the conversations. It begins in the "traditional" dwelling of forgiveness, the interpersonal and pietistic realms, and reaches out into the public space. We have already seen how acknowledgment follows a similar trajectory, starting from religious resources (namely in the confession of sin) and winding up as a broadly accessible strategy of reconciliation. Acknowledgment comes as the fourth stage of the CSIS typology of breaking the revenge cycle—after expressing grief, confronting fears, and re-humanizing the other ("why them?"). Only then do these facilitators fully introduce "the choice to forgive," defined somewhat poetically as giving up all hope of a better past.

Such a stage-by-stage approach of storytelling seems to address some concerns about premature forgiveness, particularly among victims of conflict. Referring to research involving trauma victims, Montville points out that people in these circumstances should not be expected to ruminate about forgiveness until they have had a chance to "take control of the story," to see a beginning, middle, and end.[56] Without some consciousness that the story is over, participants keep revisiting the original event of trauma or victimization through nightmares, panic attacks, and other symbolic triggers or reminders. What this requires is an "ethics of moral intervention," Montville argues, "a full understanding of the clinical psychological needs of victims before they can get to the point where they can voluntarily address a group, forgiving them."[57]

The choice to forgive, in the CSIS process, occasions far less acrimony than acknowledgment of wrongdoing. Still, in the experience of Steele and other facilitators, "the biggest problem we face in dealing with forgiveness is the sense or fear among people that someone will force it on them. We need to allow people to approach this sensitive topic at their own speed."[58]

This approach is altogether essential if forgiveness is to be widely accepted as a process that does not shortchange the need for truth and justice, as Shriver observes: "What people fear is that they will lose the right to moral indignation and judgment. They don't want to give up their own certainty that a wrong was done. They have a right to keep on remembering. [Otherwise] forgiveness sounds like moral softness. All of which is why an agreement on wrong has to be the first thing."[59]

While being sure to grant this space, CSIS facilitators feel it is important that people understand what forgiveness is and what it is not, in this social context. Steele explains, "It is not absolution. It is not an act of freeing other people from the consequences of their actions, including any kind of amnesty from punishment for criminals. Forgiveness is not done for the sake of the other person, but for oneself. It needs to be viewed as an individual's own journey out of the grip of the past and into an open and promising future. In the words of Jeremiah, 'it is a choice to live and not to die.'"[60]

This is fair enough in the context of personal healing, but commentators like Shriver are quick to stress that if forgiveness is to get over "the hump of the individual" and to become a force that is social as well as personal, its primary purpose must be seen as restoring relationships.[61] Yet even Steele's characterization of forgiveness above (i.e., done "for oneself") includes a slight turn to the social or secular, because here, forgiveness—together with repentance—has ventured well beyond the precincts of sectarian and interpersonal discourse. It has journeyed toward a new home, where forgiveness meets with methods of social trauma recovery, for example, as well as with the secular imperative of justice and restoration (ultimately also a religious imperative). Repentance, meanwhile, has developed into a more public language of acknowledgment, which enters again into the service of truth rendering.

In that way, forgiveness turns toward the public arena. The CSIS seminars begin to cast light onto a wider process that sets the stage for sociopolitical forgiveness. For example, "Why them?" is a question of empathy, opening a door to questions about the truth of the matter, which perhaps finds its most difficult expression in the work of acknowledgment.

The fluid conditions of social forgiveness include—in addition to truth, forbearance, and empathy—the determination to heal broken relationships. This phase is illustrated most clearly by the last two stages of the CSIS process, in which participants envision a kind of justice in society that goes beyond revenge, restores relationships in society, and engages in problem solving or joint planning (normally in that order). Some offshoots of the seminars help to illustrate these further levels of forgiveness.

For instance, Steele notes that one such exercise in Fonica, Bosnia, in 1996, led directly to a refugee project headed by a Muslim imam that returned more than 1,600 families to their homes—most of them Croats. More recently, a Serb-Albanian seminar in southeastern Kosovo produced a proposal for an irrigation project and led a Serb to accept the post of agriculture director in the largely Albanian-ethnic regional government. "Here you were dealing with people who knew each other before the war, so they weren't total strangers. But there had been a total breakdown of communication. These people literally had not spoken since the ethnic cleansing and the bombing campaign and now we were about a year after that," Steele recalls, adding that the outcome would have been impossible without building trust and renewing relationships.[62]

Such collaborative projects provide concrete symbols of the will to reconcile, which includes the desire to turn relationships "alongside" into relationships "with."

Making Public Space for Forgiveness: The WCRP

The word "forgiveness" has turned up frequently enough in the inter-religious experiment of the World Conference of Religions for Peace, through statements by religious leaders and scholars. More substantially, the WCRP's overall strategy addresses the prerequisites of a religious role in promoting public forgiveness. One such requisite is for religious institutions to transcend purely sectarian horizons, including those of language (which requires the "differentiation of consciousness" mentioned earlier in this chapter). This is necessary if organized religion is to bring us closer to finding a "new home" for forgiveness in the political world.

One question has to do with the ability of highly visible religious institutions, in the grip of extreme conflict, to achieve this level of social transcendence. Notwithstanding an utterly integrated notion of religious community, the WCRP's work in the Balkans does ease well enough into the "institutional" space or model, according to Hehir's arrangement of religious resources for improving international relations. (Like the CSIS model, which fits well in the communal category, the WCRP strategy also draws heavily on the resource of religious ideas.) As already mentioned, one drawback to the institutional approach is the tendency of religious authorities to "isolate themselves behind their theological language," in Steele's succinct wording.[63] However, the WCRP's intervention shows the potential for hierarchies to come out from under that shelter, with a crucial hand from neutral third parties.

Whatever differences they might have masked, the high-level "Statement of Shared Moral Commitment" and its offspring illustrate the transposition of "cares" or concerns from the isolating mode of sectarianism to public discourse. This transposition has made it possible for the religious leaders to reintroduce forgiveness as a concept of political import. Consider, for example, the invocation of forgiveness by theologians who issued a follow-up statement in support of the "Statement of Shared Moral Commitment." The theologians asked for "sincere repentance, forgiveness and reconciliation, because we believe that this is one of the most reliable ways for people to free themselves from war trauma and from pathological fear of the other and of difference."[64] At the same time (in yet another sign that forgiveness is not oblivious to justice), the scholars called for the prosecution of war criminals and stressed the rights guarantees that formed an integral part of the 1995 Dayton Accords, which set a general framework for peace in Bosnia.

Together with the notion of repentance, forgiveness has unique theological expressions within each of the four traditions represented by the theologians (that is, Serbian Orthodox, Roman Catholic, Jewish, and Muslim); and the differences within a sectarian mode are quite likely irreducible. The stance of the theologians was not to seek out a lowest common denominator of forgiveness, but rather to let it loose in an environment where forgiveness must be mediated by political values such as freedom, justice, and human rights. By mingling forgiveness with shared concerns about war trauma and "pathological fear of the other,"[65] as well as rights guarantees and peace accords, the scholars gave a sign that these communities had at least begun to transcend exclusive horizons.

Clearly this transcendance is part of the task of finding a new dwelling for forgiveness in the political realm, while keeping its primary or exclusive meanings within each religious "house." Likewise, the project of rewriting communist-era legal codes (which govern religious and other mediating organizations) casts light on social conditions of forgiveness, including the need for a strong civil society. These initiatives underscore the wider reality that justice and human rights form the moral core of forgiveness and reconciliation.

Questions remain about the degree to which such gestures and utterances at elite ecclesiastical levels can help to build forgiving communities. Perhaps these high-level initiatives are usefully viewed as events of forgiveness, many of which are required to counter the forces of unforgiveness. Depending on the cultures and circumstances, these and other voices can help to resist the "hothead factor" that propels many conflicts, even after fair swaths of the population desire reconciliation or simply forbearance from revenge. Further, if the creation of scalable (or accessible), sustainable, multi-religious infrastructures is an asset for peacebuilding, it is impossible to imagine a strategy that excludes the existing leadership structures.

At the same time, it is possible to be too admiring of the ordering of things in religious communities. Honoring the structures more or less as they exist is reasonable, but some third parties should find ways of helping people to bypass (or surpass) their structures, at times. For transcending structures is, too, part of the dynamic of religious communities, where one might plausibly expect to be forgiven for such an offense.

⌒‒‒‒

The record of religious conflict transformation in the former Yugoslavia sheds further light on observations (cited at the beginning of the previous chapter) that religion is capable but not committed, or compromised but capable. Most deeply, perhaps, the utility of religion in this whole field is grounded not only in its own assets, but also in the basic wiring of human consciousness. Robert T. Hennemeyer, a career Foreign Service officer and former U.S. ambassador to The Gambia who coordinated the Woodstock project "Forgiveness in Conflict Resolution: Reality and Utility," points out,

> In his poem, "The Star-Splitter," Robert Frost writes, "To be social is to be forgiving." Does this suggest that a wish to seek an eventual solution to a conflict situation is a natural consequence of being social? There may be a basic "peace" or compromise vocabulary to which all humans—religious or not—respond. One could argue that all major faiths have built on this primal vocabulary to make the advantages of peace in efficient social interaction more explicit—and supremely ordained. At least some of this teaching may be implanted in all of us. If so, how can it be tapped and utilized in conflict resolution, reconciliation, and ultimately forgiveness?[66]

We have already seen how religion's communal, institutional, and intellectual assets can contribute to a sociopolitical process of forgiveness. Among lessons learned from the experiences of religious communities and third parties in the former Yugoslavia, Hennemeyer cites "the crucial importance of time in creating an atmosphere in which reconciliation is possible—time for people to get away from the immediate trauma of conflict and personal loss."[67] He also relates the importance of crafting reasonably objective histories and common school curricula, the absence of which contributes to the mytho-histories that fuel ethnic antagonism. And he notes that in spite of their often compromised stance, local religious frequently enjoy a degree of influence and credibility that eludes their political counterparts. Still, he writes,

> while it is very important for the conflict resolution practitioners to appreciate the importance of understanding the power of belief systems and their significance for diplomatic strategies and peacebuilding, many religious leaders have shown extreme moral cowardice in failing to stand up to their own flocks and their political leadership and denounce acts of ethnic hatred.[68]

Other lessons learned more generally from the intersection of forgiveness and conflict resolution are related in the conclusion to this book. First, however, the significance of religion in the cultural matrix of conflict and peacemaking is worth a broader elaboration—as the subject of the next chapter.

NOTES

1   Bernard Lonergan, *Method in Theology* (New York: Herder & Herder, 1972), 265.
2   Lonergan, *Method in Theology*, 265.
3   William Vendley, "Religious Differences and Shared Care: The Need for Primary and Secondary Language," *WCRP Report* (occasional papers), September 1992, 5-6.
4   William Bole's notes from presentation by Vendley, United States Institute of Peace workshop "Peacemaking Roles of Faith-based NGOs," June 20, 2001.
5   Vendley, telephone interview with Bole, July 2001.
6   Vendley, "Religious Differences and Shared Care: The Need for Primary and Secondary Language," 1-2. This summary is also based on Bole, notes from Vendley presentation, and on Vendley, interview.
7   Vendley, interview.
8   Vendley, interview.

9   In that general direction, one could also see the relevance of Lonergan's observation that ecumenical encounter thrives on the distinction between belief and faith. Belief tends toward the sectarian realm of doctrines; faith is embedded in the universal realm of religious experience, which can lead to a common articulation of moral cares. Cf. Lonergan, "Religious Belief" (Chapter 4, section 8), in *Method in Theology*.

10 World Conference on Religions for Peace, "Healing the Wounds of War in Bosnia-Herzegovina," press release, December 1996.

11 William Vendley, in Woodstock Colloquium *Forgiveness in Conflict Resolution: Reality and Utility—The Bosnia Experience* (October 24, 1997) (Washington, DC: Woodstock Theological Center, n.d.), 9-10.

12 World Conference on Religions for Peace, "Healing the Wounds of War in Bosnia-Herzegovina."

13 This was formally announced three months later by the World Conference on Religions for Peace in "Bosnia's Religious Leaders Meet for the First Time Since Outbreak of the War," press release, January 1997.

14 World Conference on Religions for Peace, "Bosnia's Religious Leaders Sign a Statement of Shared Moral Commitment and Form Inter-Religious Council of Bosnia," press release, August 1997.

15 Vendley, interview.

16 Vendley, interview.

17 Vendley, interview.

18 World Conference of Religions for Peace, "Declaration on the Right to Freedom of Religious Practice in Bosnia and Herzegovina," press release, September 5, 1998.

19 Vendley, interview.

20 Vendley, interview.

21 Vendley, interview.

22 Vendley, interview.

23 Vendley, interview.

24 Vendley, interview.

25 Gerard F. Powers, telephone interview with Bole, June 2001.

26 Powers, interview.

27 Powers, interview.

28 Vendley, interview.

29 David Steel, telephone interview with Bole, June 2001.

30 Powers, interview.

31 Powers, interview.

32 Vendley, interview.

33 Vendley, interview.

34 Cf. Marc Gopin, *Between Eden and Armageddon: The Future of World Religions, Violence, and Peacemaking* (New York, Oxford: Oxford University Press, 2000), 40.

35 Steele, interview.

36 Bole's notes from presentation by Steele, United States Institute of Peace workshop, "Peacemaking Roles of Faith-based NGOs," June 20, 2001.

37 Steele, "Ecumenical Community Building and Conflict Resolution Training in the Balkans," in *Training to Promote Conflict Management*, ed. David Smock (Washington, DC: United States Institute of Peace, 1999), 26.

38 Steele interview; also described in Steele, "Ecumenical Community Building and Conflict Resolution Training in the Balkans," 23-24.

39   Steele, "Practical Approaches to Inter-Religious Dialogue and the Empowerment of Religious Communities as Agents of Reconciliation," in *Inter-Religious Dialogue as a Way of Reconciliation in South Eastern Europe*, ed. Milan Vukomanovi'c and Marinko Vucini'c (Beograd: Izdavac, 2001), 100.

40   Steele, "Ecumenical Community Building and Conflict Resolution Training in the Balkans," 24.

41   Steele, "Practical Approaches to Inter-Religious Dialogue and the Empowerment of Religious Communities as Agents of Reconciliation," 100.

42   Steele, "Practical Approaches to Inter-Religious Dialogue and the Empowerment of Religious Communities as Agents of Reconciliation," 102.

43   Steele, "Ecumenical Community Building and Conflict Resolution Training in the Balkans," 25.

44   Steele, interview.

45   Steele, interview.

46   Steele, interview.

47   Steele, interview.

48   Steele, interview.

49   Steele, interview.

50   Bole's notes from presentation by Elham Atashi, United States Institute of Peace workshop "Peacemaking Roles of Faith-based NGOs," June 20, 2001.

51   Joseph Montville, interview with Bole, Washington, DC, May 2001.

52   Steele, interview.

53   Steele, interview.

54   Steele, interview.

55   Smock, "Religion and International Peacemaking" (lecture, Foreign Policy Research Institute, Philadelphia, PA, December 6, 2000).

56   Montville, interview.

57   Montville, interview.

58   Steele, interview.

59   Donald Shriver Jr., interview with Bole, Washington, DC, May 2002.

60   Steele, "Practical Approaches to Inter-Religious Dialogue and the Empowerment of Religious Communities as Agents of Reconciliation," 103.

61   Shriver, interview.

62   Shriver, interview.

63   Shriver, interview.

64   World Conference of Religions for Peace, "Declaration on the Right to Freedom of Religious Practice in Bosnia and Herzegovina."

65   World Conference of Religions for Peace, "Declaration on the Right to Freedom of Religious Practice in Bosnia and Herzegovina."

66   Robert T. Hennemeyer, "Forgiveness in Conflict Resolution: Reality and Utility—The Bosnian Experience," in *Three Dimensions of Peacebuilding in Bosnia: Findings from USIP-Sponsored Research and Field Projects*, ed. Steven Riskin (Washington, DC: United States Institute of Peace, 1999), 38.

67   Hennemeyer, "Forgiveness in Conflict Resolution: Reality and Utility—The Bosnian Experience," 39.

68   Hennemeyer, "Forgiveness in Conflict Resolution: Reality and Utility—The Bosnian Experience," 39.

CHAPTER 8

Interlude:
Religion, Culture, and Forgiveness

As systems of meaning and interpretation,
religion and culture require sympathetic and
systematic attention from practitioners of conflict resolution.
Yet forgiveness belongs to neither religion nor culture.

T he last two chapters, concerning religion, began by relating skepticism about religion's potential for peacemaking and a touch of sentiment that secularization is the surer path to international stability. Also aired was the minority view that universal values such as human rights are preferable to reinforcing religion. These perspectives found an echo in popular culture after the U.S. tragedy of September 11, 2001. At the time, radio stations suddenly began playing John Lennon's song "Imagine," in which the late pop icon bids us to "imagine . . . no religion." Instead, the song lifts up universal values such as peace and brotherhood.

One can argue about how well religion has performed in the regional and international conflicts of our age; and that performance has provided mixed material for this discussion. The point here is that the "no religion" that the former Beatle asked us to imagine is really unimaginable. This is only partly for sociological reasons, which are increasingly compelling. As Chapter 6 discussed, in recent years doubts have intensified about the adequacy of the so-called secularization thesis—which, in its most familiar strain, holds that the more advanced a society becomes, the more religion fades as a force in personal as well as public life. In fact, the striking development of the past two decades has been what sociologist Jose Casanova calls the "de-privatization" of religion in many parts of the world. Yet, religious resurgence aside, what makes "no religion" unimaginable is human culture.

Renowned anthropologist Clifford Geertz describes culture as "an ordered system of meaning and symbols . . . in terms of which individuals define their world, express their feelings and make their judgments"—that is, the human person is a "meaning-seeking animal."[1] Likewise, Jesuit philosopher and theologian Bernard Lonergan defines culture as "the set of meanings and values that informs a way of life."[2] It becomes increasingly clear from any reasonable definition that culture is suffused with religion. For Lonergan, "religion enters the world mediated by meaning and regulated by values. . . . It endows that world with its deepest meaning and its highest value."[3]

Yet what is religion? The question is scarcely asked in such practical discussions, which might help explain why "no religion" could be viewed as a serious option in the world. Religion can be understood as several things, including the communities or institutions that represent a given faith, or the dogmas and doctrines of that faith. This is what people seem to have in mind when they debate the relative merits of religion versus those of no religion in the arena of international conflict. Yet deeper than all that is the human response to a reality deemed as sacred or transcendent. In this light, religion is our ultimate concern, and primarily in this sense it endows the world with its highest value and becomes embedded in the ordered system of symbols and meaning that constitute culture. Imagining no religion is not exactly the same as conceiving of no culture, but it comes close.

Theologian Paul Tillich enumerated the qualities of ultimate concern, which is "unconditional, independent of any conditions of character, desire, or circumstance. The unconditional concern is total: no part of ourselves or of our world is excluded from it; there is no 'place' to flee from it."[4] From such a perspective, it is not unreasonable to cast religion—the human response to the sacred—as a frequently neutral or ambivalent force in human affairs. Making all other concerns relative, religion becomes the utmost lever of human energies, hinging on which concerns are deemed ultimate, which are seen as preliminary or secondary, and whether we understand the radical difference between these two orders of concern. In this connection, perhaps right on point is H. Richard Niebuhr's distinction between monotheism, which is faith in the one God, and henotheism, which is faith in an ultimate that is not God.[5]

To illustrate, in the Balkans, national identity has often taken on infinite significance, though it is rightly seen as a finite value. Tillich, writing long ago, saw religious nationalism as the clearest example of a "preliminary concern . . . elevated to ultimacy," an essentially partial value "boosted into universality."[6] Such confusion paves the way for what Tillich called a "conflict of ultimates."[7] This is not so much the clash of civilizations or religions theorized by Samuel P. Huntington,[8] but rather a conflict between religion (as ultimate concern) and a faux ultimacy. Or, in Niebuhr's terms, it could be a conflict between monotheism and henotheism—"that social faith which makes a finite society, whether cultural or religious, the object of trust as well as loyalty and which tends to subvert even officially monotheistic institutions, such as churches."[9] In this way of thinking, the battle lies between authentic religion and its varieties of distortion; the question becomes how—not whether—to channel the higher values into culture.

These are high concepts, but they offer some directions for dialogue about religion's role in social conflicts. Perhaps most usefully, they point to culture as a promising nexus for conversations about religion, secularization, and international relations. "Culture is the doorway in which religion meets society and the institutions of society," notes James L. Connor, SJ: "You can't talk about justice without talking about culture and its various institutions, such as business, family, and government. And you really can't talk about culture without averting to the religious dimension."[10]

For years, some experts in conflict resolution have worried about the lack of in-depth attention to the religious and cultural dynamics of conflict and resolution, and those anxieties are all the more justified in light of today's permanent war on terrorism. Rabbi Marc Gopin writes, "Good conflict resolution strategy requires a method of reaching out to even the most intractable and parochial religious adherents by engaging in a serious examination of their values and culture."[11]

In Gopin's view, analyzing the values of a given religious culture is a necessary challenge for practitioners as well as theorists. For example, he sees, in virtually every major religion, embedded "prosocial values," such as empathy, humility, forgiveness, and repentance—potential assets for reconciliation. But before tapping those values, reconcilers have to take seriously the teachings and sacred symbolism of religious traditions, especially the most militant ones, and they must do so from within these cultural contexts. Raising the question of whether acts of forgiveness and repentance can be incorporated into conflict-resolution strategies, Gopin gives a qualified yes—"if the challenge is presented equally to both sides of a conflict, and if it speaks to profound cultural and religious metaphors of both adversaries."[12]

CULTURES, INSTITUTIONS, AND FAITH

From his experience as a Track II negotiator in the Middle East, Gopin has concluded that forgiveness in such an extreme clash might have to begin with deeds, gestures, and other symbolic acts, not necessarily with formal dialogue on universal principles. Perhaps that is another way of saying that peacebuilders can reach the radical religious through the doorway of culture, through the "ordered system of meaning and symbols" (to use Geertz's words quoted at the start of this chapter). In the months leading up to the second *intifida*, Gopin and others suggested that American mediators use this doorway to encourage the kinds of symbolic gestures that could resonate with the masses of religious believers. That might mean visits to holy places where Israeli and Palestinian officials would express regret for past acts of violence and dishonor to each other's people. By Gopin's account, some religious leaders made moves in this direction, but the efforts were either ignored or undermined by Israeli and Palestinian political leaders.

These Track II initiatives depend heavily on Track I representatives, who have their own cultural assumptions that can lead to profound skepticism of religious initiatives. As related in Chapter 6, Douglas Johnston observed in the mid-1990s that most in the diplomatic realm have a "learned repugnance to contending intellectually with anything that is religious or spiritual in nature."[13] More recently, Johnston noted in an interview that this hostile reception has eased over the years, but that religion and its strategic role in peacemaking remains a "hard sell" in such quarters.[14] It is not diplomatic business as usual, but many circles have demonstrated a greater openness toward what some have dubbed *moralpolitik*, as illustrated by Henry Kissinger's part in honoring the peace work of the St. Egidio community (related at the beginning of Chapter 6). It is not that Kissinger would have no *realpolitik* reasons for encouraging communities like St. Egidio, perhaps with a thought of leaving the conflicts in strategically "unimportant" places to sundry religious voluntary associations. The encouragement here is that *realpolitik* at its uppermost levels has felt called upon to at least nod in the direction of faith-based conflict transformation.

Practitioners of conflict resolution should indeed engage sympathetically with religion, but this engagement should not be confused with harboring illusions about religion and peacemaking. During a workshop on faith-based NGOs (non-governmental organizations) sponsored by the United States Institute on Peace, William Recant, of the American Jewish Joint Distribution Committee, held up a photograph of a devastated mosque in Kosovo. He announced that two months hence, Jews, Muslims, and Christians would hold a ceremony kicking off a campaign to rebuild it and six other mosques destroyed during hostilities between ethnic Albanians and Serbs. Recant also was quick to say, "More people have died [violently] in the name of God over the centuries than for any other reason."[15] Nobody quibbled with the observation or noted the dreadful toll taken by secular ideologies like Nazism and communism in the twentieth century. Yet at that point, William Vendley, as noted in previous chapters, made his argument that in some regions, it is actually a lack of solid religious identity that succumbs to hyper-ethnic-nationalism.[16] In other words, it is too little religion, not too much, in those instances. That aside, both he and Recant are examples of peacebuilders who harbor no illusions.

They have measured religion's assets as well as liabilities in the field of conflict resolution. They are alert to religion's distortions without sharing the cultural repugnance of religion that Johnston found in the diplomatic corps (cited at the beginning of this section).

While entrenched in culture, each religion has its own particular cultures and institutions. And some recent experiments suggest that by drawing self-consciously on the resources of faith, including intellectual assets, religious communities and institutions can provide fresh openings to forgiveness among religious institutions. Consider the lessons learned by one type of religious institutional actor: international humanitarian agencies, which are a concrete part of almost every particular religious culture. Look, for example, at Catholic Relief Services (CRS), the relief and development arm of the Catholic Church in the United States. For three decades in Rwanda, CRS did what a "good" relief and development agency was supposed to do: it extended aid to refugees and lent a hand to small farmers, among other projects, recalls Fr. William Headley of CRS. Then came the 1994 genocide in Rwanda, which he notes was not entirely unforeseen. All of the good work was wiped away, and many of the people served by the agency were suddenly among "the well-fed dead," as Headley puts it.[17]

That catastrophe eventually led CRS to put on what it calls a "justice lens." Rooted in Catholic social teaching, the approach has brought into focus the need to explore unfamiliar realms, like promoting peace and cooperation among antagonists.

CRS is not the only faith-based humanitarian organization that has taken on the new mission of helping to ease intergroup tensions and to build relationships in places like the Middle East, the Balkans, and Africa. The 1994 tragedy in Rwanda served as a sharp turning point for both that agency and the U.S. evangelical Protestant-sponsored relief agency World Vision. By their own admission, these relief agencies had gone about the usual business of humanitarian assistance while overlooking the warning signs of brutal carnage— which eventually undid all their humanitarian work. CRS has produced a handbook cataloguing peacebuilding projects in more than forty countries. For example, in Rwanda, the agency invites young people from formerly warring tribes to attend "solidarity camps." In Mindanao, Philippines, CRS started a bakery where Muslims and Christians work side by side, amid wider friction between their groups. The business is solvent, but the real bottom line is fostering intergroup relationships.[18]

For CRS and World Vision, as well as Church World Service and most other religious voluntary organizations, this work can be fairly classified as *terra incognita*, so it is too early to gauge the impacts of these and other faith-based undertakings. At the same time, these institutions clearly enjoy multiple assets and capabilities, including familial ties to local communities and cultures in regions of conflict. This means that they can operate closer to the ground than many other international actors—and normally do. International faith-based agencies are one tangible reason why religion demands sympathetic, though not uncritical, attention from peacemakers and reconcilers.

⌒—

Projects like those undertaken by the faith-based NGOs give tangible expression to the possibilities of public forgiveness, particularly the desire to repair fractured relationships. By rooting such deeds in the intellectual resources of faith, religious actors also send out an effective message that the values of peacebuilding come from within their traditions and cultures, not from without. This message counters the propaganda of both religious extremists, who thrive on popular suspicion of universalism, and secular skeptics, who might say that any hope of peacebuilding within religions lies in moving away from their traditions, not more deeply, if critically, into them.

In that sense, the "new home" of forgiveness is not a vast distance from the major religions, yet it is also apparent that these religious traditions have rarely visited this place. They have seldom envisioned themselves as helping to build a broad culture of forgiveness, because their idea of forgiveness, as such, has rarely transcended sectarian boundaries. Only partly for that reason, they cannot claim exclusive ownership of forgiveness, which is really another way of saying they do not own the quest for truth, forbearance, empathy, and restored relationships—the components of Donald Shriver Jr.'s definition. These dynamics are hard-wired into the operations of human and social consciousness, which make it possible to transcend ourselves intellectually, morally, and religiously.

Of forgiveness, we can say what the political philosopher Paul Woodruff says about another virtue, reverence:[19] Forgiveness does not belong to religion; "it belongs, rather, to community."

NOTES

1   Clifford Geertz, *The Interpretation of Cultures* (New York: Basic Books, 2000), 68. Reference by way of James L. Connor, SJ, conversations with William Bole.
2   Bernard Lonergan, *Method in Theology* (New York: Herder & Herder, 1972), xi. Reference by way of James L. Connor, SJ, conversations with William Bole.
3   Lonergan, *Method in Theology*, 112.
4   Paul Tillich, "Ultimate Concern," in *Systematic Theology*, vol. 1, *Foundations of Theological Study*, ed. Richard Viladesau and Mark Massa (New York and Mahwah: Paulist Press, 1991), 13.
5   H. Richard Niebuhr, *Radical Monotheism and Western Culture: With Supplemental Essays* (New York: Harper & Rowe, 1970), especially 65-68.
6   Tillich, "Ultimate Concern," 13.
7   Tillich, "Ultimate Concern," 13.
8   Cf. Samuel P. Huntington, *The Clash of Civilizations and the Remaking of World Order* (New York: Simon and Schuster, 1999).
9   Niebuhr, *Radical Monotheism and Western Culture*, 65-68.
10   Connor, interview with Bole, Washington, DC, March 2001.
11   Marc Gopin, *Between Eden and Armageddon: The Future of World Religions, Violence, and Peacemaking* (New York, Oxford: Oxford University Press, 2000), 199.
12   Gopin, *Between Eden and Armageddon*, 20.
13   Douglas Johnston, cited in Robert T. Hennemeyer, Martin Van Heuven, Ralph Stuart Smith, and Thomas M. F. Timberman, *Religion in World Affairs: The Findings of a Conference Organized by the DACOR Bacon House Foundation* (Washington, DC: DACOR Bacon House Foundation, 1995), 64.
14   Johnston, interview with Bole, Washington, DC, March 2001.
15   Bole's notes on William Recant presentation, United States Institute of Peace workshop "Peacemaking Roles of Faith-based NGOs," June 20, 2000.
16   Bole's notes on William Vendley presentation, United States Institute of Peace workshop, "Peacemaking Roles of Faith-based NGOs," June 20, 2000.
17   Bole's notes on William Headley presentation, United States Institute of Peace workshop, "Peacemaking Roles of Faith-based NGOs," June 20, 2001.
18   Headley presentation; Headley, telephone interview with Bole, June 2001.
19   Paul Woodruff, *Reverence: Renewing a Forgotten Virtue* (New York, Oxford: Oxford University Press, 2001), 5: "It is a natural mistake to think that reverence belongs to religion. It belongs, rather, to community."

Lessons Learned

I n late 1995, the Woodstock Theological Center at Georgetown University in Washington held a forum featuring Donald W. Shriver Jr., whose book *An Ethic for Enemies: Forgiveness in Politics* had been released earlier that year. That forum launched the project "Forgiveness in Conflict Resolution: Reality and Utility," which included four daylong colloquia, held in the following three years, plus continued meetings, dialogues, and research up to the writing of this book. From the beginning, the study has moved forward with two core audiences in mind: (1) those who study or pursue conflict resolution along the first track of official diplomacy, on behalf of governmental agencies, and (2) those who do so as representatives of non-governmental organizations or, more broadly, civil society. As this text has taken shape, however, another type of reader has emerged in the design: those from communities, namely religious communities, who may be familiar with the language of forgiveness but not with the specialized arena of peacebuilding and conflict transformation.

For each of these audiences, the essential task has been to translate forgiveness into the idiom of contemporary international relations. To a degree, this involves mediation between religion and culture—that is, between the historically spiritual grounding of forgiveness and the role of forgiveness in the cultural matrix of today's intergroup conflicts, especially clashes of ethnic and religious identity. The aim of this study is thus not only to communicate a mediated form of forgiveness to the secular and political world of practitioners and policymakers. The aim is also to help reintroduce forgiveness—in its public dimensions of peacebuilding and conflict resolution—to religious communities. In other words, the concept of forgiveness should not only act upon the secular policy world but also "act back" upon the explicitly religious world.

The question of efficacy remains. While forgiveness can be clearly shown to be a "reality" in settings of intergroup conflict, "utility" is a more elusive proposition. Consider the Northern Ireland experience, in which the language of forgiveness seemed to pervade the political dialogue in months leading up to the Good Friday peace agreement. This represents what R. Scott Appleby calls a "saturation model," in which religious peacebuilders are active over the long run at the elite levels as well as the middle management and grassroots levels of society. "It's difficult to prove how important these people are because it's difficult to prove a negative," Appleby commented at one Woodstock forum in March 2002: "In Northern Ireland, there are more peacebuilders per capita than anywhere else in the world. The cynic will say, 'Well you still had over three thousand deaths since 1970.' And the correct answer is: 'You should see what it would have been like if we hadn't had thousands of people dedicated to peacebuilding.'"[1] In that conflict between Catholics and Protestants, forgiveness has been real enough, but its utility in resolving the conflict is harder to prove or pinpoint.

Appleby was speaking more broadly of peacemaking efforts, but part of the difficulty here is that forgiveness in politics is not readily seen or recognized. "In Northern Ireland, there's a lot of forgiveness going on, but if you ask George Mitchell how much of a role forgiveness has played there, he would probably say, 'Not much,'"[2] notes Gerard F. Powers, who directs the Office of International Justice and Peace of the United States Conference of Catholic Bishops, referring to the American statesman who mediated between Protestant loyalists and Catholic unionists. As Powers notes, there are legitimate questions about where forgiveness lies in the course of peacemaking and conflict resolution: "People don't necessarily see forgiveness as the next step. There's a timing question. Where is forgiveness? Is it at the beginning? When a war is over?"[3]

These are indeed legitimate questions, and useful answers depend on a clear and particular grasp of what forgiveness means in a political context. As conceived through the work of Shriver and the Woodstock Theological Center's project, forgiveness is not a single act in which one or more people seek or extend forgiveness—it is not a transaction that can be discerned simply by hearing someone say, "You're forgiven." As we have seen in these accounts, such a literal transaction of forgiveness can and does occur in the midst or aftermath of violent intergroup conflict, usually at the initiative of individual victims or their family members who choose to engage in such a prophetic witness. However, forgiveness in politics is better understood not principally as an act, but rather as a process, one that includes truth, forbearance, empathy, and the desire to repair a fractured relationship, all of which add up to and define forgiveness (which does not include full reconciliation). In this sense, instances of forgiveness can certainly be located within a process of conflict resolution (for example, in Nelson Mandela's gesture of forbearance at his presidential inauguration). Yet the broader proposition in these pages has been that forgiveness might itself be a process of conflict resolution or a way of conceiving the task of peacemaking.

This is not to get around the question of efficacy, which is crucial. Understanding forgiveness as a process, we can cull lessons from the work of experts and practitioners in the field and from the experiences of communities locked in or emerging from conflict. From these strivings and tragedies has come what might be called, without stretching a point, "wisdom." As Shriver explains, in the Hebrew Scriptures wisdom is not as "highfalutin as truth, and it's not as lowdown as common sense." It is captured nicely in the Book of Proverbs, which says in a counsel of forbearance, "A soft answer turneth away wrath."[4]

What "soft answers" have come from those seeking to make forgiveness a reality amid conflicts, and something useful in managing or transforming those conflicts? The Woodstock project and this text have worked with a certain range of cases examined during a limited stage of history. It would be overreaching to claim that many universal or "highfalutin" truths could readily flow from such experiences, yet these have provided adequate data for a process of reflection that makes assumptions about how to understand forgiveness in political life. The discussions rendered in this text have pointed to certain themes usually prominent in most places where practitioners of conflict resolution have worked in recent years. So, in a spirit of modesty and tentativeness, we encapsulate some operational themes of which practitioners and peacebuilders should be cognizant—some ideas to try or to avoid, some lessons learned.

- **The importance of a serious effort to establish historical truth and to disseminate it widely in society cannot be underestimated.** Such an effort may ultimately require the crafting of common school curricula for communities in conflict. Official truth finding counters "mytho-history," which nurtures an exaggerated sense of victimization and thus feeds the cycle of revenge.

- **Memory matters, especially in ethnic and other clashes of group identity.** Remembrances of past misdeeds can either perpetuate conflict or set societies on the path of post-conflict recovery. The problem is not memory itself, but rather the distortions that give rise to mytho-history. Practitioners can help communities to manage these memories through such vehicles as intergroup dialogue and the various ways to truthfully account for the past, ways embodied in truth and reconciliation commissions.

- **Political forgiveness should not be confused with general amnesty.** A limited, conditional amnesty can advance an agenda of forgiveness, especially if its condition is that perpetrators provide truthful testimony about their political crimes (which is what the Truth and Reconciliation Commission in South Africa required). However, unconditional amnesty may have the effect of keeping truth hidden and acknowledgment withheld (as happened in Chile), a consequence that may, in turn, undermine eventual social healing. Further, general amnesty may contribute to the misconception that forgiveness in politics is incompatible with justice.

- Similarly suspect are amnesties granted in effect by perpetrators to themselves. These include, for example, the self-amnesties (*auto-amnestías*) secured by Chile's former Pinochet regime. A social amnesty must instead be adopted through deliberative and democratic channels, and even then it must take into account the rights of victims as well as the requirements of justice and eventual national reconciliation.

- Victims of political crimes should never feel pressured to forgive. Such pressure may deny victims their status as privileged interpreters of the crimes against them and in a sense may re-victimize them. It would also undercut the important notion that forgiveness in politics is a process that allows victims and societies to express their anger and share their memories of offense.

- One can forgive but also seek to punish for the sake of society. Punishment in this case comes out of a sense of justice, not out of revenge.

- While embracing justice, the concept of political forgiveness rejects a notion of justice as reduced simply to punishment. Punishment or retributive justice may be necessary but does not address the primary need of the victim, which is healing. For that reason, restorative justice—aimed at redressing wrongs and renewing relationships—is the justice most compatible with forgiveness.

- An instantaneous forgiveness may be too quick or superficial. One advantage of the process-oriented view of forgiveness is that it gives people and communities permission to be patient and to work out deep differences.

- Generally speaking, leaders can seek or extend forgiveness on behalf of their constituencies. While they should not presume to forgive a misdeed committed against someone else, they can effectively engage in a process of forgiveness that may include acknowledgment of historical wrongdoing or symbolic deeds that signal hope of reconciliation. Such acts of repentance or forgiveness may be more credible if a leader is somehow connected to the misdeeds as either a responsible agent or a victim.

- **Public apologies for political misdeeds are important transactions of social forgiveness, yet they are a process in themselves.** Agents of forgiveness can help advance an apology process by fulfilling three main conditions: clear acknowledgment, sincere repentance, and steps toward restitution.

- **Third-party facilitators can play a critical role in creating a "safe environment" for dialogue between enemies.** Sensitive, knowledgeable, and humble facilitators can help members of clashing communities listen to each other, develop initial trust, and reach mutual understandings. At the grassroots level in small groups, those working with religious communities have also helped congregants begin inner healing through sharing grief and acknowledging offenses.

- **In post-conflict societies, eventual reconciliation requires atmospheres of forgiveness at the societal level as well as of healing at the interpersonal levels.** These are separate though overlapping endeavors. A truth commission can help to nurture an atmosphere of forgiveness and national reconciliation, especially if it has powers to elicit testimony and perhaps to grant or deny amnesty. Facilitated small groups are usually better at promoting interpersonal healing and reconciliation, especially when they can bring members of opposing communities to a mutual acknowledgment of collective misdeeds and then conduct extensive follow-up work.

- **A culture of forgiveness ultimately requires more than good conflict resolution.** It depends on institutions and social-legal mechanisms that facilitate respect for human rights, social peace, and equitable development. In post-conflict settings, reparations may be an essential means of bringing about personal or social healing and eventual reconciliation.

- **Forgiveness in politics occurs *in politics*.** The transactions of forgiveness may derive from transcendent values such as truth and empathy; but once transported to the political realm, they become subject to the uncertainties of that realm, the ambiguities of judgment and possibilities of miscalculation or unintended consequences. For that reason, agents of forgiveness can expect few "free rides" in the back-and-forth of political argument and policymaking.

- **Even when they are co-opted and corrupted, religious communities can play a constructive role in resolving or preventing intergroup conflicts.** In spite of their often compromised stance, local religious groups frequently enjoy a degree of influence and credibility that eludes their political counterparts.

- **Practitioners of conflict resolution have made progress by holding religious groups to their own teachings and commitments.** Ideas and beliefs, such as those encouraging acknowledgment of wrongdoing, are intellectual assets that organized religion can bring to bear in conflicts. Religions also have communal and institutional assets that can be tapped for peacemaking purposes.

These lessons or themes—and others that could be culled from the text—do not lend themselves easily to hard and fast rules of conflict resolution. There are no guarantees, only partly because forgiveness in politics takes place, as already said, in politics, and thus is vulnerable to the limitations and contingencies of any political project. Guaranteed remedies are elusive also because the elements of forgiveness are largely intangible, its results hard to measure or verify. Yet that elusiveness may also be part of what makes forgiveness a fitting framework for many of today's conflicts, immersed as they are in the intangibles of social identity and the immaterial interests of long-aggrieved parties.

Forgiveness may be "subtle and unpredictable," as psychologist Olga Botcharova points out (Chapter 5), but these investigations suggest that it has a strategic value in politics. Forgiveness should be seen as part of a larger notion of security (as articulated by Douglas Johnston in Chapter 5) that includes the building of trust and relationships across dangerously divisive political lines. A few years ago, retired U.S. diplomat Robert T. Hennemeyer offered an assessment that more or less holds today. "Our conclusions are tentative and our study is only a beginning," he wrote on behalf of the forgiveness project, "but we are persuaded that forgiveness is real, it can be inspired and encouraged, and it has a genuine role in conflict resolution."[5]

NOTES

1   R. Scott Appleby, in Woodstock Theological Center Forum "Being Radically Religious in Public Life" (March 14, 2002), *Woodstock Report* (June 2002), http://www.george-town.edu/centers/woodstock/report/r-fea70b.htm (accessed in January 2004.

2   Gerard F. Powers's remarks during meeting of Forgiveness Working Group, Woodstock Theological Center, Washington, DC, May 2002.

3   Powers's remarks during meeting of Forgiveness Working Group, May 2002.

4   Quoted in Donald Shriver Jr.'s comments during meeting of Forgiveness Working Group, May 2002.

5   Robert T. Hennemeyer, "Forgiveness in Conflict Resolution: Reality and Utility—The Bosnian Experience," in *Three Dimensions of Peacebuilding in Bosnia: Findings from USIP-Sponsored Research and Field Projects*, ed. Steven M. Riskin (Washington, DC: United States Institute of Peace, 1999), 42.

Some Organizational Resources

T his book draws on the experiences of not only individuals but also organizations, foundations, projects, and other institutions and initiatives. What follows, in alphabetical order, is a summary sampling of non-governmental organizations (NGOs), culled from their own materials and websites. Most of these organizations played no formal part in the project that led to this report, and a few were largely unknown to participants until recently—but all have arrived in the wide field of forgiveness, to one extent or another.

The American Friends Service Committee (AFSC) (Philadelphia, Pennsylvania)

The American Friends Service Committee (AFSC) is a Quaker organization that includes people of various faiths who are committed to social justice, peace, and humanitarian service. Its work is based on the Religious Society of Friends (Quaker) belief in the worth of every person and faith in the power of love to overcome violence and injustice. Founded in 1917 to provide conscientious objectors with an opportunity to aid civilian victims during World War I, today the AFSC has programs that focus on issues related to economic justice, peacebuilding and demilitarization, social justice, and youth and is located in the United States, Africa, Asia, Latin America, and the Middle East.

> **CONTACT**
> American Friends Service Committee
> 1501 Cherry Street
> Philadelphia, PA 19102
> phone: (215) 241-7000

fax: (215) 241-7275
e-mail: *afscinfo@afsc.org*
website: *www.afsc.org*

Appeal of Conscience Foundation (New York, New York)

The Appeal of Conscience Foundation, founded by Rabbi Arthur Schneier in 1965, has worked on behalf of religious freedom and human rights throughout the world. This ecumenical coalition of business and religious leaders promotes mutual understanding, peace, and tolerance in areas of ethnic conflict. The foundation believes that freedom, democracy, and human rights are the fundamental values that give nations of the world their best hope for peace, security, and shared prosperity.

Appeal of Conscience delegations have met with religious and government leaders in Albania, Argentina, Armenia, Bulgaria, the People's Republic of China, the Commonwealth of Independent States (CIS), Cuba, Czech Republic, El Salvador, Germany, Hungary, India, Indonesia, Ireland, Japan, Morocco, Panama, Poland, Romania, Russia, Slovak Republic, Switzerland, Spain, Turkey, Ukraine, United Kingdom, the former Yugoslavia, and the Holy See. The foundation also hosts delegations from abroad to acquaint them with the diversity of American religious life and its contribution to a civil society.

CONTACT
Rabbi Arthur Schneier, President
Appeal of Conscience Foundation
119 West 57th Street
New York, NY 10019-2401
phone: (212) 535-5800
fax: (212) 628-2513
e-mail: *appealofconscience@msn.com*
website: *www.appealofconscience.org*

A Campaign for Forgiveness Research (Richmond, Virginia)

Funded in part by the John Templeton Foundation, A Campaign for Forgiveness Research supports scientific studies that can deepen the understanding of forgiveness and begin the process of building many different roads to reconciliation. The campaign has funded forty-six research projects that investigate the many ways forgiveness and reconciliation take place. Particular research studies give us insight into the biology of forgiveness in humans and how forgiveness operates among chimpanzee and baboon groups.

Under the heading "forgiveness among nations," at least six projects have studied how a formal political process can advance reconciliation and whether one is more likely to forgive someone of one's own group. These projects have included studies of the Truth and Reconciliation Commission in South Africa, interpersonal healing and forgiveness in Rwanda, and the role of forgiveness in coping with combat trauma.

CONTACT
Robert Coles, MD, Co-Chair
A Campaign for Forgiveness Research
P.O. Box 842018
Richmond, VA 23284-2018
phone: (804) 828-1193
fax: (804) 828-1193
website: *www.forgiving.org*

Catholic Relief Services (CRS) (Baltimore, Maryland)

Founded in 1943 by the Catholic bishops of the United States, Catholic Relief Services provides assistance to the poor and disadvantaged outside the country. CRS offers direct aid to the poor and involves people in their own development. It also educates the people of the United States about how they can fulfill their moral responsibilities by helping the poor, working to remove the causes of poverty, and promoting social justice.

Peacebuilding is one of the priorities of CRS. This work involves education and training, conflict prevention and "early warning" systems, collaboration with Catholic justice and peace commissions abroad, business and micro-enterprise development, conflict intervention (e.g., third-party mediation), trauma healing, and post-conflict reconstruction, among other initiatives.

CONTACT
Catholic Relief Services
209 West Fayette St.
Baltimore, MD 21201-3443
phone: (410) 625-2220
fax: (410) 685-1635
e-mail: *webmaster@catholicrelief.org*
website: *www.catholicrelief.org*

Center for Strategic and International Studies: Former Yugoslavia—Project on Improving Religious-Ethnic Relations (Washington, D.C.)

In its sixth year, this project is underway in the former Yugoslavia, where conflict-resolution training workshops are being conducted for religious leaders and lay representatives from the Catholic, Muslim, Orthodox, Jewish, and Protestant faiths.

In Serbia, Croatia, and Bosnia-Herzegovina, the CSIS commitment to local capacity building has resulted in the creation of indigenous organizations with which CSIS now cooperates. In Kosovo and Montenegro, the project is just beginning. In Macedonia, the possibility of implementing the project is being carefully reviewed in cooperation with potential partner organizations.

In addition to these activities with religious communities, the project director helps to lead conflict-resolution training workshops for other organizations working in the former Yugoslavia—for example, the United States Institute of Peace and the Organization for Security and Cooperation in Europe. Finally, back-channel efforts at Track II or unofficial diplomacy are pursued in order to present creative options for addressing critical social and political problems.

CONTACT

David A. Steele, PhD

Director, Religion and Conflict Resolution Project

Center for Strategic and International Studies

1800 K Street, NW

Washington, DC 20006

phone: (202) 775-3154

fax: (202) 775-3199

e-mail: *dsteele@csis.org*

website: *www.csis.org/prevdip/cp_index.htm#fy*

Center for Strategic and International Studies: Preventive Diplomacy Program (Washington, D.C.)

The CSIS preventive diplomacy program aims to help establish an ethic of prevention in the Washington foreign affairs community and to advance this ethic in the international community. Through its own research, publications, and third-party involvement in ethnic and sectarian conflicts, the program highlights the critical area of non-governmental intervention that deals with the unacknowledged historic hurts in such conflicts—the burdens of history that nourish the instinct toward continued violence.

There are certain tasks in conflict resolution that Track I representatives (diplomats and other government officials) are not yet able to carry out. These involve the fostering of relationships among adversaries in ethnic and sectarian conflicts through mediated dialogue. In undertaking these tasks, the CSIS has paid particular attention to the role of religious actors in promoting conflict and the significant potential of religion in reconciliation and peacemaking.

CONTACT

Joseph Montville

Preventive Diplomacy Program

Center for Strategic and International Studies

1800 K Street, NW

Washington, DC 20006

phone: (202) 775-3179
fax: (202) 775-3190
e-mail: *hpaulson@csis.org*
website: *www.csis.org/prevdip*

Centre for Study of Forgiveness and Reconciliation, Coventry University (United Kingdom)

How do we move beyond cycles of hatred and violence in conflict situations? How can we build community out of division and distrust after a formal peace settlement has been agreed? What is the role of forgiveness in such processes? What do we mean by reconciliation? Is reconciliation compatible with justice? These are some of the questions that inform the work of the Center for Study of Forgiveness and Reconciliation. The Center draws its inspiration from a horrifying moment of history: the night of November 14, 1940, when more than four thousand firebombs were dropped by German planes on Coventry, killing hundreds, devastating large parts of the city, and destroying the medieval cathedral in the heart of the city. In the wake of that terror, the provost of the cathedral urged people to banish all thought of revenge. A new cathedral was subsequently built and dedicated to the pursuit of reconciliation.

In this same spirit of forgiveness and reconciliation the city was twinned with other devastated and "martyred" cities throughout the world—including Dresden, Hiroshima, Stalingrad, Warsaw, Lidice, and Caen. So Coventry's global reputation as a city dedicated to reconciliation and peace has grown.

In light of this history and mission, Coventry University established this academic center with a director in 1999. The three emerging research areas of interest are approaches to forgiveness in Asian religions, the role of the arts in reconciliation, and dealing with the past as a basis for sustainable peace.

CONTACT
Centre for Study of Forgiveness and Reconciliation
Coventry University

Priory Street
Coventry
CV1 5FB DC
United Kingdom
e-mail: *a.rigby@coventry.ac.uk*
website: *www.coventry-isl.org.uk/forgive*

Children's Friendship Project for Northern Ireland (CFPNI) (Warrenton, Virginia)

The CFPNI is a peace- and friendship-building program that fosters understanding and promotes interaction between Catholic and Protestant teenagers in Northern Ireland, their families, and their friends. In an effort to break the cycle of fear and mistrust, teenagers who show the potential to be future leaders are selected and paired in crosscultural teams to spend six weeks together during the summer in an American home, where they can become friends in a neutral environment and can focus on their commonalities rather than their differences. CFPNI sponsors numerous gatherings in Northern Ireland, both before and after the summer, to build and sustain the friendships of the pairs, as well as to broaden crosscultural contacts with other teens in the program, other family members, and friends.

CONTACT
John Chadsey, President
CFPNI
340 Church Street
Warrenton, VA 22186
e-mail: *jchadsey@mnsinc.com*
website: *www.cfpni.org*

Church World Service (CWS) (New York)

Founded in 1946, CWS is the relief, development, and refugee assistance ministry of thirty-six Protestant, Orthodox, and Anglican denominations in the United States. Working in partnership with indigenous organizations in more than eighty countries, CWS works worldwide to meet human needs and foster self-reliance. The agency's Social and Economic Development Program encourages enterprise and collaboration as ways of tapping local ingenuity and promoting self-respect.

CONTACT
Church World Service
475 Riverside Drive
New York, NY 10115
phone: (212) 870-2061
fax: (212) 870-3523
e-mail: *info@churchworldservice.org*
website: *www.churchworldservice.org*

Conflict Transformation Program (CTP), Eastern Mennonite University (Harrisonburg, Virginia)

The CTP was established in 1994 and is designed to support the personal and professional development of peacebuilders and to strengthen the peacebuilding capacities of the institutions they serve. The program encourages the building of a just peace at all levels of society, in situations of violence or potential violence in the United States and abroad. The premise of CTP is that conflict transformation approaches must address root causes of conflict, must be developed strategically, and must promote healing of relationships and restoration of the torn fabric of human community. The organization's Summer Peacebuilding Institute provides specialized, intensive training in peacebuilding, conflict transformation, trauma healing, and restorative justice to practitioners around the world.

CONTACT
Conflict Transformation Program
1200 Park Road
Harrisonburg, VA 22802
phone: (540) 432-4490 or (800) 710-7871
fax: (540) 432-4449 or (540) 432-4444
e-mail: *ctprogram@emu.edu*

website: *www.emu.edu/ctp/ctp.html*

Institute for Conflict Analysis and Resolution (ICAR), George Mason University (Fairfax, Virginia)

The ICAR is a community of scholars, graduate students, alumni, practitioners, and organizations in the field of peacemaking and conflict resolution. Through the organization, faculty members and students in particular commit themselves to the development of theory, research, and practice to interrupt cycles of violence.

CONTACT
Institute for Conflict Analysis and Resolution
4260 Chain Bridge Road (Route 123)
Fairfax, VA 22030
phone: (703) 993-1300
fax: (703) 993-1302
website: *web.gmu.edu/departments/ICAR*

Institute for Justice and Reconciliation (Cape Town, South Africa)

The Institute for Justice and Reconciliation was launched in May 2000 and is self-consciously located in post-TRC (Truth and Reconciliation Commission) South Africa. The institute is committed to using the insights generated through its work in South Africa to engage in dialogue with other African countries. It is founded on the assumption that two inseparable and equally important challenges face this nation and others: namely, justice and reconciliation.

CONTACT
Institute for Justice and Reconciliation
P.O. Box 205
Rondebosch
Cape Town
7700
South Africa

phone: 021-686-5070
fax: 021-686-5079
e-mail: *ijr@grove.uct.ac.za*
website: *www.ijr.org.za*

International Center for Religion and Diplomacy (ICRD) (Washington, D.C.)

The mission of the International Center for Religion and Diplomacy (ICRD) is to facilitate increased understanding and collaboration between policymakers and diplomats, on one hand, and religious leaders (both clergy and laity), on the other, in resolving differences between people, communities, and nation-states.

ICRD's unconventional approach to peacemaking is captured in the book *Religion, the Missing Dimension of Statecraft*, edited by Douglas Johnston and Cynthia Sampson (New York, Oxford: Oxford University Press, 1994). This book illustrates through a series of case studies the positive role that religious or spiritual factors can play in preventing or resolving conflict while advancing social change based on justice and reconciliation. The book is now in its tenth printing and second foreign language translation.

CONTACT

Douglas Johnston, PhD, President and Founder
International Center for Religion and Diplomacy
1156 Fifteenth St. NW, Suite 910
Washington, DC 20005
phone: (202) 331-9404
fax: (202) 872-9137
e-mail: *postmaster@icrd.org*
website: *www.icrd.org*

International Forgiveness Institute (IFI) (Madison, Wisconsin)

Established in 1994, the International Forgiveness Institute was an outgrowth of the social scientific research done at the University of

Wisconsin–Madison since 1985 by Robert Enright and his colleagues. Enright was looking for a way to disseminate the findings of that research, and the research and writings by others exploring forgiveness, to interested people in all walks of life. The IFI has served as that forum ever since. For the first couple of years, the IFI primarily answered scholars' inquiries about setting up their own research programs on forgiveness. Occasionally, it also helped people to gather information about how they themselves can forgive certain people who have offended them.

More recently, the institute has published three times a year *The World of Forgiveness*, which highlights work on forgiveness in such varied domains as the peace movement, the legal profession, education, and psychotherapy. In the field of international diplomacy, the institute played a role, together with the Rev. Jesse Jackson, in freeing U.S. soldiers in Kosovo in 1999.

CONTACT

International Forgiveness Institute
Communications Center
6313 Landfall Drive
Madison, WI 53705
phone: (608) 231-9117
fax: (608) 262-9407
website: *www.forgiveness-institute.org*

The Kroc Institute for International Peace Studies, University of Notre Dame (Notre Dame, Indiana)

Founded in 1986, the Institute conducts research, education, and outreach programs on the causes of violence and the conditions for sustainable peace. The Institute's research agenda focuses on the religious and ethnic dimensions of conflict and peacebuilding; the ethics of the use of force; and the peacemaking role of international norms, policies and institutions.

In addition to offering a unique MA program and an innovative undergraduate supplementary major and interdisciplinary minor in peace studies, the Institute reaches out to national and international communities through media commentary, online and print publications, and workshops for non-governmental and religious organizations.

CONTACT

The Joan B. Kroc Institute for International Peace Studies
University of Notre Dame
100 Hesburgh Center for International Studies
P.O. Box 639
Notre Dame, IN 46556
phone: (574) 631-6970
website: *www.nd.edu/~krocinst*

Moral Re-Armament: Initiatives of Change (IC) (United Kingdom)

IC is an international network of people who work towards far-reaching change locally and globally by starting with change in their own lives. Its purpose is to encourage people to find their unique contribution to the transformation needed in the world. This often means taking risks for the common good. In the international field, current initiatives include forging networks among people from different faiths and cultures committed to work for reconciliation, justice, and peace.

CONTACT

IC National Office
1156 Fifteenth St. NW, Suite 910
Washington, DC 20005
phone: (202) 872-9077
fax: (202) 872-9137
e-mail: *Info@us.initiativesofchange.org*
website: *www.us.initiativesofchange.org*

United States Institute of Peace (USIP): Religion and Peacemaking Initiative (Washington, D.C.)

The USIP launched its Religion and Peacemaking Initiative in July 2000. Its purpose is to enhance the capacity of faith communities to be forces for peace. The Religion and Peacemaking Initiative builds upon the institute's earlier initiative, Religion, Ethics, and Human Rights. That program's primary focus was on the role of religion in world conflicts and the applicability of human rights norms to such conflicts. In the late 1990s the religion program gave particular attention to religion and peacebuilding in Bosnia, including support for Bosnia's Inter-Religious Council. The program produced a wide array of research findings and publications, including books on Sri Lanka, Ukraine, and Islamic activism, under the direction of David Little, now a professor at Harvard Divinity School. The Institute now focuses more directly on the increasingly significant role of faith-based peacemaking efforts. The overarching goal of the religion program is to facilitate the resolution of international disputes through aiding the efforts of faith-based organizations. The program has an electronic listserv for those engaged in the field of religion and peacemaking. Those interested in subscribing can do so by sending an e-mail to *peacemaking-subscribe@usip.org.*

CONTACT
David Smock, MDiv, PhD
Director, Religion and Peacemaking Initiative
United States Institute of Peace
1200 Seventeenth St. NW, Suite 200
Washington, DC 20036-3011
phone: (202) 429-3843
e-mail: *ds@usip.org*
website: *www.usip.org/religion/religion.html*

United States Institute of Peace (USIP): Rule of Law Program (Washington, D.C.)

Research suggests that societies governed by the rule of law are less likely to be international aggressors and more likely to contribute to international peace. To address this issue, in 1990 the USIP created its Rule of Law initiative, which became a full-fledged program in 1999. The program seeks to build upon and refine principles of the rule of law articulated by various international bodies and to provide practical guidance for their implementation. This effort is based on the premise that adherence to the rule of law entails far more than the mechanical application of static legal technicalities; it requires an evolutionary search for those institutions and processes that will best bring about authentic stability through justice.

CONTACT

Neil J. Kritz
Director, Rule of Law Program
United States Institute of Peace
1200 Seventeenth St. NW, Suite 200
Washington, DC 20036-3011
phone: (202) 457-1700
fax: (202) 429-6063
website: *www.usip.org/rol/rol.html*

World Conference of Religions for Peace (WCRP) (New York)

The WCRP was founded in 1970 to provide leaders of the world's many religions with a forum in which they can share common concerns, address collective challenges, and express their hopes for the future. Since then, WCRP has brought together hundreds of key religious leaders every five years (most recently in Amman, Jordan, in 1999) for World Assemblies in which people of many faiths discuss the great issues of our time and affirm their shared commitment to multi-religious cooperation and common living.

The organization aims to help religious communities to unleash their potential for common action. Its multi-religious initiatives have included mediating dialogue between warring factions in Sierra Leone, building a new climate of reconciliation in Bosnia and Kosovo, organizing an international network of religious women's organizations, and launching a program to assist the millions of children affected by Africa's AIDS pandemic, the Hope for African Children Initiative.

CONTACT
World Conference of Religions for Peace
777 United Nations Plaza
New York, NY 10017
phone: (212) 687-2163
fax: (212) 983-0566
e-mail: *info@wcrp.org*
website: *www.wcrp.org*

Worldwide Forgiveness Alliance (Mill Valley, California)

The Worldwide Forgiveness Alliance is dedicated to the establishment of the first global holiday, International Forgiveness Day, celebrated on the first Sunday of every August. The group honors and acknowledges individuals and organizations as "heroes of forgiveness." It also provides detailed material and seminars on the power of forgiveness.

CONTACT
International Forgiveness Day
20 Sunnyside Ave., Suite A268
Mill Valley, CA 94941
phone: (415) 381-3372
website: *www.forgivenessday.org*

terrorism, 1, 11-12, 24, 33, 121
victimhood, 11, 12, 16, 18-21, 26, 36, 48-49, 50, 62-66, 105-109, 152-154, 162-163, 182

U.S. State Department, 78, 133-134; see also *Diplomacy*.

W

Woodstock Theological Center, xi, 3, 5, 8, 12-13, 44-45, 71, 123-125, 135-136, 153, 179, 181

World Conference of Religions for Peace, 14, 24, 134, 137, 142-152, 156, 161-170, 200-201

World Vision, 176-177

Y

Yugoslavia (former), 13, 14, 24, 54, 82, 104, 113, 117, 118, 128-134, 142, 151-152, 153-154, 167, 168, 188, 190

Balkans, 2, 3, 12, 21, 24-25, 34-35, 54, 70, 72, 75, 109, 120, 127, 128-137, 146-150, 159-160, 161, 165-166, 173, 176-177

Croatia, 25, 41, 42, 49-51, 127, 128, 130-131, 132-134, 154, 156-157, 164, 190

Kosovo, 14, 15, 41-42, 48-49, 54, 127, 134-135, 147-148, 149, 154, 158, 164, 175-176, 190, 197, 200

Serbia, 25, 41-42, 48-49, 122, 128, 130-132, 156-158, 164

See also *Bosnia-Herzegovina*.

ABOUT THE AUTHORS

WILLIAM BOLE is a fellow of the Woodstock Theological Center at Georgetown University and a Massachusetts-based journalist whose articles have appeared in the *Washington Post, Commonweal,* and other publications. He co-authored, with the late Msgr. George Higgins, *Organized Labor and the Church: Reflections of a "Labor Priest."*

DREW CHRISTIANSEN, SJ, is counselor for international affairs to the United States Conference of Catholic Bishops (USCCB) and associate editor of *America.* A former Woodstock senior fellow, he formerly directed the USCCB Office of International Justice and Peace. He has co-edited several books and written more than ninety articles.

ROBERT T. HENNEMEYER is a Woodstock fellow and career foreign service officer who served in several countries including The Gambia, where he was U.S. ambassador. He coordinated Woodstock's project "Forgiveness in Conflict Resolution: Reality and Utility," and formerly directed the USCCB Office of International Justice and Peace.